HAROLD OREL earned [...]
University of New Ham[...]
Michigan. He is currently [...]
fessor of English at the U[...]
the Royal Society of Lite[...]
of twenty books, several of which deal with late-
Victorian figures such as Thomas Hardy, Rudyard
Kipling, and William Butler Yeats. His history of the
Victorian short story was published by Cambridge Uni-
versity Press in 1986. Professor Orel is also editor of
Victorian Short Stories: An Anthology, which was
published in Everyman in 1987.

To Charles Newton Kimball
and Mary Louise Theis Kimball

Victorian Short Stories 2
The Trials of Love

Selected and introduced by
Harold Orel
University Distinguished Professor of English
University of Kansas

J. M. Dent & Sons Ltd: London
EVERYMAN'S LIBRARY

© Selection, introduction and notes, J. M. Dent & Sons Ltd, 1990

Phototypeset in Linotron Sabon at
The Spartan Press Ltd,
Lymington, Hants
Made in Great Britain by
Guernsey Press Co. Ltd, Guernsey, C. I. for
J. M. Dent & Sons Ltd
91 Clapham High Street, London SW4 7TA

First published in Everyman 1990

British Library Cataloguing in Publication Data
The Trials of love. – (Victorian short stories; 2)
   1. Short stories in English 1837–1900. Anthologies
I. Orel, Harold 1926– II. Series
823′.01′08 [FS]

ISBN 0–460–87007–6

Contents

Introduction

'Reader, I married him.'

Thus Charlotte Brontë's heroine begins her thirty-eighth chapter in *Jane Eyre*. The reader who has followed the surprising course of her life may well wonder whether marriage to Mr Rochester will turn out to be a miserable affair. This question will not remain unanswered for long. 'I have now been married ten years,' Jane continues. 'I know what it is to live entirely for and with what I love best on earth. I hold myself supremely blest – blest beyond what language can express; because I am my husband's life as fully as he is mine. No woman was ever nearer to her mate than I am: ever more absolutely bone of his bone, and flesh of his flesh. I know no weariness of my Edward's society: he knows none of mine, any more than we each do of the pulsation of the heart that beats in our separate bosoms; consequently, we are ever together. To be together is for us to be at once as free as in solitude, as gay as in company. We talk, I believe, all day long: to talk to each other is but a more animated and an audible thinking. All my confidence is bestowed on him, all his confidence is devoted to me; we are precisely suited in character – perfect concord is the result.' After Mr Rochester's vision returns to one eye, he is able to see his first-born, and, at novel's end, he acknowledges that God has 'tempered judgment with mercy'.

The use of marriage as a convenient way of ending a novel, with a brief chapter, only 'one word' more, to sketch what happens next, is a commonplace of Victorian novels. The reader's expectation is that married couples will live happily ever after, and I have quoted Jane Eyre's description of felicity at some length because it explicitly sets forth an ideal relationship (unlike that of Mr Rochester's doomed first marriage). Jane Eyre does not romanticize or minimize the problems troubling men and women who find themselves attracted to each other – for example, one is never allowed to forget Jane's plainness of feature – yet the happy marriage that solves all problems is a plot element in several of Charlotte Brontë's novels. Recall the marriages made by Crimsworth in *The Professor*, and by Robert and Louis Moore in *Shirley*, as well as Jane's to Mr Rochester in *Jane Eyre*.

Charles Dickens desexualized his women in order to idealize them: Little Dorrit, Lizzie Hexam, Florence, Esther Summerson. There is something incomplete, and consequently unsatisfying, about George Eliot's treatment of the sexual passion in the Gwendolen–Grandcourt relationship in *Daniel Deronda*, and something stagey in the use of a violent storm to dramatize the declaration of love between Ladislaw and Dorothea in *Middlemarch*. The popular Victorian novels written by Mrs Oliphant, Ouida, Miss Braddon, Mrs Humphry Ward, and Marie Corelli, told the truth only intermittently about what women could and could not do in Victorian society.

It was Thomas Hardy, George Moore, and George Gissing who were the pioneers in bringing to the English novel a set of frank attitudes toward courtship, marriage, and its aftermath, attitudes that had already marked for fifty years much of the serious fiction of France. It is no accident that these late Victorian novelists encountered stiff opposition from the gods of the lending library, W. H. Smith's and Mudie's in particular, or that their fictional representations of women coincided with the startling increase in the number of new periodicals fostering the rapid development of short-story talents. A word about each development is in order before we examine more closely the particular examples chosen for this collection.

The growing popularity of the middle-class novel was a by-product of population growth in England and Wales, a phenomenon that tripled the number of people between 1750 and 1850 (6,250,000 to 18,000,000). One capitalist who appreciated early on the financial gain to be derived from marketing middle-class values in three-volume novels ('three-deckers') was Charles Edward Mudie. By the mid-1860s he was earning some £40,000 a year in subscriptions, at the rate of a guinea a year per client, taken in at his New Oxford Street emporium. In 1861 he owned 800,000 volumes; in 1900, 7,500,000; and the percentage of volumes that were novels, over this remarkable half-century, remained remarkably constant, fairly close to half his stock.[1] The variety of these novels was impressive. The three-deckers included stories of sensation, religion, adventure, sports, and military life.

By far the largest number had to do with domestic life, with homes, families, and romantic love (usually culminating in marriage). Mudie ran his main store and branches as a business; he did not intend to act as a spokesman for the Higher Literature. He was concerned about the sensibilities of his readers, and sometimes censored (by not purchasing) the novels of those writers whom he believed might offend customers. Two examples: George Meredith's *The Ordeal of Richard Feverel: A History of a Father and Son* (1859), was withdrawn because some clients complained of its frankness. Rhoda Broughton was considered unacceptable until the mid-1870s.

There was opposition from some authors, of course. Charles Reade hated Mudie's power, and Henry James spoke of the 'tyranny' of the three-decker form (which Mudie liked largely because a reader was obliged to come to his shop three times to read a single novel). Wilkie Collins called Mudie and Smith the 'twin tyrants of literature'. George Gissing attacked them in a letter to the *Pall Mall Gazette* (1884), and George Moore's pamphlet, *Literature at Nurse; or, Circulating Morals* (1885), signalled the rise of a strong revulsion that commercial considerations should control what serious novelists might want to say. The Society of Authors, founded in 1884, fought against an exploitative system that forced most novelists to pay to have their work published; for a majority of them, the returns over and above their investment were fairly paltry.

Other representative cases of censorship by the use of economic boycott occurred when George Moore's *A Mummer's Wife* (1884) and Thomas Hardy's *Tess of the d'Urbervilles* (1891) were banned. If Mudie's 'Select Library' did not carry a novel, the novel's price of 31s. 6d. was too high for the average reader, and sales tended to be very poor. Moore's anger at the 'illiterate censorship of a librarian' did not sway William Faux, the head of Smith's library department, who was impervious to the moral outrage of a banned author. But William Gladstone's praise of the anti-betting scenes in *Esther Waters* (another banned novel written by Moore) proved more useful in Moore's campaign to break the power of the censor; by Moore's calculation, Mudie's lost £1,500 by refusing to stock his novel. *Esther Waters* was published in 1894, a key year in the history of the Victorian novel.

The sensational trial and imprisonment of Henry Vizetelly, who published expurgated translations of Zola's novels, George Bernard Shaw's intense campaigning, and the rapid-fire slogan-eering of Gissing and Moore, plus a number of changing market-place realities, smashed the monopolistic system.[2] In 1894 there were 184 new three-volume novels circulated; in 1895, fifty-two; in 1897, only four.

Mudie's and Smith's primarily opposed fictional treatments that raised disturbing questions about the sanctity of marriage. Radical political and religious convictions were less likely to invite censorship. Mudie himself died in 1890, and during the 1880s and 1890s hundreds of general-interest, lively magazines came into existence which provided home for shorter fiction, ranging in length from two or three pages to one-hundred-page novellas. Rudyard Kipling's earliest efforts, published in *Plain Tales from the Hills* (1888), and the stories of Wells, Conrad, Stevenson, Hardy, and James found their audience – newly created, and weary beyond measure at the overstuffed and often badly written novels that had so dominated the era through the vehicle of periodicals and inexpensive paperbacks. The rate of pay for the most successful authors was rising exponentially. Arthur Conan Doyle, in large part because of his Sherlock Holmes stories, may have been the best-remunerated author in England by the end of the century. H. G. Wells, even more canny than Doyle in negotiating high royalties with publishers, was only a short distance behind.

The sense of relief that authors experienced when the obliga-tion to write enough to fill three volumes (or twenty monthly instalments, or eight bi-monthly parts) evaporated can scarcely be exaggerated. Trollope, Rhoda Broughton, and Mrs Oliphant were not alone in their irritation at being forced to write to lengths rigidly prescribed in advance by publishing practice: the irritation was very widespread.

*

It was not until late in the century that writers of fiction analysed in detail several unpleasant truths about the importance of property in defining a woman's place in society. A man could pass on his estate to a descendant of his own blood only if he could be sure his wife had been faithful to him alone. From 1697 onwards, men of the upper classes could be divorced by an Act of Parliament in order to 'safeguard the inheritance of property and family succession endangered by a wife's adultery'. (Premarital pregnancy sometimes confused the issue.) In 1857 the Matrimonial Causes Act extended to the middle class the same principle as a cause for divorce. The fact that a father of an unmarried woman could sue a man who seduced her – because the father had lost her 'services' – suggests strongly that he thought of his daughter as a piece of property. When the daughter married, her husband immediately took possession of everything she owned, and everything she might earn. The law would not touch him, indeed could not touch him, if he beat her (he could not endanger her life, however); if he took away her children from her, and refused visitation rights; or even if he imprisoned her. So far as the courts were concerned, marrying him had nullified her separateness as a person. The legal consequences were severe. She could not sue him; she could not bring a case against him for physical abuse. If she wanted to institute a lawsuit against someone else, her husband had to be the plaintiff; she had to defer to his wishes as to whether the lawsuit could be instituted at all. Since she was married, her husband, by definition, did not 'rape' her when he exercised his marital rights. The distinction between marital rights and property rights were fairly opaque.[3]

The founding of Queen's and Bedford Colleges in 1848, of Cheltenham Ladies College in 1853, and of Girton in 1869 helped women to feel more dignified and self-worthy as they gained access to higher education, but so long as the legal view of women as property remained strong, even the passage of the first restriction on working hours for women (1849) seemed controversial. The first Parliamentary Bill to give married women the right to own their own property was introduced in 1856, but not passed until 1870, and not given teeth until 1882.[4] Nevertheless, numbers were beginning to weigh more heavily in the balance. The census of 1851 counted 2,765,000 single women over the age of fifteen; twenty years later there were 3,228,700. Harriet Martineau, writing in the *Edinburgh Review* (April 1859), noted that at mid-century a third of all females over twenty were independently supporting themselves and their households, and that this percentage was growing with the number of 'surplus' women (widows as well as those who never married). There were half a million more women than men, and the latter often married late or not at all. Many of the more enterprising bachelors emigrated to the colonies. Women who married faced the terrors of child-bearing at much too frequent intervals; many of their children were born dead or died within a year; wives were not able to practise contraception, and frequently were ignorant of how to do so, until the mid-1870s.[5] Spinsters, taken all in all, were better off; they could own and acquire possessions, enter into contracts, take responsibility for their own finances, and be responsible for themselves.

In 1857, the year that the *English Women's Journal* began publishing, a new divorce law was passed, facilitating less complicated and expensive procedures than those which had required a Parliamentary decision. The new legislation allowed a husband to get a divorce simply on the evidence that his wife had committed adultery. However, if a wife acted as a plaintiff, in addition to proving her husband's adultery, she had to show that her husband had either deserted her for an uninterrupted period of two years, or that he had treated her with brutality. The sexes, in brief, were still unequal before the law.[6] Still, the passage of the Matrimonial Causes Act represented progress. More laws, beginning in the 1860s, helped to clear the way for the universal suffrage embodied in the Acts of 1918 and 1928. The Second Reform Act of 1867, which still insisted on property qualifications, granted the franchise to the lower middle class and to a small privileged section of the working class. Members of Parliament were beginning to speak of 'persons' rather than 'men' (partly because of John Stuart Mill's vigorous initiative). In 1867–68 a commission inquiring into schools recommended accelerating improvements in secondary and higher education for women. The Factory Acts regulating the work of women and children were extended to non-textile industries and craft occupations. Lord and Lady Amberley confronted the problem of birth-control in a series of courses on hygiene. Perhaps the stormiest reaction was set off by the furtive hastening through Parliament of the Contagious Diseases Prevention Acts in 1864, 1866, and 1869. British laws protecting the rights of the individual were cavalierly pushed to one side so that the high incidence of venereal disease among soldiers and sailors could be reduced. Special police could arrest women on mere suspicion. Prostitutes were registered and supervised. Compulsory medical examinations of women could lead to detention in hospitals if infection were proved. At the same time, penalties for men were either light or non-existent. 'The Great Crusade', a feminist counter-offensive, was led by Josephine Butler to eliminate the odious double standard promulgated by the Acts; these were suspended in 1883, and repealed in 1886. The first association for female suffrage was formed; and John Stuart Mill published *The Subjection of Women*, the key propositions of which were much talked about.[7]

In 1870 for the first time English law nullified the complete control of a wife's assets and person by the husband. The Married Women's Property Act guaranteed that a wife could own her earnings, investments, inheritance, rents, revenues, and any money gifts over £200. The intolerable situation whereby a husband possessed unlimited rights over his children — for example, the right to take a daughter away from a wife who had committed no wrong, and entrust her to his mistress — was seriously modified by the new position (1873) of the courts, which now said that a divorced mother could be entrusted with the custody of children up to the age of sixteen.[8]

Agitation for reform of the divorce law grew more intense during the final years of the century. Perhaps the most effective society pushing in this direction, rallying to its cause Gilbert Murray, Thomas Hardy, E. S. P. Haynes, Sir Frederick Pollock, Sir John Cockburn, Sir Clifford Cory, and Sir Arthur Conan Doyle as president, was the Divorce Law Reform Union which led to the creation of a Royal Commission of Inquiry under the presidency of Lord Gorell. In November, 1912, the principle that 'the cause for divorce should be the same between the sexes' was clearly set forth. The opposition of the Church finally ended in 1923. The recommendations of the Gorell Commission, extending the right to divorce where either party had been deserted for an uninterrupted period of at least three years, became law in 1937.[9]

*

I have traced this history well into the twentieth century to show how long it took for self-evident truths about the double standard to be accepted in law. Whenever Victorian women sought to assert their 'rights', they faced ridicule, abuse, even physical violence. Not until the 1880s did either Cambridge or Oxford admit women students to the same examinations as men. Women were accepted only as clerks, shorthand writers, and typists in the legal professions. They encountered very strong opposition whenever they attempted to enter the field of medicine. Only in 1856 did the first woman register as a medical student. Approximately 100 earned their medical degrees by 1891. Middle-class women interested in a profession went – for the most part – into teaching: 94,229 in 1871, and 123,995 in 1881. Many others worked in the Post Office and in various public services. And even though many intellectuals like T. H. Huxley strenuously argued the case for the liberation of women, politicians like Gladstone vigorously campaigned against all Bills that sought to grant women the suffrage, particularly in the late 1860s and again in 1884, when the projected Reform Bill broadened the franchise.[10]

Traditionalists who opposed women's rights kept returning to three arguments: a woman's place was in the home (the domestic theory); women were meant to be chiefly, perhaps even exclusively, mothers (the 'intention of Nature' theory); and women were goddesses, albeit of a minor order, and had to be worshipped from afar (the 'pedestal' or 'pinnacle' theory).[11]

Small wonder, then, that novelists and an ever-widening circle of readers became impatient with the conventions of a genre that denied women their very identity as human beings, their sexuality, their capacity for intellectual development. In 'The Science of Fiction', a contribution submitted to a symposium printed in the *New Review* (April 1891), Thomas Hardy wrote, 'The materials of Fiction being human nature and circumstances, the science thereof may be dignified by calling it the codified law of things as they really are. No single pen can treat exhaustively of this. The Science of Fiction is contained in the large work, the cyclopaedia of life.' The artificial narrowing of subject-matter necessitated by compromises with the spirit of Grundyism meant that only a few articles of the cyclopaedia, and those bowdlerized, could be printed. Although Hardy did not wish to be regarded as a trail-blazer in his final novels, *Jude the Obscure* – published in 1895 as his last novel – exhibits a 'particular savagery' (such is Jenni Calder's phrasing) in the way it binds together 'the frustrations of class, the tyranny of institutions, and established Christianity into a devastating vicious circle'. It is no wonder that in this bleak rendering of the anti-marriage theme 'aspirations and ideals are self destructive'.[12]

From the 1880s on short stories treated love and marriage with growing freedom, though two qualifications must be made at once to this generalization. Authors working in both genres – the short story and the novel – grouped women into the over-simplified 'pure' and 'fallen' categories until disgracefully late into the century. Moreover, major novelists (Dickens, Collins, Mrs Gaskell, Trollope, Gissing, Moore, and Hardy) examined with sympathy particular examples of the fallen woman sooner, and perhaps more daringly, than the writers of most short stories. To illustrate the richness of the variety of approaches taken to the intertwining of the destinies of men and women, I have chosen fifteen stories, five in each of three categories: courtship, troubled marriages, and happy marriages. All but two were published after 1880. I have spared the reader samples from the Christmas annuals, and from the literally thousands of saccharine, sentimental, and stereotypical stories that entertained without seriously disturbing the preconceptions about romance held by the mass reading audience. These fifteen stories still speak to us; the problems confronted by these lovers – and by those who have fallen out of love – are for the most part contemporary as well as Victorian; and the solutions worked out then may not be all that inferior to solutions to parallel problems encountered during our own moment in history.

*

The first story, by William Schwenck Gilbert, speaks of a courtship too frail to develop fully. The language of 'Angela' may seem courtly, even over-refined, but the sustaining metaphor – the blindness of love to the realities of a given situation – provides an early and important reminder that the heart obeys its own imperatives. It does not pay to define too rigorously the conditions under which love (however mistaken in its assumptions) will flourish. 'Angela' also depicts the problems created by an unreturned love: Angela never knows of the narrator's passion for her.

Courtships that do not come to much intrigued Victorian short-story writers. Anthony Trollope's 'The Parson's Daughter of Oxney Colne', George Egerton's 'A Little Grey Glove', and Israel Zangwill's 'The Woman Beater' are eloquent in their portrayals of romances that end before the taking of vows at a marriage altar. In Trollope's story, Patience Woolsworthy's acceptance of Captain Broughton's proposal has about it the air of inevitability; the two are eminently suited for one another, at least as the world sees them; and there exist no serious obstacles to prevent them from living happily ever after. The objections which Patty raises – the second thoughts which prevent her from beginning what George Eliot, in the Finale of *Middlemarch*, called 'the home epic – the gradual conquest or irremediable loss of that complete union which makes the advancing year a climax, and age the harvest of sweet memories in common' – are not all that far from the objections to forswearing bachelorhood that immediately plague the Captain. He is all too conscious of his superior social class, of the fact that his family has more money than hers. Another consideration gnaws at him, the very fact of her acceptance: 'When you have your plaything how much of the anticipated pleasure vanishes, especially if it have been won easily!' He will have to educate her in the ways of London; he must think of his own sister's probable reaction; he may have 'sold himself too cheaply'. As time passes, these objections loom larger. Trollope feels compelled to anticipate his reader's reaction: ' "Then he was a brute," you say, my pretty reader. I have never said that he was not a brute. But this I remark, that many such brutes are to be met with in the beaten paths of the world's high highway.' It thus becomes inevitable that pride and prejudice will drive them asunder: her pride rejecting the view that class distinctions must be weighed in the balance as well as love; his prejudice that her marriage to him will be 'a leap upwards'. Destiny demands that in their later years they remain true to themselves. We are not surprised to learn that Patty, deprived of 'romance', dedicates herself to selfless service for others, or that Captain Broughton marries a 'great heiress' and turns into 'a useful member of Parliament, working on committees three or four days a week with zeal that is indefatigable'.

'A Little Grey Glove' is told by a 'sex-shy' young man whose 'book of life' began with a frustrated yearning for a barmaid; he is spared the disillusionment of a marriage that could not have succeeded: she jilts him in favour of a pork butcher. He remains an innocent, unable to move far beyond the novels about women which he studies 'in order to get some definite data before venturing amongst them'. George Egerton, who wrote some of the most searingly candid short stories of her generation, insists that we recognize the splendid diversity of women. It does not take long for her 'hero' to realize that the division made by Victorian authors of all women 'into good-uns and bad-uns' has limited utility (in other words, there is still some hope for him). For years he pursues 'the Eternal Feminine', only to give up the chase as hopeless. For twelve years he wanders the world, a confirmed bachelor. He meets unexpectedly an interesting woman; more precisely, she casts a fly while fishing, and the hook catches in the lobe of his ear; and he falls in love. But the circumstances of her married life – which has but recently ended in divorce – prevent her from responding with a light heart to his advances. George Egerton suggests, however obliquely, that the status of a divorced woman in Victorian England is very ill-defined. The lady with a grey glove (we never learn her name) orders her priorities in a way that can only disconcert the middle-aging protagonist. She intends, first of all, to redefine her existence as 'a free woman' before she will think again of marriage. She likes, but does not love, the narrator. As in Trollope's story, the heroine chooses not to commit herself.

'The Woman Beater' presents us with a marvellously precise picture of a 'tease'. Zangwill, popular at the turn of the century but perhaps never to be so again, was often less than subtle in sketching characters, but not in this story. The romance between John Lefolle and Winifred Glamorys is more one-sided than Lefolle realizes. The reader will not fully appreciate the hopelessness of his aspirations until the story's surprising twist at the end. The chosen point of view, that of an Oxford tutor hopelessly besotted over a sophisticated woman with a somewhat mysterious background ('She was better than a poetess, she was a poem') brings us again to a sense of the awesome difficulties inherent in explaining why some courtships succeed and others do not. Some readers will enjoy the running anecdote about the woefully prepared student who finally collapses under the ferocity of his three grand inquisitors. Others will want to re-read Mrs Glamorys's comments on marriage and divorce in order to appreciate better her seven types of ambiguity. Yet others will trace still one more time the stages in a hero's growing perception of a failed courtship. Again, the man is helpless in the face of a woman's determination to make her own way in the world.

Yet, as we know, courtships often do end in marriage, that 'great beginning'. I have selected as an example of one courtship that will turn out well for both man and woman – at least we have grounds for believing that it will do so – one of Hubert Crackanthorpe's most successful stories, 'Anthony Garstin's Courtship'. Altogether grimmer as a figure than Hardy's Gabriel Oak in *Far from the Madding Crowd*, Garstin is described uncompromisingly when we first see him herding his sheep in treeless country. It takes some time before his more attractive features, his vulnerability, and his humanness, become visible. He is an intriguing example of the new subject-matter that moved in with the techniques of naturalistic story-telling. His troubled relationship to his mother is premonitory of the difficulties he will encounter in wooing Rosa Blencarn. Since his is a joyless existence, he has no right to expect Rosa, already entangled with the brutish peasant Luke Stock, to love him, particularly since she knows of Mrs Garstin's bitter disdain for her. This is a story of a forty-six-year-old man who, against the odds, inherits his true love. It is salutary to compare his vision of married domesticity, dreamed after he receives Mr Blencarn's blessing, with Jane Eyre's description of two hearts beating as one (quoted at the beginning of this Introduction): the grittier honesty of the former may serve to counter the extraordinary gush of the latter.

Courtships that end unsuccessfully or with a certain prospect of continuing married friction should depress us. Curiously, however, this should not be our reaction after reading these five stories. Rather, a conviction of the value of self-determination – of the capability to work out one's destiny as a man or as a woman – becomes exhilarating by story's end in each case. These are all ordinary people, ungifted, obscurely resident in their respective corners of England, anxiously seeking love, but increasingly self-aware as they define the reasons why a given relationship can endure, or why it must be ended.

The middle section, which deals with five failed marriages, is representative of a very large number of short stories that diagnose the problems of inequality of the sexes in late Victorian England. Rudyard Kipling's 'turn-over' for the newspaper *Civil and Military Gazette* of Lahore, India (a 'turn-over' is a short journalistic piece that begins on page one and continues inside the issue), comes at the very beginning of his astonishing career. It introduces us to the policeman Strickland, whose exploits in disguises of various kinds are recounted in six stories as well as in *Kim*. It is not one of the more well-known stories in the Kipling canon, but the manner of its telling is very characteristic of the early Kipling ('The Bronckhorst Divorce-Case' is one of the stories in *Plain Tales from the Hills*), and the ending, with its unanswerable question, 'How do women like Mrs Bronckhorst come to marry men like Bronckhorst?', may serve as signature for the other four stories of unsuccessful marriages. It is a puzzlement (as the King of Siam more than once remarked), and a puzzlement for marriages in the West as well as in the inscrutable East. The Bronckhorsts are married when the story begins, and Mrs Bronckhorst is already desperately unhappy. Kipling does not speculate either why she at one time thought her suitor sufficiently attractive to accept his proposal of marriage, or why he now behaves so much like a cur and blackguard toward her.

Ella D'Arcy's 'Irremediable' sketches for us the probable outcome of the marriage that George Egerton's undergraduate might have contracted with a barmaid (in 'A Little Grey Glove'). Willoughby's range of experience is not sufficiently wide that he can identify in Esther the evidences of a slattern that will inevitably destroy his marriage. D'Arcy makes a strong point of Willoughby's naivety: 'Like many intelligent young men, he had dabbled a little in Socialism, and at one time had wandered among the dispossessed; but since then, had caught up and held loosely the new doctrine – it is a good and fitting thing that Woman also should earn her bread by the sweat of her brow.' Theory divorced from common sense ill-prepares any young man for the stern realities of marriage. His affection for Esther, based on his admiration of her as a 'working daughter of the people', will not survive (he himself earns only £130 a year). Anton Chekhov, in 'The Lady with a Dog', has recorded a comparable moment of realization for the greying hero of an adulterous affair, who comes to see that he is locked forever into a hopeless situation. D'Arcy underscores the poignance of the hero's coming to understand that Love itself has turned into Hatred – he is only twenty-six years old, with perhaps another half-century to go.

Arthur Morrison's *Tales of Mean Streets* (1894) is a compulsively readable collection of stories that depict London slums with an unrelenting honesty. '"A Poor Stick"', about one man's 'courtship-blindness', tells us perhaps more than we wish to know about a woman (his wife) who 'stayed out or came home as she chose, and cooked a dinner or didn't, as her inclination stood'. Morrison is almost clinical in his sketching of a workingman's grim condition after a full decade of marriage. Robert Jennings will never see 'Jinnins', his wife, for what she is. He will remain till the day of his death 'a poor stick', in the eyes of his wife and in those of the entire community. The interest of the story may lie in our attempt to understand why, after being deserted by a wife who has run off with the lodger, Bob still clings to his remembered image of a beautiful, good-hearted woman who 'ought to married a swell' instead of himself. Why does he continue to believe in her? Again, we receive no answer from the author, whose primary responsibility is discharged when he convinces us that such people really do exist, and have their own reasons for behaving as they do.

Arthur Conan Doyle's story about an adventure of Sherlock Holmes was written before its author began his ten-year presidency of the society for the reform of the divorce law, but no reader can escape Doyle's intense conviction that Sir Eustace Brackenstall (the murdered victim) has no moral right to brutalize his wife; if the laws of England allowed him to do so, there was something dreadfully wrong with them, and they should be changed. (This is one of two stories in which Holmes allows the murderer to escape justice.) Sir Eustace was a confirmed drunkard, his wife tells Holmes and Watson. 'To be with such a man for an hour is unpleasant. Can you imagine what it means for a sensitive and high-spirited woman to be tied to him for day and night? It is a sacrilege, a crime, a villainy to hold that such a marriage is binding. I say that these monstrous laws of yours will bring a curse upon the land – God will not let such wickedness endure.' Her eyes blaze 'from under the terrible mark upon her brow' (Sir Eustace was a wife-beater), and Holmes's indignation at the pain she has suffered is correspondingly intense.

Mr Archibald Jordan, the supposedly permanent bachelor of 'The Prize Lodger', by George Gissing, is one of a very large number of single men in lodging-houses. Like them, he seeks to control his fate by moving, at regular intervals, from one lodging to another, so that he will not be beholden to any single landlady. For a full quarter of a century he escapes matrimonial entanglements. But when he meets Mrs Elderfield, the 'admirable land-lady', his fate is sealed. She seems to satisfy his every need almost before he becomes conscious of it; her bills are moderate; she cooks well; she maintains a clean establishment. I leave to the reader the series of discoveries – each more horrendous than the next – which Mr Jordan makes after he marries, but hasten to assure those who are still unfamiliar with the formidable talents of George Gissing that the humour of the situation, though grim, is genuine, and that this failed marriage exhibits an engaging sardonic wit.

It would be mischievous to suggest the existence of a wide-spread conviction, on the part of story-tellers, that the truths about marriage were uniformly bleak. Statistically, the number of failed Victorian marriages, whether they led to divorce proceed-ings or not, cannot be said to have been greater than the number of marriages in which necessary accommodations were made, children were brought into the world and raised with tender loving care, and husbands enjoyed the company of their wives. This collection concludes with five stories about marriages that worked reasonably well, or even better than that. The first such tale, 'The Manchester Marriage', is particularly interesting. It appeared in a Christmas number of *Household Words*, the periodical edited by Charles Dickens. It is a commercially crafted statement of the good intentions of a representative merchant hailing from Lancashire, who has come to London to run a warehouse for his manufacturing firm. Mr Openshaw will impress many readers as a bully who dominates his gentle wife Alice, and who is all too conscious of his own virtues as head of the household.

Mrs Gaskell works with a situation familiar to all readers of Victorian fiction, that of the sailor-husband who disappears at sea and is not heard from for many years, and who turns up disconcertingly after his 'widow' has remarried. But Mrs Gaskell's chief interest does not reside there. She concerns herself first with the delight that overcomes Mr Openshaw when he discovers that his landlady is diligent and solicitous of his comfort; then with his growing tenderness for Alice's child by her first husband, who is presumed dead; and with his benevolence for Norah, Alice's servant. All this kindness lies hidden beneath a gruff exterior. But the reappearance of Alice's first husband in the child's bedroom (at night) under suspicious circumstances, while the Openshaws are away from home, and the disappearance of a valuable brooch that instantly creates in Mr Openshaw's mind a suspicion of Norah, provides a test of character that in turn becomes a means of testing the strength of the Manchester marriage. The specific details of how Mr Openshaw comes through with flying colours may be left to the reader, but never once does Mr Openshaw suspect or accuse his wife of committing a serious transgression. His concern at all times is the protection of his family. Having learned the error of his ways and the unjustness of his suspicions of Norah, he finds that his love for Alice becomes transmuted into something even finer: 'Towards Alice he could hardly be more kind than he had always been; but he now seemed to look upon her as someone sacred, and to be treated with reverence, as well as tenderness.'

Thomas Hardy's 'A Mere Interlude' describes marriage in two ways immediately recognizable to readers of the Wessex novels: as a romantic fantasy, no more substantial than a dream, and as a set of compromises by both husband and wife, compromises that must be mutually accepted if the relationship is to endure. Baptista Trewthen (the name is an interesting variant of 'truth') is a young woman temperamentally unsuited for teaching. She becomes entangled in an unfortunate first marriage that, by a series of convincing details, she learns to forget. Later, after she marries David Hedeggan, whom she does not love, she reconciles herself to the task of educating his four daughters. In Hardy's memorable language, she enters her 'serener season' with a 'chastened spirit', and her marriage develops into 'a sterling friendship at least, between a pair in whose existence there had threatened to be neither friendship nor love'. That, Hardy implies, may be the best possible outcome; more may not reasonably be expected or demanded.

'A Faithful Heart' may depict a situation more common in Victorian society than many readers appreciate: the husband who keeps his wife very much like a mistress, largely because his family does not approve of the woman in question, and partly because he is not a wholly admirable character. George Moore sensitively, with even-handed sympathy, shows us how a married and impoverished couple can learn to live under intolerable pressures. Major Charles Shepherd, his wife, and his little daughter are unimportant in any larger scheme of things, and perhaps somewhat colourless as personalities; but there can be no question of the strength of the love ties here. 'She had noticed that her economies endeared her to the Major, and it was pleasant to please him. Hers was a kind-hearted, simple nature, that misfortune had brought down in the world; but, as is not uncommon with persons of weak character, she possessed a clear, sensible mind which allowed her to see things in their true lights, and without difficulty she recognized the unalterable nature of her case.'

The last two stories deal with deception, the necessary lies that make marriage possible. Walter Besant's 'The Solid Gold Reef Company, Limited' is the most cheerfully cynical story in this anthology. Besant, though more than half-forgotten today, was a well-known personality in the fading years of his century, and his novel *All in a Garden Fair* was the direct cause of Rudyard Kipling's becoming inspired to leave India in order to make a run at success in England. Rosie is determined to marry well (her father wants all his money for himself), and has already rejected several suitors who, for one reason or another, have proved unsatisfactory. The last, Lord Evergreen, had a title; Rosie would have enjoyed that; but he was too old, and science could not keep him alive long enough for the wedding. Rosie's father, through an unscrupulous financial manœuvre, insures the ability of his daughter's current suitor – an 'impulsive, emotional nature' who, in Rosie's shrewd assessment, 'doesn't understand the City' – to provide Rosie with the life-style she demands. Reggie marries Rosie. The last we hear from him are the words, 'I wish all the world were as happy as you and me.' But Rosie, who knows better than he about the 'poor devils' of the world, will shield Reggie from learning more about them.

Henry James also seems to suggest that for some marriages a decent series of lies is needed to keep them afloat. 'The Tree of Knowledge' presents us with familiar Jamesian types: the honourable bachelor who loves another man's wife, but will not declare himself, the husband who fatuously believes in his own (non-existent) talent, the wife who knows how to measure reality and who, like the bachelor, keeps silent about what she knows. The complicating factor here is the son Lance, whose discovery of Peter Brench's silent, long-suffering love for his mother leads in turn to Peter's discovery that Mrs Mallow has known all along. The wonder of it all is that nothing significant in any relationship delineated here will change. The Brenches, we feel sure, will continue happily as before, nourished by the deceptions that politeness and social habit require.

Courtship and marriage, then, are limned in Victorian short stories with a surprising candour, not to mention art. In the last quarter-century of the Queen's reign especially do the number of women characters expand – delightfully, excitingly – beyond a few shopworn images. These are not merely New Women, as that term was used in the sunset years of Victorianism, but rather women who, in their complexity of motive and action, more accurately mirror the kinds of people who were fighting to assert their individuality throughout the second half of the century. As the lot of women generally improved, so did the variety and literary value of short stories dealing with romance and its ensuing complications.

1. R. C. Terry, *Victorian Popular Fiction, 1860–80* (London: Macmillan Press, 1983), is particularly good on Mudie's Select Library of Fiction, but all of Chapter 1, 'Reading Mania', and Chapter 2, 'The

Fiction Industry', provides useful background information about reading habits in Victorian England.

2. George Watt, *The Fallen Woman in the Nineteenth-Century English Novel* (London: Croom Helm, 1984), pp. 172–80.

3. Sally Mitchell, *The Fallen Angel/Chastity, Class and Women's Reading, 1835–1880* (Bowling Green, Ohio: Bowling Green University Popular Press, 1981), pp. x–xi.

4. Patricia Stubbs, *Women and Fiction/Feminism and the Novel 1880—1920* (Sussex: Harvester Press, 1979), p. 4.

5. Shirley Foster, *Victorian Women's Fiction: Marriage, Freedom, and the Individual* (London: Croom Helm, 1985), p. 7.

6. Pierre Nordon, *Conan Doyle/A Biography* (New York: Holt, Rinehart and Winston, 1967), pp. 67–9.

7. Françoise Basch, *Relative Creatures/Victorian Women in Society and the Novel* (New York: Holt, Rinehart and Winston, 1967), pp. xvi–xvii.

8. ibid., pp. 21–2.

9. Nordon, op. cit.

10. Lloyd Fernando, *'New Women' in the late Victorian Novel* (University Park: Pennsylvania State University Press, 1977), pp. 4–5.

11. ibid., p. 2.

12. Jenni Calder, *Women and Marriage in Victorian Fiction* (London: Thames and Hudson, 1976), p. 195.

STORIES OF COURTSHIP

ANGELA
An Inverted Love Story

(*The Century Magazine*, September 1890)

I am a poor paralysed fellow who, for many years past, has been confined to a bed or a sofa. For the last six years I have occupied a small room, giving on to one of the side canals of Venice, and having no one about me but a deaf old woman, who makes my bed and attends to my food; and there I eke out a poor income of about thirty pounds a year by making water-colour drawings of flowers and fruit (they are the cheapest models in Venice), and these I send to a friend in London, who sells them to a dealer for small sums. But, on the whole, I am happy and content.

It is necessary that I should describe the position of my room rather minutely. Its only window is about five feet above the water of the canal, and above it the house projects some six feet, and overhangs the water, the projecting portion being supported by stout piles driven into the bed of the canal. This arrangement has the disadvantage (among others) of so limiting my upward view that I am unable to see more than about ten feet of the height of the house immediately opposite to me, although, by reaching as far out of the window as my infirmity will permit, I can see for a considerable distance up and down the canal, which does not exceed fifteen feet in width. But, although I can see but little of the material house opposite, I can see its reflection upside down in the canal, and I take a good deal of inverted interest in such of its inhabitants as show themselves from time to time (always upside down) on its balconies and at its windows.

When I first occupied my room, about six years ago, my attention was directed to the reflection of a little girl of thirteen or so (as nearly as I could judge), who passed every day on a balcony just above the upward range of my limited field of view. She had a glass of flowers and a crucifix on a little table by her side; and as she sat there, in fine weather, from early morning until dark,

working assiduously all the time, I concluded that she earned her
living by needle-work. She was certainly an industrious little girl,
and, as far as I could judge by her upside-down reflection, neat in
her dress and pretty. She had an old mother, an invalid, who, on
warm days, would sit on the balcony with her, and it interested me
to see the little maid wrap the old lady in shawls, and bring pillows
for her chair, and a stool for her feet, and every now and again lay
down her work and kiss and fondle the old lady for half a minute,
and then take up her work again.

Time went by, and as the little maid grew up, her reflection
grew down, and at last she was quite a little woman of, I suppose,
sixteen or seventeen. I can only work for a couple of hours or so in
the brightest part of the day, so I had plenty of time on my hands
in which to watch her movements, and sufficient imagination to
weave a little romance about her, and to endow her with a beauty
which, to a great extent, I had to take for granted. I saw – or
fancied that I could see – that she began to take an interest in *my*
reflection (which, of course, she could see as I could see hers); and
one day, when it appeared to me that she was looking right at it –
that is to say when her reflection appeared to be looking right at
me – I tried the desperate experiment of nodding to her, and to my
intense delight her reflection nodded in reply. And so our two
reflections became known to one another.

It did not take me very long to fall in love with her, but a long
time passed before I could make up my mind to do more than nod
to her every morning, when the old woman moved me from my
bed to the sofa at the window, and again in the evening, when the
little maid left the balcony for that day. One day, however, when I
saw her reflection looking at mine, I nodded to her, and threw a
flower into the canal. She nodded several times in return, and I
saw her direct her mother's attention to the incident. Then every
morning I threw a flower into the water for 'good morning', and
another in the evening for 'goodnight', and I soon discovered that
I had not altogether thrown them in vain, for one day she threw a
flower to join mine, and she laughed and clapped her hands when
she saw the two flowers join forces and float away together. And
then every morning and every evening she threw her flower when I
threw mine, and when the two flowers met she clapped her hands,
and so did I; but when they were separated, as they sometimes

were, owing to one of them having met an obstruction which did not catch the other, she threw up her hands in a pretty affectation of despair, which I tried to imitate but in an English and unsuccessful fashion. And when they were rudely run down by a passing gondola (which happened not unfrequently) she pretended to cry, and I did the same. Then, in pretty pantomime, she would point downwards to the sky to tell me that it was Destiny that had caused the shipwreck of our flowers, and I, in pantomime, not nearly so pretty, would try to convey to her that Destiny would be kinder next time, and that perhaps tomorrow our flowers would be more fortunate – and so the innocent courtship went on. One day she showed me her crucifix and kissed it, and thereupon I took a little silver crucifix that always stood by me, and kissed that, and so she knew that we were one in religion.

One day the little maid did not appear on her balcony, and for several days I saw nothing of her; and although I threw my flowers as usual, no flower came to keep it company. However, after a time, she reappeared, dressed in black, and crying often, and then I knew that the poor child's mother was dead, and, as far as I knew, she was alone in the world. The flowers came no more for many days, nor did she show any sign of recognition, but kept her eyes on her work, except when she placed her handkerchief to them. And opposite to her was the old lady's chair, and I could see that, from time to time, she would lay down her work and gaze at it, and then a flood of tears would come to her relief. But at last one day she roused herself to nod to me, and then her flower came, day by day, and my flower went forth to join it, and with varying fortunes the two flowers sailed away as of yore.

But the darkest day of all to me was when a good-looking young gondolier, standing right end uppermost in his gondola (for I could see *him* in the flesh), worked his craft alongside the house, and stood talking to her as she sat on the balcony. They seemed to speak as old friends – indeed, as well as I could make out, he held her by the hand during the whole of their interview which lasted quite half an hour. Eventually he pushed off, and left my heart heavy within me. But I soon took heart of grace, for as soon as he was out of sight, the little maid threw two flowers growing on the same stem – an allegory of which I could make nothing, until it broke upon me that she meant to convey to me that he and she were brother and sister, and that I had no cause to be sad. And thereupon I nodded to her cheerily, and she nodded to me, and laughed aloud, and I laughed in return, and all went on again as before.

Then came a dark and dreary time, for it became necessary that I should undergo treatment that confined me absolutely to my bed for many days, and I worried and fretted to think that the little maid and I should see each other no longer, and worse still, that she would think that I had gone away without even hinting to her that I was going. And I lay awake at night wondering how I could let her know the truth, and fifty plans flitted through my brain, all appearing to be feasible enough at night, but absolutely wild and impracticable in the morning. One day – and it was a bright day indeed for me – the old woman who tended me told me that a gondolier had inquired whether the English signor had gone away or had died; and so I learnt that the little maid had been anxious about me, and that she had sent her brother to inquire, and the brother had no doubt taken to her the reason of my protracted absence from the window.

From that day, and ever after during my three weeks of bed-keeping, a flower was found every morning on the ledge of my window, which was within easy reach of anyone in a boat; and when at last a day came when I could be moved, I took my accustomed place on my sofa at the window, and the little maid saw me, and stood on her head (so to speak) and clapped her hands upside down with a delight that was as eloquent as my right-end-up delight could be. And so the first time the gondolier passed my window I beckoned to him, and he pushed alongside, and told me, with many bright smiles, that he was glad indeed to see me well again. Then I thanked him and his sister for their many kind thoughts about me during my retreat, and I then learnt from him that her name was Angela, and that she was the best and purest maiden in all Venice, and that anyone might think himself happy indeed who could call her sister, but that he was happier even than her brother, for he was to be married to her, and indeed they were to be married the next day.

Thereupon my heart seemed to swell to bursting, and the blood rushed through my veins so that I could hear it and nothing else for a while. I managed at last to stammer forth some words of awkward congratulation, and he left me, singing merrily, after asking permission to bring his bride to see me on the morrow as they returned from church.

'For', said he, 'my Angela has known you very long – ever since she was a child, and she has often spoken to me of the poor Englishman who was a good Catholic, and who lay all day long for years and years on a sofa at a window, and she had said over and over again how dearly she wished she could speak to him and comfort him; and one day, when you threw a flower into the canal, she asked me whether she might throw another, and I told her yes, for he would understand that it meant sympathy for one sorely afflicted.'

And so I learned that it was pity, and not love, except indeed such love as is akin to pity, that prompted her to interest herself in my welfare, and there was an end of it all.

For the two flowers that I thought were on one stem were two flowers tied together (but I could not tell that), and they were meant to indicate that she and the gondolier were affianced lovers, and my expressed pleasure at this symbol delighted her, for she took it to mean that I rejoiced in her happiness.

And the next day the gondolier came with a train of other gondoliers, all decked in their holiday garb, and on his gondola sat Angela, happy, and blushing at her happiness. Then he and she entered the house in which I dwelt, and came into my room (and it was strange indeed, after so many years of inversion, to see her with her head above her feet!), and then she wished me happiness and a speedy restoration to good health (which could never be); and I in broken words and with tears in my eyes, gave her the little silver crucifix that had stood by my bed or my table for so many years. And Angela took it reverently, and crossed herself, and kissed it, and so departed with her delighted husband.

And as I heard the song of the gondoliers as they went their way – the song dying away in the distance as the shadows of the sundown closed around me – I felt that they were singing the requiem of the only love that had ever entered my heart.

Anthony Trollope

THE PARSON'S DAUGHTER OF OXNEY COLNE

(*London Review*, 2 March 1861)

The prettiest scenery in all England – and if I am contradicted in that assertion, I will say in all Europe – is in Devonshire, on the southern and southeastern skirts of Dartmoor, where the rivers Dart and Avon and Teign form themselves, and where the broken moor is half cultivated, and the wild-looking uplands fields are half moor. In making this assertion I am often met with much doubt, but it is by persons who do not really know the locality. Men and women talk to me on the matter who have travelled down the line of railway from Exeter to Plymouth, who have spent a fortnight at Torquay, and perhaps made an excursion from Tavistock to the convict prison on Dartmoor. But who knows the glories of Chagford? Who has walked through the parish of Manaton? Who is conversant with Lustleigh Cleeves and Withycombe in the moor? Who has explored Holne Chase? Gentle reader, believe me that you will be rash in contradicting me unless you have done these things.

There or thereabouts – I will not say by the waters of which little river it is washed – is the parish of Oxney Colne. And for those who would wish to see all the beauties of this lovely country a sojourn in Oxney Colne would be most desirable, seeing that the sojourner would then be brought nearer to all that he would delight to visit, than at any other spot in the country. But there is an objection to any such arrangement. There are only two decent houses in the whole parish, and these are – or were when I knew the locality – small and fully occupied by their possessors. The larger and better is the parsonage in which lived the parson and his daughter; and the smaller is the freehold residence of a certain Miss Le Smyrger, who owned a farm of a hundred acres which was rented by one Farmer Cloysey, and who also possessed some thirty acres round her own house which she managed herself, regarding herself to be quite as great in cream as Mr Cloysey, and altogether superior to him in the article of cider. 'But yeu has to pay no rent, Miss,' Farmer Cloysey would say, when Miss Le Smyrger expressed this opinion of her art in a manner too defiant. 'Yeu pays no rent, or yeu couldn't do it.' Miss Le Smyrger was an old maid, with a pedigree and blood of her own, a hundred and thirty acres of fee-simple land on the borders of Dartmoor, fifty years of age, a constitution of iron, and an opinion of her own on every subject under the sun.

And now for the parson and his daughter. The parson's name was Woolsworthy – or Woolathy as it was pronounced by all those who lived around him – the Rev. Saul Woolsworthy; and his daughter was Patience Woolsworthy, or Miss Patty, as she was known to the Devonshire world of those parts. That name of Patience had not been well chosen for her for she was a hot-tempered damsel, warm in her convictions, and inclined to express them freely. She had but two closely intimate friends in the world, and by both of them this freedom of expression had been fully permitted to her since she was a child. Miss Le Smyrger and her father were well accustomed to her ways, and on the whole well satisfied with them. The former was equally free and equally warm-tempered as herself, and as Mr Woolsworthy was allowed by his daughter to be quite paramount on his own subject – for he had a subject – he did not object to his daughter being paramount on all others. A pretty girl was Patience Woolsworthy at the time of which I am writing, and one who possessed much that was worthy of remark and admiration had she lived where beauty meets with admiration, or where force of character is remarked. But at Oxney Colne, on the borders of Dartmoor, there were few to appreciate her, and it seemed as though she herself had but little idea of carrying her talent further afield, so that it might not remain for ever wrapped in a blanket.

She was a pretty girl, tall and slender, with dark eyes and black hair. Her eyes were perhaps too round for regular beauty, and her hair was perhaps too crisp; her mouth was large and expressive; her nose was finely formed, though a critic in female form might have declared it to be somewhat broad. But her countenance altogether was very attractive – if only it might be seen without that resolution for dominion which occasionally marred it, though sometimes it even added to her attractions.

It must be confessed on behalf of Patience Woolsworthy that the circumstances of her life had peremptorily called upon her to exercise dominion. She had lost her mother when she was sixteen, and had had neither brother nor sister. She had no neighbours near her fit either from education or rank to interfere in the conduct of her life, excepting always Miss Le Smyrger. Miss Le Smyrger would have done anything for her, including the whole management of her morals and of the parsonage household, had Patience been content with such an arrangement. But much as Patience had ever loved Miss Le Smyrger, she was not content with this, and therefore she had been called on to put forth a strong hand of her own. She had put forth this strong hand early, and hence had come the character which I am attempting to describe. But I must say on behalf of this girl that it was not only over others that she thus exercised dominion. In acquiring that power she had also acquired the much greater power of exercising rule over herself.

But why should her father have been ignored in these family arrangements? Perhaps it may almost suffice to say, that of all living men her father was the man best conversant with the antiquities of the county in which he lived. He was the Jonathan Oldbuck of Devonshire, and especially of Dartmoor, – but without that decision of character which enabled Oldbuck to keep his womenkind in some kind of subjection, and probably enabled him also to see that his weekly bill did not pass their proper limits. Our Mr Oldbuck, of Oxney Colne, was sadly deficient in these respects. As a parish pastor with but a small cure he did his duty with sufficient energy to keep him, at any rate, from reproach. He was kind and charitable to the poor, punctual in his services, forbearing with the farmers around him, mild with his brother clergymen, and indifferent to aught that bishop or archdeacon might think or say of him. I do not name this latter attribute as a virtue, but as a fact. But all these points were as nothing in the known character of Mr Woolsworthy, of Oxney Colne. He was the antiquarian of Dartmoor. That was his line of life. It was in that capacity that he was known to the Devonshire world; it was as such that he journeyed about with his humble carpetbag, staying away from his parsonage a night or two at a time; it was in that character that he received now and again stray visitors in the single spare bedroom – not friends asked to see him and his girl because of their friendship – but men who knew something as to this buried stone, or that old land-mark. In all these things his daughter let him have his own way, assisting and encouraging him. That was his line of life, and therefore she respected it. But in all other matters she chose to be paramount at the parsonage.

Mr Woolsworthy was a little man, who always wore, except on Sundays, grey clothes – clothes of so light a grey that they would hardly have been regarded as clerical in a district less remote. He had now reached a goodly age, being full seventy years old; but still he was wiry and active, and shewed but few symptoms of decay. His head was bald, and the few remaining locks that surrounded it were nearly white. But there was a look of energy about his mouth, and a humour in his light grey eye, which forbade those who knew him to regard him altogether as an old man. As it was, he could walk from Oxney Colne to Priestown, fifteen long Devonshire miles across the moor; and he who could do that could hardly be regarded as too old for work.

But our present story will have more to do with his daughter than with him. A pretty girl, I have said, was Patience Woolsworthy; and one, too, in many ways remarkable. She had taken her outlook into life, weighing the things which she had and those which she had not, in a manner very unusual, and, as a rule, not always desirable for a young lady. The things which she had not were very many. She had not society; she had not a fortune; she had not any assurance of future means of livelihood; she had not high hope of procuring for herself a position in life by marriage; she had not that excitement and pleasure in life which she read of in such books as found their way down to Oxney Colne Parsonage. It would be easy to add to the list of the things which she had not; and this list against herself she made out with the utmost vigour. The things which she had, or those rather which she assured herself of having, were much more easily counted. She had the birth and education of a lady, the strength of a healthy woman, and a will of her own. Such was the list as she made it out for herself, and I protest that I assert no more than the truth in saying that she never added to it either beauty, wit, or talent.

I began these descriptions by saying that Oxney Colne would, of all places, be the best spot from which a tourist could visit those parts of Devonshire, but for the fact that he could obtain there none of the accommodation which tourists require. A brother antiquarian might, perhaps, in those days have done so, seeing that there was, as I have said, a spare bedroom at the parsonage. Any intimate friend of Miss Le Smyrger's might be as fortunate, for she was also so provided at Oxney Combe, by which name her house was known. But Miss Le Smyrger was not given to extensive hospitality, and it was only to those who were bound to her, either by ties of blood or of very old friendship, that she delighted to open her doors. As her old friends were very few in number, as those few lived at a distance, and as her nearest relations were higher in the world than she was, and were said by herself to look down upon her, the visits made to Oxney Combe were few and far between.

But now, at the period of which I am writing, such a visit was about to be made. Miss Le Smyrger had a younger sister who had inherited a property in the parish of Oxney Colne equal to that of the lady who lived there; but this younger sister had inherited beauty also, and she therefore, in early life, had found sundry lovers, one of whom became her husband. She had married a man even then well to do in the world, but now rich and almost mighty; a Member of Parliament, a Lord of this and that board, a man who had a house in Eaton Square, and a park in the north of England; and in this way her course of life had been very much divided from that of our Miss Le Smyrger. But the Lord of the Government board had been blessed with various children, and perhaps it was now thought expedient to look after Aunt Penelope's Devonshire acres. Aunt Penelope was empowered to leave them to whom she pleased; and though it was thought in Eaton Square that she must, as a matter of course, leave them to one of the family, nevertheless a little cousinly intercourse might make the thing more certain. I will not say that this was the sole cause for such a visit, but in these days a visit was to be made by Captain Broughton to his aunt. Now Captain John Broughton was the second son of Alfonso Broughton, of Clapham Park and

Eaton Square, Member of Parliament, and Lord of the aforesaid Government Board.

And what do you mean to do with him? Patience Woolsworthy asked of Miss Le Smyrger when that lady walked over from the Combe to say that her nephew John was to arrive on the following morning.

'Do with him? Why, I shall bring him over here to talk to your father.'

'He'll be too fashionable for that, and papa won't trouble his head about him if he finds that he doesn't care for Dartmoor.'

'Then he may fall in love with you, my dear.'

'Well, yes; there's that resource at any rate, and for your sake I dare say I should be more civil to him than papa. But he'll soon get tired of making love to me, and what you'll do then I cannot imagine.'

That Miss Woolsworthy felt no interest in the coming of the Captain I will not pretend to say. The advent of any stranger with whom she would be called on to associate must be matter of interest to her in that secluded place; and she was not so absolutely unlike other young ladies that the arrival of an unmarried young man would be the same to her as the advent of some patriarchal pater-familias. In taking that outlook into life of which I have spoken she had never said to herself that she despised those things from which other girls received the excitement, the joys, and the disappointment of their lives. She had simply given herself to understand that very little of such things would come in her way, and that it behoved her to live – to live happily if such might be possible – without experiencing the need of them. She had heard, when there was no thought of any such visit to Oxney Colne, that John Broughton was a handsome clever man – one who thought much of himself and was thought much of by others – that there had been some talk of his marrying a great heiress, which marriage, however had not taken place through unwillingness on his part, and that he was on the whole a man of more mark in the world than the ordinary captains of ordinary regiments.

Captain Broughton came to Oxney Combe, stayed there a fortnight – the intended period for his projected visit having been fixed at three or four days – and then went his way. He went his way back to his London haunts, the time of the year then being the close of the Easter holy-days; but as he did so he told his aunt that he should assuredly return to her in the autumn.

'And assuredly I shall be happy to see you, John – if you come with a certain purpose. If you have no such purpose, you had better remain away.'

'I shall assuredly come,' the Captain had replied, and then he had gone on his journey.

The summer passed rapidly by, and very little was said between Miss Le Smyrger and Miss Woolsworthy about Captain Broughton. In many respects – nay, I may say, as to all ordinary matters, – no two women could well be more intimate with each other than they were; and more than that, they had the courage each to talk to the other with absolute truth as to things concerning themselves – a courage in which dear friends often fail. But, nevertheless, very little was said between them about Captain John Broughton. All that was said may be here repeated.

'John says that he shall return here in August,' Miss Le Smyrger said as Patience was sitting with her in the parlour at Oxney Combe, on the morning after that gentleman's departure.

'He told me so himself,' said Patience; and as she spoke her round dark eyes assumed a look of more than ordinary self-will. If Miss Le Smyrger had intended to carry the conversation any further she changed her mind as she looked at her companion. Then, as I said, the summer ran by, and towards the close of the warm days of July, Miss Le Smyrger, sitting in the same chair in the same room, again took up the conversation.

'I got a letter from John this morning. He says that he shall be here on the third.'

'Does he?'

'He is very punctual to the time he named.'

'Yes; I fancy that he is a punctual man,' said Patience.

'I hope that you will be glad to see him,' said Miss Le Smyrger.

'Very glad to see him,' said Patience, with a bold clear voice; and then the conversation was again dropped, and nothing further was said till after Captain Broughton's second arrival in the parish.

Four months had then passed since his departure, and during that time Miss Woolsworthy had performed all her usual daily duties in their accustomed course. No one could discover that she had been less careful in her household matters than had been her wont, less willing to go among her poor neighbours, or less assiduous in her attentions to her father. But not the less was there a feeling in the minds of those around her that some great change had come upon her. She would sit during the long summer evenings on a certain spot ouside the parsonage orchard, at the top of a small sloping field in which their solitary cow was always pastured, with a book on her knees before her, but rarely reading. There she would sit, with the beautiful view down to the winding river below her, watching the setting sun, and thinking, thinking, thinking – thinking of something of which she had never spoken. Often would Miss Le Smyrger come upon her there, and sometimes would pass her even without a word; but never – never once did she dare to ask of the matter of her thoughts. But she knew the matter well enough. No confession was necessary to inform her that Patience Woolsworthy was in love with John Broughton – ay, in love, to the full and entire loss of her whole heart.

On one evening she was so sitting till the July sun had fallen and hidden himself for the night, when her father came upon her as he returned from one of his rambles on the moor. 'Patty,' he said, 'you are always sitting there now. Is it not late? Will you not be cold?'

'No papa,' she said, 'I shall not be cold.'

'But won't you come to the house? I miss you when you come in so late that there's no time to say a word before we go to bed.'

She got up and followed him into the parsonage, and when they were in the sitting-room together, and the door was closed, she came up to him and kissed him. 'Papa,' she said, 'would it make you very unhappy if I were to leave you?'

'Leave me!' he said, startled by the serious and almost solemn tone of her voice. 'Do you mean for always?'

'If I were to marry, papa?'

'Oh, marry! No; that would not make me unhappy. It would make me very happy, Patty, to see you married to a man you would love; – very, very happy; though my days would be desolate without you.'

'That is it, papa. What would you do if I went from you?'

'What would it matter, Patty? I should be free, at any rate, from a load which often presses heavy on me now. What will you do when I shall leave you? A few more years and all will be over with me. But who is it, love? Has anybody said anything to you?'

'It was only an idea, papa. I don't often think of such a thing; but I did think of it then.' And so the subject was allowed to pass by. This had happened before the day of the second arrival had been absolutely fixed and made known to Miss Woolsworthy.

And then that second arrival took place. The reader may have understood from the words with which Miss Le Smyrger authorized her nephew to make his second visit to Oxney Combe that Miss Woolsworthy's passion was not altogether unauthorized. Captain Broughton had been told that he was not to come unless he came with a certain purpose; and having been so told, he still persisted in coming. There can be no doubt but that he well understood the purport to which his aunt alluded. 'I shall assuredly come,' he had said. And true to his word, he was now there.

Patience knew exactly the hour at which he must arrive at the station at Newton Abbot, and the time also which it would take to travel over those twelve up-hill miles from the station to Oxney. It need hardly be said that she paid no visit to Miss Le Smyrger's house on that afternoon; but she might have known something of Captain Broughton's approach without going thither. His road to the Combe passed by the parsonage-gate, and had Patience sat even at her bedroom window she must have seen him. But on such an evening she would not sit at her bedroom window; – she would do nothing which would force her to accuse herself of a restless longing for her lover's coming. It was for him to seek her. If he chose to do so, he knew the way to the parsonage.

Miss Le Smyrger – good, dear, honest, hearty Miss Le Smyrger, was in a fever of anxiety on behalf of her friend. It was not that she wished her nephew to marry Patience, – or rather that she had entertained any such wish when he first came among them. She was not given to match-making, and moreover thought, or had thought within herself, that they of Oxney Colne could do very well without any admixture from Eaton Square. Her plan of life had been that when old Mr Woolsworthy was taken away from Dartmoor, Patience should live with her, and that when she also shuffled off her coil, then Patience Woolsworthy should be the maiden-mistress of Oxney Combe – of Oxney Combe and of Mr Cloysey's farm – to the utter detriment of all the Broughtons. Such had been her plan before nephew John had come among them – a plan not to be spoken of till the coming of that dark day which should make Patience an orphan. But now her nephew had been there, and all was to be altered. Miss Le Smyrger's plan would have provided a companion for her old age; but that had not been her chief object. She had thought more of Patience than of herself, and now it seemed that a prospect of a higher happiness was opening for her friend.

'John,' she said, as soon as the first greetings were over, 'do you remember the last words that I said to you before you went away?' Now, for myself, I much admire Miss Le Smyrger's heartiness, but I do not think much of her discretion. It would have been better, perhaps, had she allowed things to take their course.

'I can't say that I do,' said the Captain. At the same time the Captain did remember very well what those last words had been.

'I am so glad to see you, so delighted to see you, if – if – if –,' and then she paused, for with all her courage she hardly dared to ask her nephew whether he had come there with the express purport of asking Miss Woolsworthy to marry him.

To tell the truth – for there is no room for mystery within the limits of this short story, – to tell, I say, at a word the plain and simple truth, Captain Broughton had already asked that question. On the day before he left Oxney Colne he had in set terms proposed to the parson's daughter, and indeed the words, the hot and frequent words, which previously to that had fallen like sweetest honey into the ears of Patience Woolsworthy, had made it imperative on him to do so. When a man in such a place as that has talked to a girl of love day after day, must not he talk of it to some definite purpose on the day on which he leaves her? Or if he do not, must he not submit to be regarded as false, selfish, and almost fraudulent? Captain Broughton, however, had asked the question honestly and truly. He had done so honestly and truly, but in words, or, perhaps, simply with a tone, that had hardly sufficed to satisfy the proud spirit of the girl he loved. She by that time had confessed to herself that she loved him with all her heart; but she had made no such confession to him. To him she had spoken no word, granted no favour, that any lover might rightfully regard as a token of love returned. She had listened to him as he spoke, and bade him keep such sayings for the drawing-rooms of his fashionable friends. Then he had spoken out and had asked for that hand, —not, perhaps, as a suitor tremulous with hope,—but as a rich man who knows that he can command that which he desires to purchase.

'You should think more of this,' she had said to him at last. 'If you would really have me for your wife, it will not be much to you to return here again when time for thinking of it shall have passed by.' With these words she had dismissed him, and now he had again come back to Oxney Colne. But still she would not place herself at the window to look for him, nor dress herself in other than her simple morning country dress, nor omit one item of her daily work. If he wished to take her at all, he should wish to take her as she really was, in her plain country life, but he should take her also with full observance of all those privileges which maidens are allowed to claim from their lovers. He should curtail no ceremonious observance because she was the daughter of a poor country parson who would come to him without a shilling, whereas he stood high in the world's books. He had asked her to give him all that she had, and that all she was ready to give, without stint. But the gift must be valued before it could be given or received. He also was to give her as much, and she would accept it as being beyond all price. But she would not allow that that which was offered to her was in any degree the more precious because of his outward worldly standing.

She would not pretend to herself that she thought he would come to her that afternoon, and therefore she busied herself in the kitchen and about the house, giving directions to her two maids as though the day would pass as all other days did pass in that household. They usually dined at four, and she rarely, in these summer months, went far from the house before that hour. At four precisely she sat down with her father, and then said that she was going up as far as Helpholme after dinner. Helpholme was a solitary farmhouse in another parish, on the border of the moor, and Mr Woolsworthy asked her whether he should accompany her.

'Do, papa,' she said, 'if you are not too tired.' And yet she had thought how probable it might be that she should meet John Broughton on her walk. And so it was arranged; but, just as dinner was over, Mr Woolsworthy remembered himself.

'Gracious me,' he said, 'how my memory is going! Gribbles, from Ivybridge, and old John Poulter, from Bovey, are coming to meet here by appointment. You can't put Helpholme off till tomorrow?'

Patience, however, never put off anything, and therefore at six o'clock, when her father had finished his slender modicum of toddy, she tied on her hat and went on her walk. She started forth with a quick step, and left no word to say by which route she would go. As she passed up along the little lane which led towards Oxney Combe she would not even look to see if he was coming towards her; and when she left the road, passing over a stone stile into a little path which ran first through the upland fields, and then across the moor ground towards Helpholme, she did not look back once, or listen for his coming step.

She paid her visit, remaining upwards of an hour with the old bedridden mother of the farmer of Helpholme. 'God bless you, my darling!' said the old lady as she left her; 'and send you someone to make your own path bright and happy through the world.' These words were still ringing in her ears with all their significance as she saw John Broughton waiting for her at the first stile which she had to pass after leaving the farmer's haggard.

'Patty,' he said, as he took her hand, and held it close within both his own, 'what a chase I have had after you!'

'And who asked you, Captain Broughton?' she answered, smiling. 'If the journey was too much for your poor London strength, could you not have waited till tomorrow morning, when you would have found me at the parsonage?' But she did not draw her hand away from him, or in any way pretend that he had not a right to accost her as a lover.

'No, I could not wait. I am more eager to see those I love than you seem to be.'

'How do you know whom I love, or how eager I might be to see them? There is an old woman there whom I love, and I have thought nothing of this walk with the object of seeing her.' And now, slowly drawing her hand away from him, she pointed to the farmhouse which she had left.

'Patty,' he said, after a minute's pause, during which she had looked full into his face with all the force of her bright eyes; 'I have come from London today, straight down her to Oxney, and from my aunt's house close upon your footsteps after you to ask you that one question. Do you love me?'

'What a Hercules?' she said, again laughing. 'Do you really mean that you left London only this morning? Why, you must have been five hours in a railway carriage and two in a post-chaise, not to talk of the walk afterwards. You ought to take more care of yourself, Captain Broughton!'

He would have been angry with her, – for he did not like to be quizzed, – had she not put her hand on his arm as she spoke, and the softness of her touch had redeemed the offence of her words.

'All that have I done,' said he, 'that I may hear one word from you.'

'That any word of mine should have such potency! But, let us walk on, or my father will take us for some of the standing stones of the moor. How have you found your aunt? If you only knew the cares that have sat on her dear shoulders for the last week past, in order that your high mightyness might have a sufficiency to eat and drink in these desolate half-starved regions.'

'She might have saved herself such anxiety. No one can care less for such things than I do.'

'And yet I think I have heard you boast of the cook of your club.' And then again there was silence for a minute or two.

'Patty,' said he, stopping again in the path; 'answer my question. I have a right to demand an answer. Do you love me?'

'And what if I do? What if I have been so silly as to allow your perfections to be too many for my weak heart? What then, Captain Broughton?'

'It cannot be that you love me, or you would not joke now.'

'Perhaps not, indeed,' she said. It seemed as though she were resolved not to yield an inch in her own humour. And then again they walked on.

'Patty,' he said once more, 'I shall get an answer from you tonight, – this evening; now, during this walk, or I shall return tomorrow, and never revisit this spot again.'

'Oh, Captain Broughton, how should we ever manage to live without you?'

'Very well,' he said; 'up to the end of this walk I can bear it all; – and one word spoken then will mend it all.'

During the whole of this time she felt that she was ill-using him. She knew that she loved him with all her heart; that it would nearly kill her to part with him; that she had heard his renewed offer with an ecstasy of joy. She acknowledged to herself that he was giving proof of his devotion as strong as any which a girl could receive from her lover. And yet she could hardly bring herself to say the word he longed to hear. That word once said, and then she knew that she must succumb to her love for ever! That word once said, and there would be nothing for her but to spoil him with her idolatry! That word once said, and she must continue to repeat it into his ears, till perhaps he might be tired of hearing it! And now he had threatened her, and how could she speak it after that? She certainly would not speak it unless he asked her again without such threat. And so they walked on again in silence.

'Patty,' he said at last. 'By the heavens above us you shall answer me. Do you love me?'

She now stood still, and almost trembled as she looked up into his face. She stood opposite to him for a moment, and then placing her two hands on his shoulders, she answered him. 'I do, I do, I do,' she said, 'with all my heart; with all my heart – with all my heart and strength.' And then her head fell upon his breast.

Captain Broughton was almost as much surprised as delighted by the warmth of the acknowledgment made by the eager-hearted passionate girl whom he now held within his arms. She had said it now; the words had been spoken; and there was nothing for her but to swear to him over and over again with her sweetest oaths, that those words were true – true as her soul. And very sweet was the walk down from thence to the parsonage gate. He spoke no more of the distance of the ground, or the length of his day's journey. But he stopped her at every turn that he might press her arm the closer to his own, that he might look into the brightness of her eyes, and prolong his hour of delight. There were no more gibes now on her tongue, no raillery at his London finery, no laughing comments on his coming and going. With downright honesty she told him everything: how she had loved him before her heart was warranted in such a passion; how, with much thinking, she had resolved that it would be unwise to take him at his first word, and had thought it better that he should return to

London, and then think over it; how she had almost repented of her courage when she had feared, during those long summer days, that he would forget her; and how her heart had leapt for joy when her old friend had told her that he was coming.

'And yet,' said he, 'you were not glad to see me!'

'Oh, was I not glad? You cannot understand the feelings of a girl who has lived secluded as I have done. Glad is no word for the joy I felt. But it was not seeing you that I cared for so much. It was the knowledge that you were near me once again. I almost wish now that I had not seen you till tomorrow.' But as she spoke she pressed his arm, and this caress gave the lie to her last words.

'No, do not come in tonight,' she said, when she reached the little wicket that led up the parsonage. 'Indeed you shall not. I could not behave myself properly if you did.'

'But I don't want you to behave properly.'

'Oh! I am to keep that for London, am I? But, nevertheless, Captain Broughton, I will not invite you either to tea or to supper tonight.'

'Surely I may shake hands with your father.'

'Not tonight – not till –. John, I may tell him, may I not? I must tell him at once.'

'Certainly,' said he.

'And then you shall see him tomorrow. Let me see – at what hour shall I bid you come?'

'To breakfast.'

'No, indeed. What on earth would your aunt do with her broiled turkey and the cold pie? I have got no cold pie for you.'

'I hate cold pie.'

'What a pity! But, John, I should be forced to leave you directly after breakfast. Come down – come down at two, or three; and then I will go back with you to Aunt Penelope. I must see her tomorrow.' And so at last the matter was settled, and the happy Captain, as he left her, was hardly resisted in his attempt to press her lips to his own.

When she entered the parlour in which her father was sitting, there still were Gribbles and Poulter discussing some knotty point of Devon lore. So Patience took off her hat, and sat herself down, waiting till they should go. For full an hour she had to wait, and then Gribbles and Poulter did go. But it was not in such matters as this that Patience Woolsworthy was impatient. She could wait, and wait, and wait, curbing herself for weeks and months, while the thing waited for was in her eyes good; but she could not curb her hot thoughts or her hot words when things came to be discussed which she did not think to be good.

'Papa,' she said, when Gribbles' long-drawn last word had been spoken at the door. 'Do you remember how I asked you the other day what you would say if I were to leave you?'

'Yes, surely,' he replied, looking up at her in astonishment.

'I am going to leave you now,' she said. 'Dear, dearest father, how am I to go from you?'

'Going to leave me,' said he, thinking of her visit to Helpholme, and thinking of nothing else.

Now there had been a story about Helpholme. That bedridden old lady there had a stalwart son, who was now the owner of the Helpholme pastures. But though owner in fee of all those wild acres and of the cattle which they supported, he was not much above the farmers around him, either in manners or education. He had his merits, however; for he was honest, well to do in the world, and modest withal. How strong love had grown up, springing from neighbourly kindness, between our Patience and his mother, it needs not here to tell; but rising from it had come another love – or an ambition which might have grown to love. The young man, after much thought, had not dared to speak to Miss Woolsworthy, but he had sent a message by Miss Le Smyrger. If there could be any hope for him, he would present himself as a suitor – on trial. He did not owe a shilling in the world, and had money by him – saved. He wouldn't ask the parson for a shilling of fortune. Such had been the tenor of his message, and Miss Le Smyrger had delivered it faithfully. 'He does not mean it,' Patience had said with her stern voice. 'Indeed he does, my dear. You may be sure he is in earnest,' Miss Le Smyrger had replied; 'and there is not an honester man in these parts.'

'Tell him,' said Patience, not attending to the latter portion of her friend's last speech, 'that it cannot be, – make him understand, you know – and tell him also that the matter shall be thought of no more.' The matter had, at any rate, been spoken of no more, but the young farmer still remained a bachelor, and

Helpholme still wanted a mistress. But all this came back upon the parson's mind when his daughter told him that she was about to leave him.

'Yes, dearest,' she said; and as she spoke, she now knelt at his knees. 'I have been asked in marriage, and I have given myself away.'

'Well, my love, if you will be happy –'

'I hope I shall; I think I shall. But you, papa?'

'You will not be far from us.'

'Oh, yes; in London.'

'In London.'

'Captain Broughton lives in London generally.'

'And has Captain Broughton asked you to marry him?'

'Yes, papa – who else? Is he not good? Will you not love him? Oh, papa, do not say that I am wrong to love him?'

He never told her his mistake, or explained to her that he had not thought it possible that the high-placed son of the London great man shall have fallen in love with his undowered daughter; but he embraced her, and told her, with all his enthusiasm, that he rejoiced in her joy, and would be happy in her happiness. 'My own Patty,' he said, 'I have ever known that you were too good for this life of ours here.' And then the evening wore away into the night, with many tears but still with much happiness.

Captain Broughton, as he walked back to Oxney Combe, made up his mind that he would say nothing on the matter to his aunt till the next morning. He wanted to think over it all, and to think it over, if possible, by himself. He had taken a step in life, the most important that a man is ever called on to take, and he had to reflect whether or no he had taken it with wisdom.

'Have you seen her?' said Miss Le Smyrger, very anxiously, when he came into the drawing-room.

'Miss Woolsworthy you mean,' said he. 'Yes, I've seen her. As I found her out I took a long walk and happened to meet her. Do you know, aunt, I think I'll go to bed; I was up at five this morning, and have been on the move ever since.'

Miss Le Smyrger perceived that she was to hear nothing that evening, so she handed him his candlestick and allowed him to go to his room.

But Captain Broughton did not immediately retire to bed, nor when he did so was he able to sleep at once. Had this step that he had taken been a wise one? He was not a man who, in worldly matters, had allowed things to arrange themselves for him, as is the case with so many men. He had formed views for himself, and had a theory of life. Money for money's sake he had declared to himself to be bad. Money, as a concomitant to things which were in themselves good, he had declared to himself to be good also. That concomitant in this affair of his marriage, he had now missed. Well; he had made up his mind to that, and would put up with the loss. He had means of living of his own, though means not so extensive as might have been desirable. That it would be well for him to become a married man, looking merely to that state of life as opposed to his present state, he had fully resolved. On that point, therefore, there was nothing to repent. That Patty Woolsworthy was good, affectionate, clever, and beautiful, he was sufficiently satisfied. It would be odd indeed if he were not so satisfied now, seeing that for the last four months he had declared to himself daily that she was so with many inward asseverations. And yet though he repeated now again that he was satisfied, I do not think that he was so fully satisfied of it as he had been throughout the whole of those four months. It is sad to say so, but I fear – I fear that such was the case. When you have your plaything how much of the anticipated pleasure vanishes, especially if it have been won easily!

He had told none of his family what were his intentions in this second visit to Devonshire, and now he had to bethink himself whether they would be satisfied. What would his sister say, she who had married the Honourable Augustus Gumbleton, gold-stick-in-waiting to Her Majesty's Privy Council? Would she receive Patience with open arms, and make much of her about London? And then how far would London suit Patience, or would Patience suit London? There would be much for him to do in teaching her, and it would be well for him to set about the lesson without loss of time. So far he got that night, but when the morning came he went a step further, and began mentally to criticize her manner to himself. It had been very sweet, that warm, that full, that ready declaration of love. Yes; it had been very sweet; but – but –; when, after her little jokes, she did confess her love, had she not been a little too free for feminine excellence? A man likes to be told that he is loved, but he hardly wishes that the girl he is to marry should fling herself at his head!

Ah me! yes; it was thus he argued to himself as on that morning he went through the arrangements of his toilet. 'Then he was a brute,' you say, my pretty reader. I have never said that he was not a brute. But this I remark, that many such brutes are to be met with in the beaten paths of the world's high highway. When Patience Woolsworthy had answered him coldly, bidding him go back to London and think over his love; while it seemed from her manner that at any rate as yet she did not care for him; while he was absent from her, and, therefore, longing for her, the possession of her charms, her talent, and bright honesty of purpose had seemed to him a thing most desirable. Now they were his own. They had, in fact, been his own from the first. The heart of this country-bred girl had fallen at the first word from his mouth. Had she not so confessed to him? She was very nice, – very nice indeed. He loved her dearly. But had he not sold himself too cheaply?

I by no means say that he was not a brute. But whether brute or no he was an honest man, and had no remotest dream, either then, on that morning, or during the following days on which such thoughts pressed more thickly on his mind – of breaking away from his pledged word. At breakfast on that morning he told all to Miss Le Smyrger, and that lady, with warm and gracious intentions, confided to him her purpose regarding her property. 'I have always regarded Patience as my heir,' she said, 'and shall do so still.'

'Oh, indeed,' said Captain Broughton.

'But it is a great, great pleasure to me to think that she will give back the little property to my sister's child. You will have your mother's, and thus it will all come together again.'

'Ah!' said Captain Broughton. He had his own ideas about property, and did not, even under existing circumstances, like to hear that his aunt considered herself at liberty to leave the acres away to one who was by blood quite a stranger to the family.

'Does Patience know of this?' he asked.

'Not a word,' said Miss Le Smyrger. And then nothing more was said upon the subject.

On that afternoon he went down and received the parson's benediction and congratulations with a good grace. Patience said very little on the occasion, and indeed was absent during the greater part of the interview. The two lovers then walked up to Oxney Combe, and there were more benedictions and more congratulations. 'All went merry as a marriage bell', at any rate as far as Patience was concerned. Not a word had yet fallen from that dear mouth, not a look had yet come over that handsome face, which tended in any way to mar her bliss. Her first day of acknowledged love was a day altogether happy, and when she prayed for him as she knelt beside her bed there was no feeling in her mind that any fear need disturb her joy.

I will pass over the next three or four days very quickly, merely saying that Patience did not find them so pleasant as that first day after her engagement. There was something in her lover's manner – something which at first she could not define – which by degrees seemed to grate against her feelings. He was sufficiently affectionate, that being a matter on which she did not require much demonstration; but joined to his affection there seemed to be –; she hardly liked to suggest to herself a harsh word, but could it be possible that he was beginning to think that she was not good enough for him? And then she asked herself the question – was she good enough for him? If there were doubt about that, the match should be broken off, though she tore her own heart out in the struggle. The truth, however, was this, – that he had begun that teaching which he had already found to be so necessary. Now, had any one essayed to teach Patience German or mathematics, with that young lady's free consent, I believe that she would have been found a meek scholar. But it was not probable that she would be meek when she found a self-appointed tutor teaching her manners and conduct without her consent.

So matters went on for four or five days, and on the evening of the fifth day, Captain Broughton and his aunt drank tea at the parsonage. Nothing very especial occurred; but as the parson and Miss Le Smyrger insisted on playing backgammon with devoted perseverance during the whole evening, Broughton had a good opportunity of saying a word or two about those changes in his lady-love which a life in London would require – and some word he said also – some single slight word, as to the higher station in life to which he would exalt his bride. Patience bore it – for her father and Miss Le Smyrger were in the room – she bore it well, speaking no syllable of anger, and enduring, for the moment, the implied scorn of the old parsonage. Then the evening broke up, and Captain Broughton walked back to Oxney Combe with his aunt. 'Patty,' her father said to her before they went to bed, 'he seems to me to be a most excellent young man.' 'Dear papa,' she answered, kissing him. 'And terribly deep in love,' said Mr Woolsworthy. 'Oh, I don't know about that,' she answered, as she left him with her sweetest smile. But though she could thus smile at her father's joke, she had already made up her mind that there was still something to be learned as to her promised husband before she could place herself altogether in his hands. She would ask him whether he thought himself liable to injury from this proposed marriage; and though he should deny any such thought, she would know from the manner of his denial what his true feelings were.

And he, too, on that night, during his silent walk with Miss Le Smyrger, had entertained some similar thoughts. 'I fear she is obstinate', he had said to himself, and then he had half accused her of being sullen also. 'If that be her temper, what a life of misery I have before me!'

'Have you fixed a day yet?' his aunt asked him as they came near to her house.

'No, not yet; I don't know whether it will suit me to fix it before I leave.'

'Why, it was but the other day you were in such a hurry.'

'Ah – yes – I have thought more about it since then.'

'I should have imagined that this would depend on what Patty thinks,' said Miss Le Smyrger, standing up for the privileges of her sex. 'It is presumed that the gentleman is always ready as soon as the lady will consent.'

'Yes, in ordinary cases it is so; but when a girl is taken out of her own sphere –'

'Her own sphere! Let me caution you, Master John, not to talk to Patty about her own sphere.'

'Aunt Penelope, as Patience is to be my wife and not yours, I must claim permission to speak to her on such subjects as may seem suitable to me.' And then they parted – not in the best humour with each other.

On the following day Captain Broughton and Miss Woolsworthy did not meet till the evening. She had said, before those few ill-omened words had passed her lover's lips, that she would probably be at Miss Le Smyrger's house on the following morning. Those ill-omened words did pass her lover's lips, and then she remained at home. This did not come from sullenness, nor even from anger, but from a conviction that it would be well that she should think much before she met him again. Nor was he anxious to hurry a meeting. His thought – his base thought – was this; that she would be sure to come up to the Combe after him; but she did not come, and therefore in the evening he went down to her, and asked her to walk with him.

They went away by the path that led by Helpholme, and little was said between them till they had walked some mile together. Patience, as she went along the path, remembered almost to the letter the sweet words which had greeted her ears as she came down that way with him on the night of his arrival; but he remembered nothing of that sweetness then. Had he not made an ass of himself during these last six months? That was the thought which very much had possession of his mind.

'Patience,' he said at last, having hitherto spoken only an indifferent word now and again since they had left the parsonage, 'Patience, I hope you realize the importance of the step which you and I are about to take?'

'Of course I do,' she answered: 'what an odd question that is for you to ask!'

'Because,' said he, 'sometimes I almost doubt it. It seems to me as though you thought you could remove yourself from here to your new home with no more trouble than when you go from home up to the Combe.'

'Is that meant for a reproach, John?'

'No, not for a reproach, but for advice. Certainly not for a reproach.'

'I am glad of that.'

'But I should wish to make you think how great is the leap in the world which you are about to take.' Then again they walked on for many steps before she answered him.

'Tell me, then, John,' she said, when she had sufficiently considered what words she would speak; – and as she spoke a dark bright colour suffused her face, and her eyes flashed almost with anger. 'What leap do you mean? Do you mean a leap upwards?'

'Well, yes; I hope it will be so.'

'In one sense, certainly, it would be a leap upwards. To be the wife of the man I loved; to have the privilege of holding his happiness in my hand; to know that I was his own – the companion whom he had chosen out of all the world – that would, indeed, be a leap upward; a leap almost to heaven, if all that were so. But if you mean upwards in any other sense –'

'I was thinking of the social scale.'

'Then, Captain Broughton, your thoughts were doing me dishonour.'

'Doing you dishonour!'

'Yes, doing me dishonour. That your father is, in the world's esteem, a greater man than mine is doubtless true enough. That you, as a man, are richer than I am as a woman is doubtless also true. But you dishonour me, and yourself also, if these things can weigh with you now.'

'Patience, – I think you can hardly know what words you are saying to me.'

'Pardon me, but I think I do. Nothing that you can give me – no gifts of that description – can weigh aught against that which I am giving you. If you had all the wealth and rank of the greatest lord in the land, it would count as nothing in such a scale. If – as I have not doubted – if in return for my heart you have given me yours, then – then – then, you have paid me fully. But when gifts such as those are going, nothing else can count even as a make-weight.'

'I do not quite understand you,' he answered, after a pause. 'I fear you are a little high-flown.' And then, while the evening was still early, they walked back to the parsonage almost without another word.

Captain Broughton at this time had only one more full day to remain at Oxney Combe. On the afternoon following that he was to go as far as Exeter, and thence return to London. Of course it was to be expected, that the wedding day would be fixed before he went, and much had been said about it during the first day or two of his engagement. Then he had pressed for an early time, and Patience, with a girl's usual diffidence, had asked for some little delay. But now nothing was said on the subject; and how was it probable that such a matter could be settled after such a conversation as that which I have related? That evening, Miss Le Smyrger asked whether the day had been fixed. 'No,' said Captain

Broughton harshly; 'nothing has been fixed.' 'But it will be arranged before you go.' 'Probably not,' he said; and then the subject was dropped for the time.

'John,' she said, just before she went to bed, 'if there be anything wrong between you and Patience, I conjure you to tell me.'

'You had better ask her,' he replied. 'I can tell you nothing.'

On the following morning he was much surprised by seeing Patience on the gravel path before Miss Le Smyrger's gate immediately after breakfast. He went to the door to open it for her, and she, as she gave him her hand, told him that she came up to speak to him. There was no hesitation in her manner, nor any look of anger in her face. But there was in her gait and form, in her voice and countenance, a fixedness of purpose which he had never seen before, or at any rate had never acknowledged.

'Certainly,' said he. 'Shall I come out with you, or will you come upstairs?'

'We can sit down in the summer-house,' she said; and thither they both went.

'Captain Broughton,' she said – and she began her task the moment that they were both seated – 'You and I have engaged ourselves as man and wife, but perhaps we have been over rash.'

'How so?' said he.

'It may be – and indeed I will say more – it is the case that we have made this engagement without knowing enough of each other's character.'

'I have not thought so.'

'The time will perhaps come when you will so think, but for the sake of all that we most value, let it come before it is too late. What would be our fate – how terrible would be our misery, if such a thought should come to either of us after we have linked our lots together.'

There was a solemnity about her as she thus spoke which almost repressed him, – which for a time did prevent him from taking that tone of authority which on such a subject he would choose to adopt. But he recovered himself. 'I hardly think that this comes well from you,' he said.

'From whom else should it come? Who else can fight my battle for me; and, John, who else can fight that same battle on your behalf? I tell you this, that with your mind standing towards me as it does stand at present you could not give me your hand at the altar with true words and a happy conscience. Is it not true? You have half repented of your bargain already. Is it not so?'

He did not answer her; but getting up from his seat walked to the front of the summer-house, and stood there with his back turned upon her. It was not that he meant to be ungracious, but in truth he did not know how to answer her. He had half repented of his bargain.

'John,' she said, getting up and following him so that she could put her hand upon his arm, 'I have been very angry with you.'

'Angry with me!' he said, turning sharp upon her.

'Yes, angry with you. You would have treated me like a child. But that feeling has gone now. I am not angry now. There is my hand; — the hand of a friend. Let the words that have been spoken between us be as though they had not been spoken. Let us both be free.'

'Do you mean it?' he asked.

'Certainly I mean it.' As she spoke these words her eyes were filled with tears in spite of all the efforts she could make to restrain them; but he was not looking at her, and her efforts had sufficed to prevent any sob from being audible.

'With all my heart,' he said; and it was manifest from his tone that he had no thought of her happiness as he spoke. It was true that she had been angry with him — angry, as she had herself declared; but nevertheless, in what she had said and what she had done, she had thought more of his happiness than of her own. Now she was angry once again.

'With all your heart, Captain Broughton! Well, so be it. If with all your heart, then is the necessity so much the greater. You go tomorrow. Shall we say farewell now?'

'Patience, I am not going to be lectured.'

'Certainly not by me. Shall we say farewell now?'

'Yes, if you are determined.'

'I am determined. Farewell, Captain Broughton. You have all my wishes for your happiness.' And she held out her hand to him.

'Patience!' he said. And he looked at her with a dark frown, as though he would strive to frighten her into submission. If so, he might have saved himself any such attempt.

'Farewell, Captain Broughton. Give me your hand, for I cannot stay.' He gave her his hand, hardly knowing why he did so. She lifted it to her lips and kissed it, and then, leaving him, passed from the summer-house down through the wicket-gate, and straight home to the parsonage.

During the whole of that day she said no word to anyone of what had occurred. When she was once more at home she went about her household affairs as she had done on that day of his arrival. When she sat down to dinner with her father he observed nothing to make him think that she was unhappy, nor during the evening was there any expression in her face, or any tone in her voice, which excited his attention. On the following morning Captain Broughton called at the parsonage, and the servant-girl brought word to her mistress that he was in the parlour. But she would not see him. 'Laws miss, you ain't a quarrelled with your beau?' the poor girl said. 'No, not quarrelled,' she said; 'but give him that.' It was a scrap of paper containing a word or two in pencil. 'It is better that we should not meet again. God bless you.' And from that day to this, now more than ten years, they have never met.

'Papa,' she said to her father that afternoon, 'dear papa, do not be angry with me. It is all over between me and John Broughton. Dearest, you and I will not be separated.'

It would be useless here to tell how great was the old man's surprise and how true his sorrow. As the tale was told to him no cause was given for anger with anyone. Not a word was spoken against the suitor who had on that day returned to London with a full conviction that now at least he was relieved from his engagement. 'Patty, my darling child,' he said, 'may God grant that it be for the best!'

'It is for the best,' she answered stoutly. 'For this place I am fit; and I much doubt whether I am fit for any other.'

On that day she did not see Miss Le Smyrger, but on the following morning, knowing that Captain Broughton had gone off, – having heard the wheels of the carriage as they passed by the parsonage gate on his way to the station, – she walked up to the Combe.

'He has told you, I suppose?' said she.

'Yes,' said Miss Le Smyrger. 'And I will never see him again unless he asks your pardon on his knees. I have told him so. I would not even give him my hand as he went.'

'But why so, thou kindest one? The fault was mine more than his.'

'I understand. I have eyes in my head,' said the old maid. 'I have watched him for the last four or five days. If you could have kept the truth to yourself and bade him keep off from you, he would have been at your feet now, licking the dust from your shoes.'

'But, dear friend, I do not want a man to lick dust from my shoes.'

'Ah, you are a fool. You do not know the value of your own wealth.'

'True; I have been a fool. I was a fool to think that one coming from such a life as he has led could be happy with such as I am. I know the truth now. I have bought the lesson dearly – but perhaps not too dearly, seeing that it will never be forgotten.'

There was but little more said about the matter between our three friends at Oxney Combe. What, indeed, could be said? Miss Le Smyrger for a year or two still expected that her nephew would return and claim his bride; but he has never done so, nor has there been any correspondence between them. Patience Woolsworthy had learned her lesson dearly. She had given her whole heart to the man; and, though she so bore herself that no one was aware of the violence of the struggle, nevertheless the struggle within her bosom was very violent. She never told herself that she had done wrong; she never regretted her loss; but yet – yet! – the loss was very hard to bear. He also had loved her, but he was not capable of a love which could much injure his daily peace. Her daily peace was gone for many a day to come.

Her father is still living; but there is a curate now in the parish. In conjunction with him and with Miss Le Smyrger she spends her time in the concerns of the parish. In her own eyes she is a confirmed old maid; and such is my opinion also. The romance of her life was played out in that summer. She never sits now lonely on the hillside thinking how much she might do for one whom she really loved. But with a large heart she loves many, and, with no romance, she works hard to lighten the burdens of those she loves.

As for Captain Broughton, all the world knows that he did marry that great heiress with whom his name was once before connected, and that he is now a useful member of Parliament, working on committees three or four days a week with zeal that is indefatigable. Sometimes, not often, as he thinks of Patience Woolsworthy a smile comes across his face.

ANTHONY GARSTIN'S COURTSHIP

(*Savoy*, July 1896)

I

A stampede of huddled sheep, wildly scampering over the slaty shingle, emerged from the leaden mist that muffled the fell-top, and a shrill shepherd's whistle broke the damp stillness of the air. And presently a man's figure appeared, following the sheep down the hillside. He halted a moment to whistle curtly to his two dogs, who, laying back their ears, chased the sheep at top speed beyond the brow; then, his hands deep in his pockets, he strode vigorously forward. A streak of white smoke from a toiling train was creeping silently across the distance: the great, grey, desolate undulations of treeless country showed no other sign of life.

The sheep hurried in single file along a tiny track worn threadbare amid the brown, lumpy grass: and, as the man came round the mountain's shoulder, a narrow valley opened out beneath him – a scanty patchwork of green fields, and, here and there, a whitewashed farm, flanked by a dark cluster of sheltering trees.

The man walked with a loose, swinging gait. His figure was spare and angular: he wore a battered, black felt hat and clumsy, iron-bound boots: his clothes were dingy from long exposure to the weather. He had close-set, insignificant eyes, much wrinkled, and stubbly eyebrows streaked with grey. His mouth was close-shaven, and drawn by his abstraction into hard and taciturn lines; beneath his chin bristled an unkempt fringe of sandy-coloured hair.

When he reached the foot of the fell, the twilight was already blurring the distance. The sheep scurried, with a noisy rustling, across a flat, swampy stretch, over-grown with rushes, while the dogs headed them towards a gap in a low, ragged wall built of loosely-heaped boulders. The man swung the gate to after them, and waited, whistling peremptorily, recalling the dogs. A moment later, the animals reappeared, cringing as they crawled through the bars of the gate. He kicked out at them contemptuously, and mounting a stone stile a few yards further up the road, dropped into a narrow lane.

Presently, as he passed a row of lighted windows, he heard a voice call to him. He stopped, and perceived a crooked, white-bearded figure, wearing clerical clothes, standing in the garden gateway.

'Good-evening, Anthony. A raw evening this.'

'Ay, Mr Blencarn, it is a bit frittish,' he answered. 'I've jest bin gittin' a few lambs off t'fell. I hope ye're keepin' fairly, an' Miss Rosa too.' He spoke briefly, with a loud, spontaneous cordiality.

'Thank ye, Anthony, thank ye. Rosa's down at the church, playing over the hymns for tomorrow. How's Mrs Garstin?'

'Nicely, thank ye, Mr Blencarn. She's wonderful active, is mother.'

'Well, good night to ye, Anthony,' said the old man, clicking the gate.

'Good night, Mr Blencarn,' he called back.

A few minutes later the twinkling lights of the village came in sight, and from within the sombre form of the square-towered church, looming by the roadside, the slow, solemn strains of the organ floated out on the evening air. Anthony lightened his tread: then paused, listening; but, presently, becoming aware that a man stood, listening also, on the bridge some few yards distant, he moved forward again. Slackening his pace, as he approached, he eyed the figure keenly; but the man paid no heed to him, remaining, with his back turned, gazing over the parapet into the dark, gurgling stream.

Anthony trudged along the empty village street, past the gleaming squares of ruddy gold, starting on either side out of the darkness. Now and then he looked furtively backwards. The straight open road lay behind him, glimmering wanly: the organ seemed to have ceased: the figure on the bridge had left the parapet, and appeared to be moving away towards the church. Anthony halted, watching it till it had disappeared into the blackness beneath the churchyard trees. Then, after a moment's hesitation, he left the road, and mounted an upland meadow towards his mother's farm.

It was a bare, oblong house. In front, a whitewashed porch, and a narrow garden-plot, enclosed by a low iron railing, were dimly discernible: behind, the steep fell-side loomed like a monstrous, mysterious curtain hung across the night. He passed round the back into the twilight of a wide yard, cobbled and partially grass-grown, vaguely flanked by the shadowy outlines of long, low farm-buildings. All was wrapped in darkness: somewhere over-head a bat fluttered, darting its puny scream.

Inside, a blazing peat-fire scattered capering shadows across the smooth, stone floor, flickered among the dim rows of hams suspended from the ceiling and on the panelled cupboards of dark, glistening oak. A servant-girl, spreading the cloth for supper, clattered her clogs in and out of the kitchen: old Mrs Garstin was stooping before the hearth, tremulously turning some girdle-cakes that lay roasting in the embers.

At the sound of Anthony's heavy tread in the passage, she rose, glancing sharply at the clock above the chimney-piece. She was a heavy-built woman, upright, stalwart almost, despite her years. Her face was gaunt and sallow; deep wrinkles accentuated the hardness of her features. She wore a black widow's cap above her iron-grey hair, gold-rimmed spectacles, and a soiled, chequered apron.

'Ye're varra late, Tony,' she remarked querulously.

He unloosened his woollen neckerchief, and when he had hung it methodically with his hat behind the door, answered:

''Twas terrible thick on t' fell-top, an' them two bitches be that senseless.'

She caught his sleeve, and, through her spectacles, suspiciously scrutinized his face.

'Ye did na meet wi' Rosa Blencarn?'

'Nay, she was in church, hymn-playin', wi' Luke Stock hangin' roond door,' he retorted bitterly, rebuffing her with rough impatience.

She moved away, nodding sententiously to herself. They began supper: neither spoke: Anthony sat slowly stirring his tea, and staring moodily into the flames: the bacon on his plate lay untouched. From time to time his mother, laying down her knife and fork, looked across at him in unconcealed asperity, pursing her wide, ungainly mouth. At last, abruptly setting down her cup, she broke out:

'I wonder ye hav'na mare pride, Tony. For hoo lang are ye goin' t' continue settin' mopin' and broodin' like a seck sheep? Ye'll jest mak yessell ill, an' then I reckon what ye'll prove satisfied. Ay, but I wonder ye hav'na more pride.'

But he made no answer, remaining unmoved, as if he had not heard.

Presently, half to himself, without raising his eyes, he murmured:

'Luke be goin' South, Monday.'

'Well, ye canna tak' oop wi' his leavin's anyways. It hasna coom't that, has it? Ye doan't intend settin' all t' parish a laughin' at ye a second occasion?'

He flushed dully, and bending over his plate, mechanically began his supper.

'Wa dang it,' he broke out a minute later, 'd'ye think I heed the cacklin' o' fifty parishes? Na, not I,' and, with a short, grim laugh, he brought his fist down heavily on the oak table.

'Ye're daft, Tony,' the old woman blurted.

'Daft or na daft, I tell ye this, mother, that I be forty-six year o' age this back-end, and there be some things I will na listen to. Rosa Blencarn's bonny enough for me.'

'Ay, bonny enough – I've na patience wi' ye. Bonny enough – tricked oot in her furbelows, gallivantin' wi' every royster fra Pe'rith. Bonny enough – that be all ye think on. She's bin a proper parson's niece – the giddy, feckless creature, an she'd mak' ye a proper sort o' wife, Tony Garstin, ye great, fond booby.'

She pushed back her chair, and, hurriedly clattering the crockery, began to clear away the supper.

'T' hoose be mine, t' Lord be praised,' she continued in a loud, hard voice, 'an' as long as he spare me, Tony, I'll na see Rosa Blencarn set foot inside it.'

Anthony scowled, without replying, and drew his chair to the hearth. His mother bustled about the room behind him. After a while she asked:

'Did ye pen t' lambs in t' back field?'

'Na, they're in Hullam bottom,' he answered curtly.

The door closed behind her, and by and by he could hear her moving overhead. Meditatively blinking, he filled his pipe clumsily, and pulling a crumpled newspaper from his pocket, sat on over the smouldering fire, reading and stolidly puffing.

II

The music rolled through the dark, empty church. The last, leaden flicker of daylight glimmered in through the pointed windows, and beyond the level rows of dusky pews, tenanted only by a litter of prayer-books, two guttering candles revealed the organ pipes, and the young girl's swaying figure.

She played vigorously. Once or twice the tune stumbled, and she recovered it impatiently, bending over the key-board, showily flourishing her wrists as she touched the stops. She was bare-headed (her hat and cloak lay beside her on a stool). She had fair, fluffy hair, cut short behind her neck; large, round eyes, heightened by a fringe of dark lashes; rough, ruddy cheeks, and a rosy, full-lipped, unstable mouth. She was dressed quite simply, in a black, close-fitting bodice, a little frayed at the sleeves. Her hands and neck were coarsely fashioned: her comeliness was brawny, literal, unfinished, as it were.

When at last the ponderous chords of the Amen faded slowly into the twilight, flushed, breathing a little quickly, she paused, listening to the stillness of the church. Presently a small boy emerged from behind the organ.

'Good evenin', Miss Rosa,' he called, trotting briskly away down the aisle.

'Good night, Robert,' she answered, absently.

After a while, with an impatient gesture, as if to shake some importunate thought from her mind, she rose abruptly, pinned on her hat, threw her cloak round her shoulders, blew out the candles, and groped her way through the church, towards the half-open door. As she hurried along the narrow pathway that led across the churchyard, of a sudden, a figure started out of the blackness.

'Who's that?' she cried, in a loud, frightened voice.

A man's uneasy laugh answered her.

'It's only me, Rosa. I didna' think t' scare ye. I've bin waitin' for ye, this hoor past.'

She made no reply, but quickened her pace. He strode on beside her.

'I'm off, Monday, ye know,' he continued. And, as she said nothing,

'Will ye na stop jest a minnit? I'd like t' speak a few words wi' ye before I go, an tomorrow I hev t' git over t' Scarsdale betimes,' he persisted.

'I don't want t' speak wi' ye: I don't want ever to see ye agin. I jest hate the sight o' ye.' She spoke with a vehement, concentrated hoarseness.

'Nay, but ye must listen to me. I will na be put off wi' fratchin speeches.'

And gripping her arm, he forced her to stop.

'Loose me, ye great beast,' she broke out.

'I'll na hould ye, if ye'll jest stand quiet-like. I meant t' speak fair t' ye, Rosa.'

They stood at a bend in the road, face to face quite close together. Behind his burly form stretched the dimness of a grey, ghostly field.

'What is't ye hev to say to me? Hev done wi' it quick,' she said sullenly.

'It be jest this, Rosa,' he began with dogged gravity. 'I want t' tell ye that ef any trouble comes t'ye after I'm gone – ye know t' what I refer – I want t' tell ye that I'm prepared t' act square by ye. I've written out on an envelope my address in London. Luke Stock, care o' Purcell & Co., Smithfield Market, London.'

'Ye're a bad, sinful man. I jest hate t' sight o' ye. I wish ye were dead.'

'Ay, but I reckon what ye'd ha best thought o' that before. Ye've changed yer whistle considerably since Tuesday. Nay, hould on,' he added, as she struggled to push past him. 'Here's t' envelope.'

She snatched the paper, and tore it passionately, scattering the fragments on to the road. When she had finished, he burst out angrily:

'Ye cussed, unreasonable fool.'

'Let me pass, ef ye've nought mare t'say,' she cried.

'Nay, I'll na part wi' ye this fashion. Ye can speak soft enough when ye choose.' And seizing her shoulders, he forced her backwards against the wall.

'Ye do look fine, an' na mistake, when ye're jest ablaze wi' ragin',' he laughed bluntly, lowering his face to hers.

'Loose me, loose me, ye great coward,' she gasped, striving to free her arms.

Holding her fast, he expostulated:

'Coom, Rosa, can we na part friends?'

'Part friends, indeed,' she retorted bitterly. 'Friends wi' the likes o' you. What d'ye tak me for? Let me git home, I tell ye. An' please God I'll never set eyes on ye again. I hate t' sight o' ye.'

'Be off wi' ye, then,' he answered, pushing her roughly back into the road. 'Be off wi' ye, ye silly. Ye canna say I hav na spak fair t' ye, an', by goom, ye'll na see me shally-wallyin this fashion agin. Be off wi' ye: ye can jest shift for yerself, since ye canna keep a civil tongue in yer head.'

The girl, catching at her breath, stood as if dazed, watching his retreating figure; then starting forward at a run, disappeared up the hill, into the darkness.

III

Old Mr Blencarn concluded his husky sermon. The scanty congregation, who had been sitting, stolidly immobile in their stiff, Sunday clothes, shuffled to their feet, and the pewful of school children, in clamorous chorus, intoned the final hymn. Anthony stood near the organ, absently contemplating, while the rude melody resounded through the church, Rosa's deft manipulation of the key-board. The rugged lines of his face were relaxed to a vacant, thoughtful limpness, that aged his expression not a little: now and then, as if for reference, he glanced questioningly at the girl's profile.

A few minutes later the service was over, and the congregation sauntered out down the aisle. A gawky group of men remained loitering by the church door: one of them called to Anthony; but, nodding curtly, he passed on, and strode away down the road, across the grey upland meadows, towards home. As soon as he had breasted the hill, however, and was no longer visible from below, he turned abruptly to the left, along a small, swampy hollow, till he had reached the lane that led down from the fell-side.

He clambered over a rugged, moss-grown wall, and stood, gazing expectantly down the dark, disused roadway; then, after a moment's hesitation, perceiving nobody, seated himself beneath the wall, on a projecting slab of stone.

Overhead hung a sombre, drifting sky. A gusty wind rollicked down from the fell – huge masses of chilly grey, stripped of the last night's mist. A few dead leaves fluttered over the stones, and from off the fell-side there floated the plaintive, quavering rumour of many bleating sheep.

Before long, he caught sight of two figures coming towards him, slowly climbing the hill. He sat awaiting their approach, fidgeting with his sandy beard, and abstractedly grinding the ground beneath his heel. At the brow they halted: plunging his hands deep into his pockets, he strolled sheepishly towards them.

'Ah! good day t' ye, Anthony,' called the old man, in a shrill, breathless voice. ''Tis a long hill, an' my legs are not what they were. Time was when I'd think nought o' a whole day's tramp on t' fells. Ay, I'm gittin' feeble, Anthony, that's what 'tis. And if Rosa here wasn't the great, strong lass she is, I don't know how her old uncle'd manage;' and he turned to the girl with a proud, tremulous smile.

'Will ye tak my arm a bit, Mr Blencarn? Miss Rosa'll be tired, likely,' Anthony asked.

'Nay, Mr Garstin, but I can manage nicely,' the girl interrupted sharply.

Anthony looked up at her as she spoke. She wore a straw hat, trimmed with crimson velvet, and a black, fur-edged cape, that seemed to set off mightily the fine whiteness of her neck. Her large, dark eyes were fixed upon him. He shifted his feet uneasily, and dropped his glance.

She linked her uncle's arm in hers, and the three moved slowly forward. Old Mr Blencarn walked with difficulty, pausing at intervals for breath. Anthony, his eyes bent on the ground, sauntered beside him, clumsily kicking at the cobbles that lay in his path.

When they reached the vicarage gate, the old man asked him to come inside.

'Not jest now, thank ye, Mr Blencarn. I've that lot o' lambs t' see to before dinner. It's a grand marnin', this,' he added, inconsequently.

'Uncle's bought a nice lot o' Leghorns, Tuesday,' Rosa remarked. Anthony met her gaze; there was a grave, subdued expression on her face this morning, that made her look more of a woman, less of a girl.

'Ay, do ye show him the birds, Rosa. I'd be glad to have his opinion on 'em.'

The old man turned to hobble into the house, and Rosa, as she supported his arm, called back over her shoulder:

'I'll not be a minute, Mr Garstin.'

Anthony strolled round to the yard behind the house, and waited, watching a flock of glossy-white poultry that strutted, perkily pecking, over the grass-grown cobbles.

'Ay, Miss Rosa, they're a bonny lot,' he remarked, as the girl joined him.

'Are they not?' she rejoined, scattering a handful of corn before her.

The birds scuttled across the yard with greedy, outstretched necks. The two stood, side by side, gazing at them.

'What did he give for 'em?' Anthony asked.

'Fifty-five shillings.'

'Ay,' he assented, nodding absently.

'Was Dr Sanderson na seein' o' yer father yesterday?' he asked, after a moment.

'He came in t' forenoon. He said he was jest na worse.'

'Ye knaw, Miss Rosa, as I'm still thinkin' on ye,' he began abruptly, without looking up.

'I reckon it ain't much use,' she answered shortly, scattering another handful of corn towards the birds. 'I reckon I'll never marry. I'm jest weary o' bein' courted —'

'I would na weary ye wi' courtin',' he interrupted.

She laughed noisily.

'Ye are a queer customer, an' na mistake.'

'I'm a match for Luke Stock anyway,' he continued fiercely. 'Ye think nought o' taking oop wi' him – about as ranty, wild a young feller as ever stepped.'

The girl reddened, and bit her lip.

'I don't know what you mean, Mr Garstin. It seems to me ye're might hasty in jumpin' t' conclusions.'

'Mabbe I kin see a thing or two,' he retorted doggedly.

'Luke Stock's gone to London, anyway.'

'Ay, an' a powerful good job too, in t' opinion o' some folks.'

'Ye're jest jealous,' she exclaimed, with a forced titter. 'Ye're jest jealous o' Luke Stock.'

'Nay, but ye need na fill yer head wi' that nonsense. I'm too deep set on ye t' feel jealousy,' he answered, gravely.

The smile faded from her face, as she murmured:

'I canna mak ye out, Mr Garstin.'

'Nay, that ye canna. An' I suppose it's natural, considerin' ye're little more than a child, an' I'm a'most old enough to be yer father,' he retorted, with blunt bitterness.

'But ye know yer mother's took that dislike t' me. She'd never abide the sight o' me at Hootsey.'

He remained silent a moment, moodily reflecting.

'She'd jest ha' t' git ower it. I see nought in that objection,' he declared.

'Nay, Mr Garstin, it canna be. Indeed it canna be at all. Ye'd best jest put it right from yer mind, once and for all.'

'I'd jest best put it off my mind, had I? Ye talk like a child!' he burst out scornfully. 'I intend ye t' coom t' love me, an' I will na tak ye till ye do. I'll jest go on waitin' for ye, an', mark my words, my day 'ull coom at last.'

He spoke loudly, in a slow, stubborn voice, and stepped suddenly towards her. With a faint, frightened cry she shrank back into the doorway of the hen-house.

'Ye talk like a prophet. Ye sort o' skeer me.'

He laughed grimly, and paused, reflectively scanning her face. He seemed about to continue in the same strain; but, instead, turned abruptly on his heel, and strode away through the garden gate.

IV

For three hundred years there had been a Garstin at Hootsey: generation after generation had tramped the grey stretch of upland, in the spring-time scattering their flocks over the fell-sides, and, at the 'back-end', on dark, winter afternoons, driving them home again, down the broad bridlepath that led over the 'raise'. They had been a race of few words, 'keeping themselves to themselves', as the phrase goes; beholden to no man, filled with a dogged, churlish pride – an upright, old-fashioned race, stubborn, long-lived, rude in speech, slow of resolve.

Anthony had never seen his father, who had died one night, upon the fell-top, he and his shepherd, engulfed in the great snowstorm of 1849. Folks had said that he was the only Garstin who had failed to make old man's bones.

After his death, Jake Atkinson, from Ribblehead in Yorkshire, had come to live at Hootsey. Jake was a fine farmer, a canny bargainer, and very handy among the sheep, till he took to drink, and roystering every week with the town wenches up at Carlisle. He was a corpulent, deep-voiced, free-handed fellow: when his time came, though he died very hardly, he remained festive and convivial to the last. And for years afterwards, in the valley, his memory lingered: men spoke of him regretfully, recalling his quips, his feats of strength, and his choice breed of Herdwicke rams. But he left behind him a host of debts up at Carlisle, in Penrith, and in almost every market town – debts that he had long ago pretended to have paid with money that belonged to his sister. The widow Garstin sold the twelve Herdwicke rams, and nine acres of land: within six weeks she had cleared off every penny, and for thirteen months, on Sundays, wore her mourning with a mute, forbidding grimness: the bitter thought that, unbeknown to her, Jake had acted dishonestly in money matters, and that he had ended his days in riotous sin, soured her pride, imbued her with a rancorous hostility against all the world. For she was a very proud woman, independent, holding her head high, so folks said, like a Garstin bred and born; and Anthony, although some reckoned him quiet and of little account, came to take after her as he grew into manhood.

She took into her own hands the management of the Hootsey farm, and set the boy to work for her along with the two farm servants. It was twenty-five years now since his uncle Jake's death: there were grey hairs in his sandy beard; but he still worked for his mother, as he had done when a growing lad.

And now that times were grown to be bad (of late years the price of stock had been steadily falling; and the hay harvests had drifted from bad to worse) the widow Garstin no longer kept any labouring men; but lived, she and her son, year in and year out, in a close parsimonious way.

That had been Anthony Garstin's life – a dull, eventless sort of business, the sluggish incrustation of monotonous years. And until Rosa Blencarn had come to keep house for her uncle, he had never thought twice on a woman's face.

The Garstins had always been good church-goers, and Anthony, for years, had acted as churchwarden. It was one summer evening, up at the vicarage, whilst he was checking the offertory account, that he first set eyes upon her. She was fresh back from school at Leeds: she was dressed in a white dress: she looked, he thought, like a London lady.

She stood by the window, tall and straight and queenly, dreamily gazing out into the summer twilight, whilst he and her uncle sat over their business. When he rose to go, she glanced at him with quick curiosity; he hurried away, muttering a sheepish good night.

The next time that he saw her was in church on Sunday. He watched her shyly, with a hesitating, reverential discretion: her beauty seemed to him wonderful, distant, enigmatic. In the afternoon, young Mrs Forsyth, from Longscale, dropped in for a cup of tea with his mother, and the two set off gossiping of Rosa Blencarn, speaking of her freely, in tones of acrimonious contempt. For a long while he sat silent, puffing at his pipe; but at last, when his mother concluded with, 'She looks t' me fair stuck-oop, full o' toonish airs an' graces,' despite himself, he burst out: 'Ye're jest wastin' yer breath wi' that cackle. I reckon Miss Blencarn's o' a different clay to us folks.' Young Mrs Forsyth tittered immoderately, and the next week it was rumoured about the valley that 'Tony Garstin was gone luny over t' parson's niece.'

But of all this he knew nothing – keeping to himself, as was his wont, and being, besides, very busy with the hay harvest – until one day, at dinner-time, Henry Sisson asked if he'd started his courting; Jacob Sowerby cried that Tony'd been too slow in getting to work, for that the girl had been seen spooning in Crosby Shaws with Curbison the auctioneer, and the others (there were half-a-dozen of them lounging round the hay-waggon) burst into a boisterous guffaw. Anthony flushed dully, looking hesitatingly from the one to the other; then slowly put down his beer-can, and of a sudden, seizing Jacob by the neck, swung him heavily on the grass. He fell against the waggon-wheel, and when he rose the blood was streaming from an ugly cut in his forehead. And henceforward Tony Garstin's courtship was the common jest of all the parish.

As yet, however, he had scarcely spoken to her, though twice he had passed her in the lane that led up to the vicarage. She had given him a frank, friendly smile; but he had not found the resolution to do more than lift his hat. He and Henry Sisson stacked the hay in the yard behind the house; there was no further mention made of Rosa Blencarn; but all day long Anthony, as he knelt thatching the rick, brooded over the strange sweetness of her face, and on the fell-top, while he tramped after the ewes over the dry, crackling heather, and as he jogged along the narrow, rickety road, driving his cartload of lambs into the auction mart.

Thus, as the weeks slipped by, he was content with blunt, wistful ruminations upon her indistinct image. Jacob Sowerby's accusation, and several kindred innuendoes let fall by his mother, left him coolly incredulous; the girl still seemed to him altogether distant; but from the first sight of her face he had evolved a stolid, unfaltering conception of her difference from the ruck of her sex.

But one evening, as he passed the vicarage on his way down from the fells, she called to him, and with a childish, confiding familiarity asked for advice concerning the feeding of the poultry. In his eagerness to answer her as best he could, he forgot his customary embarrassment, and grew, for the moment, almost voluble, and quite at his ease in her presence. Directly her flow of questions ceased, however, the returning perception of her rosy, hesitating smile, and of her large, deep eyes looking straight into his face, perturbed him strangely, and, reddening, he remembered the quarrel in the hay-field and the tale of Crosby Shaws.

After this, the poultry became a link between them — a link which he regarded in all seriousness, blindly unconscious that there was aught else to bring them together, only feeling himself in awe of her, because of her schooling, her townish manners, her ladylike mode of dress. And soon, he came to take a sturdy, secret pride in her friendly familiarity towards him. Several times a week he would meet her in the lane, and they would loiter a moment together; she would admire his dogs, though he assured her earnestly that they were but sorry curs; and once, laughing at his staidness, she nick-named him 'Mr Churchwarden'.

That the girl was not liked in the valley he suspected, curtly attributing her unpopularity to the women's senseless jealousy. Of gossip concerning her he heard no further hint; but instinctively, and partly from that rugged, natural reserve of his, shrank from mentioning her name, even incidentally, to his mother.

Now, on Sunday evenings, he often strolled up to the vicarage, each time quitting his mother with the same awkward affectation of casualness; and, on his return, becoming vaguely conscious of how she refrained from any comment on his absence, and appeared oddly oblivious of the existence of parson Blencarn's niece.

She had always been a sour-tongued woman; but, as the days shortened with the approach of the long winter months, she seemed to him to grow more fretful than ever; at times it was almost as if she bore him some smouldering, sullen resentment. He was of stubborn fibre, however, toughened by long habit of a bleak, unruly climate; he revolved the matter in his mind deliberately, and when, at last, after much plodding thought, it dawned upon him that she resented his acquaintance with Rosa Blencarn, he accepted the solution with an unflinching phlegm, and merely shifted his attitude towards the girl, calculating each day the likelihood of his meeting her, and making, in her presence, persistent efforts to break down, once for all, the barrier of his own timidity. He was a man not to be clumsily driven, still less, so he prided himself, a man to be craftily led.

It was close upon Christmas time before the crisis came. His mother was just home from Penrith market. The spring-cart stood in the yard, the old grey horse was steaming heavily in the still, frosty air.

'I reckon ye've come fast. T' ould horse is over hot,' he remarked bluntly, as he went to the animal's head.

She clambered down hastily, and, coming to his side, began breathlessly:

'Ye ought t' hev coom t' market, Tony. There's bin pretty goin's on in Pe'rith today. I was helpin' Anna Forsyth t' choose six yards o' sheetin' in Dockroy, when we sees Rosa Blencarn coom oot o' t' 'Bell and Bullock' in company we' Curbison and young Joe Smethwick. Smethwick was fair reelin' drunk, and Curbison and t' girl were a-houldin' on to him, to keep him fra fallin'; and then, after a bit, he puts his arm round the girl t' stiddy hisself, and that fashion they goes off, right oop t' public street —'

He continued to unload the packages, and to carry them mechanically one by one into the house. Each time, when he reappeared, she was standing by the steaming horse, busy with her tale.

'An' on t' road hame we passed t' three on' em in Curbison's trap, with Smethwick leein' in t' bottom, singin' maudlin' songs. They were passin' Dunscale village, an' t' folks coom runnin' oot o' houses t' see 'em go past —'

He led the cart away towards the stable, leaving her to cry the remainder after him across the yard.

Half-an-hour later he came in for his dinner. During the meal not a word passed between them, and directly he had finished he strode out of the house. About nine o'clock he returned, lit his pipe, and sat down to smoke it over the kitchen fire.

'Where've ye bin, Tony?' she asked.

'Oop t' vicarage, courtin',' he retorted defiantly, with his pipe in his mouth.

This was ten months ago; ever since he had been doggedly waiting. That evening he had set his mind on the girl, he intended to have her; and while his mother gibed, as she did now upon every opportunity, his patience remained grimly unflagging. She would remind him that the farm belonged to her, that he would have to wait till her death before he could bring the hussy to Hootsey: he would retort that as soon as the girl would have him, he intended taking a small holding over at Scarsdale. Then she would give way, and for a while piteously upbraid him with her old age, and with the memory of all the years she and he had spent together, and he would comfort her with a display of brusque, evasive remorse.

But, none the less, on the morrow, his thoughts would return to dwell on the haunting vision of the girl's face, while his own rude, credulous chivalry, kindled by the recollection of her beauty, stifled his misgivings concerning her conduct.

Meanwhile she dallied with him, and amused herself with the younger men. Her old uncle fell ill in the spring, and could scarcely leave the house. She declared that she found life in the valley intolerably dull, that she hated the quiet of the place, that she longed for Leeds, and the exciting bustle of the streets; and in the evenings she wrote long letters to the girl-friends she had left behind there, describing with petulant vivacity her tribe of rustic admirers. At the harvest-time she went back on a fortnight's visit to friends; the evening before her departure she promised Anthony to give him her answer on her return. But, instead, she avoided him, pretended to have promised in jest, and took up with Luke Stock, a cattle-dealer from Wigton.

V

It was three weeks since he had fetched his flock down from the fell.

After dinner he and his mother sat together in the parlour: they had done so every Sunday afternoon, year in and year out, as far back as he could remember.

A row of mahogany chairs, with shiny, horse-hair seats, were ranged round the room. A great collection of agricultural prize-tickets were pinned over the wall; and, on a heavy, highly-polished sideboard stood several silver cups. A heap of gilt-edged shavings filled the unused grate: there were gaudily-tinted roses along the mantelpiece, and, on a small table by the window, beneath a glass-case, a gilt basket filled with imitation flowers. Every object was disposed with a scrupulous precision: the carpet and the red-patterned cloth on the centre table were much faded. The room was spotlessly clean, and wore, in the chilly winter sunlight, a rigid, comfortless air.

Neither spoke, or appeared conscious of the other's presence. Old Mrs Garstin, wrapped in a woollen shawl, sat knitting: Anthony dozed fitfully on a stiff-backed chair.

Of a sudden, in the distance, a bell started tolling. Anthony rubbed his eyes drowsily, and taking from the table his Sunday hat, strolled out across the dusky fields. Presently, reaching a rude wooden seat, built beside the bridle-path, he sat down and relit his pipe. The air was very still; below him a white filmy mist hung across the valley: the fell-sides, vaguely grouped, resembled hulking masses of sombre shadow; and, as he looked back, three squares of glimmering gold revealed the lighted windows of the square-towered church.

He sat smoking; pondering, with placid and reverential contemplation, on the Mighty Maker of the world – a world majestically and inevitably ordered; a world where, he argued, each object – each fissure in the fells, the winding course of each tumbling stream – possesses its mysterious purport, its inevitable signification. . . .

At the end of the field two rams were fighting; retreating, then running together, and, leaping from the ground, butting head to head and horn to horn. Anthony watched them absently, pursuing his rude meditations.

. . . And the succession of bad seasons, the slow ruination of the farmers throughout the country, were but punishment meted out for the accumulated wickedness of the world. In the olden time God rained plagues upon the land: nowadays, in His wrath, He spoiled the produce of the earth, which, with His own hands, He had fashioned and bestowed upon men.

He rose and continued his walk along the bridle-path. A multitude of rabbits scuttled up the hill at his approach; and a great cloud of plovers, rising from the rushes, circled overhead, filling the air with a profusion of their querulous cries. All at once he heard a rattling of stones, and perceived a number of small pieces of shingle bounding in front of him down the grassy slope.

A woman's figure was moving among the rocks above him. The next moment, by the trimming of crimson velvet on her hat, he had recognized her. He mounted the slope with springing strides, wondering the while how it was she came to be there, that she was not in church playing the organ at afternoon service.

Before she was aware of his approach, he was beside her.

'I thought ye'd be in church —' he began.

She started: then, gradually regaining her composure, answered, weakly smiling:

'Mr Jenkinson, the new schoolmaster, wanted to try the organ.'

He came towards her impulsively: she saw the odd flickers in his eyes as she stepped back in dismay.

'Nay, but I will na harm ye,' he said. 'Only I reckon what 'tis a special turn o' Providence, meetin' wi' ye oop here. I reckon what ye'll hev t' give me a square answer noo. Ye canna dilly-dally everlastingly.'

He spoke almost brutally; and she stood, white and gasping,

staring at him with large, frightened eyes. The sheep-walk was but a tiny threadlike track: the slope of the shingle on either side was very steep: below them lay the valley; distant, lifeless, all blurred by the evening dusk. She looked about her helplessly for a means of escape.

'Miss Rosa,' he continued, in a husky voice, 'can ye na coom t' think on me? Think ye, I've bin waitin' nigh upon two year for ye. I've watched ye tak oop, first wi' this young fellar, and then wi' that, till soomtimes my heart's fit t' burst. Many a day, oop on t' fell-top, t' thought o' ye's nigh driven me daft, and I've left my shepherdin' jest t' set on a cairn in t' mist, picturin' an' broodin' on yer face. Many an evenin' I've started oop t' vicarage, wi' t' resolution t' speak right oot t' ye; but when it coomed t' point, a sort o' timidity seemed t' hould me back, I was that feared t' displease ye. I knaw I'm na scholar, an' mabbe ye think I'm rough-mannered. I knaw I've spoken sharply to ye once or twice lately. But it's jest because I'm that mad wi' love for ye: I jest canna help myself soomtimes —'

He waited, peering into her face. She could see the beads of sweat above his bristling eyebrows: the damp had settled on his sandy beard: his horny fingers were twitching at the buttons of his black Sunday coat.

She struggled to summon a smile; but her underlip quivered, and her large dark eyes filled slowly with tears.

And he went on:

'Ye've coom t' mean jest everything to me. Ef ye will na hev me, I care for nought else. I canna speak t' ye in phrases: I'm jest a plain, unscholarly man: I canna wheedle ye, wi' cunnin' after t' fashion o' toon folks. But I can love ye wi' all my might, an' watch over ye, and work for ye better than any one o' em —'

She was crying to herself, silently, while he spoke. He noticed nothing, however: the twilight hid her face from him.

'There's nought against me,' he persisted. 'I'm as good a man as any one on 'em. Ay, as good a man as any one on 'em,' he repeated defiantly, raising his voice.

'It's impossible, Mr Garstin, it's impossible. Ye've been very kind to me —' she added, in a choking voice.

'Wa dang it, I didna mean t' mak ye cry, lass,' he exclaimed, with a softening of his tone. 'There's nought for ye t' cry ower.'

She sank on to the stones, passionately sobbing in hysterical and defenceless despair. Anthony stood a moment, gazing at her in clumsy perplexity: then, coming close to her, put his hand on her shoulder, and said gently:

'Coom, lass, what's trouble? Ye can trust me.'

She shook her head faintly.

'Ay, but ye can though,' he asserted, firmly. 'Come, what is't?'

Heedless of him, she continued to rock herself to and fro, crooning in her distress:

'Oh! I wish I were dead! . . . I wish I could die!'

– 'Wish ye could die?' he repeated. 'Why, whatever can 't be that's troublin' ye like this? There, there, lassie, give ower: it 'ull all coom right, whatever it be —'

'No, no,' she wailed. 'I wish I could die! . . . I wish I could die!'

Lights were twinkling in the village below; and across the valley darkness was draping the hills. The girl lifted her face from her hands, and looked up at him with a scared, bewildered expression.

'I must go home: I must be getting home,' she muttered.

'Nay, but there's sommut mighty amiss wi' ye.'

'No, it's nothing . . . I don't know – I'm not well . . . I mean it's nothing . . . it'll pass over . . . you mustn't think anything of it.'

'Nay, but I canna stand by an see ye in sich trouble.'

'It's nothing, Mr Garstin, indeed it's nothing,' she repeated.

'Ay, but I canna credit that,' he objected stubbornly.

She sent him a shifting, hunted glance.

'Let me get home . . . you must let me get home.'

She made a tremulous, pitiful attempt at firmness. Eyeing her keenly, he barred her path: she flushed scarlet, and looked hastily away across the valley.

'If ye'll tell me yer distress, mabbe I can help ye.'

'No, no, it's nothing . . . it's nothing.'

'If ye'll tell me yer distress, mabbe I can help ye,' he repeated, with a solemn, deliberate sternness. She shivered, and looked away again, vaguely, across the valley.

'You can do nothing: there's nought to be done,' she murmured drearily.

'There's a man in this business,' he declared.

'Let me go! Let me go!' she pleaded desperately.

'Who is't that's bin puttin' ye into this distress?' His voice sounded loud and harsh.

'No one, no one. I canna tell ye, Mr Garstin. . . . It's no one,' she protested weakly. The white, twisted look on his face frightened her.

'My God!' he burst out, gripping her wrist, 'an' a proper soft fool ye've made o' me. Who is't, I tell ye? Who's t' man?'

'Ye're hurtin' me. Let me go. I canna tell ye.'

'And ye're fond o' him?'

'No, no. He's a wicked, sinful man. I pray God I may never set eyes on him again. I told him so.'

'But ef he's got ye into trouble, he'll hev t' marry ye,' he persisted with a brutal bitterness.

'I will not. I hate him!' she cried fiercely.

'But is he *willin'* t' marry ye?'

'I don't know . . . I don't care . . . he said so before he went away . . . But I'd kill myself sooner than live with him.'

He let her hands fall and stepped back from her. She could only see his figure, like a sombre cloud, standing before her. The whole fell-side seemed still and dark and lonely. Presently she heard his voice again:

'I reckon what there's one road oot o' yer distress.'

She shook her head drearily.

'There's none. I'm a lost woman.'

'An' ef ye took me instead?' he said eagerly.

'I – I don't understand —'

'Ef ye married me instead of Luke Stock?'

'But that's impossible – the – the —'

'Ay, t' child. I know. But I'll tak t' child as mine.'

She remained silent. After a moment he heard her voice answer in a queer, distant tone:

'You mean that – that ye're ready to marry me, and adopt the child?'

'I do,' he answered doggedly.

'But people – your mother —?'

'Folks 'ull jest know nought about it. It's none o' their business. T' child 'ull pass as mine. Ye'll accept that?'

'Yes,' she answered, in a low, rapid voice.

'Ye'll consent t' hev me, ef I git ye oot o' yer trouble?'

'Yes,' she repeated, in the same tone.

She heard him draw a long breath.

'I said 't was a turn o' Providence, meetin' wi' ye oop here,' he exclaimed, with half-suppressed exultation.

Her teeth began to chatter a little: she felt that he was peering at her, curiously, through the darkness.

'An' noo,' he continued briskly, 'ye'd best be gettin' home. Give me ye're hand, an' I'll stiddy ye ower t' stones.'

He helped her down the bank of shingle, exclaiming: 'By goom, ye're stony cauld.' Once or twice she slipped: he supported her, roughly gripping her knuckles. The stones rolled down the steps, noisily, disappearing into the night.

Presently they struck the turf bridle-path, and, as they descended silently towards the lights of the village, he said gravely:

'I always reckoned what my day 'ud coom.'

She made no reply; and he added grimly:

'There'll be terrible work wi' mother over this.'

He accompanied her down the narrow lane that led past her uncle's house. When the lighted windows came in sight he halted.

'Good night, lassie,' he said kindly. 'Do ye give ower distressin' yeself.'

'Good night, Mr Garstin,' she answered, in the same low, rapid voice in which she had given him her answer up on the fell.

'We're man an' wife plighted now, are we not?' he blurted timidly.

She held her face to his, and he kissed her on the cheek, clumsily.

VI

The next morning the frost had set in. The sky was still clear and glittering: the whitened fields sparkled in the chilly sunlight: here and there, on high, distant peaks, gleamed dainty caps of snow. All the week Anthony was to be busy at the fell-foot, wall-building against the coming of the winter storms: the work was heavy, for he was single-handed, and the stone had to be fetched from off the fell-side. Two or three times a day he led his rickety, lumbering cart along the lane that passed the vicarage gate, pausing on each journey to glance furtively up at the windows.

But he saw no sign of Rosa Blencarn; and, indeed, he felt no longing to see her: he was grimly exultant over the remembrance of his wooing of her, and over the knowledge that she was his. There glowed within him a stolid pride in himself: he thought of the others who had courted her, and the means by which he had won her seemed to him a fine stroke of cleverness.

And so he refrained from any mention of the matter; relishing, as he worked, all alone, the days through, the consciousness of his secret triumph, and anticipating, with inward chucklings, the discomforted cackle of his mother's female friends. He foresaw without misgiving, her bitter opposition: he felt himself strong; and his heart warmed towards the girl. And when, at intervals, the brusque realization that, after all, he was to possess her swept over him, he gripped the stones, and swung them almost fiercely into their places.

All around him the white, empty fields seemed slumbering breathlessly. The stillness stiffened the leafless trees. The frosty air flicked his blood: singing vigorously to himself he worked with a stubborn, unflagging resolution, methodically postponing, till the length of the wall should be completed, the announcement of his betrothal.

After his reticent, solitary fashion, he was very happy, reviewing his future prospects, with a plain and steady assurance, and, as the week-end approached, coming to ignore the irregularity of the whole business: almost to assume, in the exaltation of his pride, that he had won her honestly; and to discard, stolidly, all thought of Luke Stock, of his relations with her, of the coming child that was to pass for his own.

And there were moments too, when, as he sauntered homewards through the dusk at the end of his day's work, his heart grew full to overflowing of a rugged, superstitious gratitude towards God in Heaven who had granted his desires.

About three o'clock on the Saturday afternoon he finished the length of wall. He went home, washed, shaved, put on his Sunday coat; and, avoiding the kitchen, where his mother sat knitting by the fireside, strode up to the vicarage.

It was Rosa who opened the door to him. On recognizing him she started, and he followed her into the dining-room. He seated himself, and began, brusquely:

'I've coom, Miss Rosa, t' speak t' Mr Blencarn.'

Then added, eyeing her closely:

'Ye're lookin' sick, lass.'

Her faint smile accentuated the worn, white look on her face.

'I reckon ye've been frettin' yeself,' he continued gently, 'leein' awake o' nights, hev'n't yee, noo?'

She smiled vaguely.

'Well, but ye see I've coom t' settle t' whole business for ye. Ye thought mabbe that I was na a man o' my word.'

'No, no, not that,' she protested, 'but – but –'

'But what then?'

'Ye must not do it, Mr Garstin . . . I must just bear my own trouble the best I can —' she broke out.

'D'ye fancy I'm takin' ye oot of charity? Ye little reckon the sort o' stuff my love for ye's made of. Nay, Miss Rosa, but ye canna draw back noo.'

'But ye cannot do it, Mr Garstin. Ye know your mother will na have me at Hootsey. . . . I could na live there with your mother. . . . I'd sooner bear my trouble alone, as best I can. . . . She's that stern is Mrs Garstin. I couldn't look her in the face. . . . I can go away somewhere. . . . I could keep it all from uncle.'

Her colour came and went: she stood before him, looking away from him, dully, out of the window.

'I intend ye t' coom t' Hootsey. I'm na lad: I reckon I can choose my own wife. Mother'll hev ye at t' farm, right enough: ye need na distress yeself on that point —'

'Nay, Mr Garstin, but indeed she will not, never. . . . I know she will not. . . . She always set herself against me, right from the first.'

'Ay, but that was different. T' case is all changed noo,' he objected doggedly.

'She'll support the sight of me all the less,' the girl faltered.

'Mother'll hev ye at Hootsey – receive ye willin' of her own free wish – of her own free wish, d'ye hear? I'll answer for that.'

He struck the table with his fist heavily. His tone of determination awed her: she glanced at him hurriedly, struggling with her irresolution.

'I knaw hoo t' manage mother. An' now,' he concluded, changing his tone, 'is yer uncle about t' place?'

'He's up the paddock, I think,' she answered.

'Well, I'll jest step oop and hev a word wi' him.'

'Ye're . . . ye will na tell him.'

'Tut, tut, na harrowin' tales, ye need na fear, lass. I reckon ef I can tackle mother, I can accommodate myself t' parson Blencarn.'

He rose, and coming close to her, scanned her face.

'Ye must git t' roses back t' yer cheeks,' he exclaimed, with a short laugh, 'I canna be takin' a ghost t' church.'

She smiled tremulously, and he continued, laying one hand affectionately on her shoulder:

'Nay, but I was but jestin'. Roses or na roses, ye'll be t' bonniest bride in all Coomberland. I'll meet ye in Hullam lane, after church time, tomorrow,' he added, moving towards the door.

After he had gone, she hurried to the backdoor furtively. His retreating figure was already mounting the grey upland field. Presently, beyond him, she perceived her uncle, emerging through the paddock gate. She ran across the poultry yard, and mounting a tub, stood watching the two figures as they moved towards one another along the brow, Anthony vigorously trudging, with his hands thrust deep in his pockets; her uncle, his wideawake tilted over his nose, hobbling, and leaning stiffly on his pair of sticks. They met; she saw Anthony take her uncle's arm: the two, turning together, strolled away towards the fell.

She went back into the house. Anthony's dog came towards her, slinking along the passage. She caught the animal's head in her hands, and bent over it caressingly, in an impulsive outburst of almost hysterical affection.

VII

The two men returned towards the vicarage. At the paddock gate they halted, and the old man concluded:

'I could not have wished a better man for her, Anthony. Mabbe the Lord'll not be minded to spare me much longer. After I'm gone Rosa'll hev all I possess. She was my poor brother Isaac's only child. After her mother was taken, he, poor fellow, went altogether to the bad, and until she came here she mostly lived among strangers. It's been a wretched sort of childhood for her – a wretched sort of childhood. Ye'll take care of her, Anthony, will ye not? . . . Nay, but I could not hev wished for a better man for her, and there's my hand on 't.'

'Thank ee, Mr Blencarn, thank ee,' Anthony answered huskily, gripping the old man's hand.

And he started off down the lane homewards.

His heart was full of a strange, rugged exaltation. He felt with a swelling pride that God had entrusted to him this great charge – to tend her; to make up to her, tenfold, for all that loving care, which, in her childhood, she had never known. And together with a stubborn confidence in himself, there welled up within him a great pity for her – a tender pity, that, chastening with his passion, made her seem to him, as he brooded over that lonely childhood of hers, the more distinctly beautiful, the more profoundly precious. He pictured to himself, tremulously, almost incredulously, their married life – in the winter, his return home at nightfall to find her awaiting him with a glad, trustful smile; their evenings, passed together, sitting in silent happiness over the smouldering logs; or, in summer-time, the midday rest in the hay-fields when, wearing perhaps a large-brimmed hat fastened with a red ribbon, beneath her chin, he would catch sight of her, carrying his dinner, coming across the upland.

She had not been brought up to be a farmer's wife: she was but a child still, as the old parson had said. She should not have to work as other men's wives worked: she should dress like a lady, and on Sundays, in church, wear fine bonnets, and remain, as she had always been, the belle of all the parish.

And, meanwhile, he would farm as he had never farmed before, watching his opportunities, driving cunning bargains, spending nothing on himself, hoarding every penny that she might have what she wanted. . . . And, as he strode through the village, he seemed to foresee a general brightening of prospects, a sobering of the fever of speculation in sheep, a cessation of the insensate glutting, year after year, of the great winter marts throughout the North, a slackening of the foreign competition followed by a steady revival of the price of fatted stocks – a period of prosperity in store for the farmer at last. . . . And the future years appeared to open out before him, spread like a distant, glittering plain, across which, he and she, hand in hand, were called to travel together. . . .

And then, suddenly, as his iron-bound boots clattered over the cobbled yard, he remembered, with brutal determination, his mother, and the stormy struggle that awaited him.

He waited till supper was over, till his mother had moved from the table to her place by the chimney corner. For several minutes he remained debating with himself the best method of breaking the news to her. Of a sudden he glanced up at her: her knitting had slipped on to her lap: she was sitting, bunched of a heap in her chair, nodding with sleep. By the flickering light of the wood fire, she looked worn and broken: he felt a twinge of clumsy compunction. And then he remembered the piteous, hunted look in the girl's eyes, and the old man's words when they had parted at the paddock gate, and he blurted out:

'I doot but what I'll hev t' marry Rosa Blencarn after all.'

She started, and blinking her eyes, said:

'I was jest takin' a wink o' sleep. What was 't ye were saying, Tony?'

He hesitated a moment, puckering his forehead into coarse rugged lines, and fidgeting noisily with his tea-cup. Presently he repeated:

'I doot but what I'll hev t' marry Rosa Blencarn after all.'

She rose stiffly, and stepping down from the hearth, came towards him.

'Mabbe I did na hear ye aright, Tony.' She spoke hurriedly, and though she was quite close to him, steadying herself with one hand clutching the back of his chair, her voice sounded weak, distant almost.

'Look oop at me. Look oop into my face,' she commanded fiercely.

He obeyed sullenly.

'Noo oot wi 't. What's yer meanin', Tony?'

'I mean what I say,' he retorted doggedly, averting his gaze.

'What d'ye mean by sayin' that ye've *got* t' marry her?'

'I tell yer I mean what I say,' he repeated dully.

'Ye mean ye've bin an' put t' girl in trouble?'

He said nothing; but sat staring stupidly at the floor.

'Look oop at me, and answer,' she commanded, gripping his shoulder and shaking him.

He raised his face slowly, and met her glance.

'Ay, that's aboot it,' he answered.

'This'll na be truth. It'll be jest a piece o' wanton trickery!' she cried.

'Nay, but 't is truth,' he answered deliberately.

'Ye will na swear t' it?' she persisted.

'I see na necessity for swearin'.'

'Then ye canna swear t' it,' she burst out triumphantly.

He paused an instant; then said quietly:

'Ay, but I'll swear t' it easy enough. Fetch t' Book.'

She lifted the heavy, tattered Bible from the chimney-piece, and placed it before him on the table. He laid his lumpish fist on it.

'Say,' she continued with a tense tremulousness, 'say, I swear t' ye, mother, that 't is t' truth, t' whole truth, and noat but t' truth, s'help me God.'

'I swear t' ye, mother, it's truth, t' whole truth, and nothin' but t' truth, s'help me God,' he repeated after her.

'Kiss t' Book,' she ordered.

He lifted the Bible to his lips. As he replaced it on the table, he burst out into a short laugh:

'Be ye satisfied noo?'

She went back to the chimney corner without a word. The logs on the hearth hissed and crackled. Outside, amid the blackness the wind was rising, hooting through the firs, and past the windows.

After a long while he roused himself, and drawing his pipe from his pocket almost steadily, proceeded leisurely to pare in the palm of his hand a lump of black tobacco.

'We'll be asked in church Sunday,' he remarked bluntly.

She made no answer.

He looked across at her.

Her mouth was drawn tight at the corners: her face wore a queer, rigid aspect. She looked, he thought, like a figure of stone.

'Ye're not feeling poorly, are ye, mother?' he asked.

She shook her head grimly: then, hobbling out into the room, began to speak in a shrill, tuneless voice.

'Ye talked at one time o' takin' a farm over Scarsdale way. But ye'd best stop here. I'll no hinder ye. Ye can have t' large bedroom in t' front, and I'll move ower to what used to be my brother Jake's room. Ye knaw I've never had no opinion of t' girl, but I'll do what's right by her, ef I break my sperrit in t' doin' on't. I'll mak' t' girl welcome here: I'll stand by her proper-like: mebbe I'll finish by findin' soom good in her. But from this day forward, Tony, ye're na son o' mine. Ye've dishonoured yeself: ye've laid a trap for me – ay, laid a trap, that's t' word. Ye've brought shame and bitterness on yer ould mother in her ould age. Ye've made me despise t' varra seet o' ye. Ye can stop on here, but ye shall niver touch a penny of my money; every shillin' of 't shall go t' yer child, or to your child's children. Ay,' she went on, raising her voice, 'ay, ye've got yer way at last, and mebbe ye reckon ye've chosen a mighty smart way. But time 'ull coom when ye'll regret this day, when ye eat oot yer repentance in doost an' ashes. Ay, Lord 'ull punish ye, Tony, chastize ye properly. Ye'll learn that marriage begun in sin can end in nought but sin. Ay,' she concluded, as she reached the door, raising her skinny hand prophetically, 'ay, after I'm deed and gone, ye mind ye o' t' words o' t' apostle – "For them that hev sinned without t' law, shall also perish without t' law." '

And she slammed the door behind her.

George Egerton
(Mary Chavelita [Dunne] Bright)

A LITTLE GREY GLOVE

(*Keynotes*, London: Elkin Mathews and John Lane, Vigo Street, 1893)

Early-Spring, 1893

The book of life begins with a man and woman in a garden and ends – with Revelations.

OSCAR WILDE

Yes, most fellows' book of life may be said to begin at the chapter where woman comes in; mine did. She came in years ago, when I was a raw undergraduate. With the sober thought of retrospective analysis, I may say she was not all my fancy painted her; indeed now that I come to think of it there was no fancy about the vermeil of her cheeks, rather an artificial reality; she had her bower in the bar of the Golden Boar, and I was madly in love with her, seriously intent on lawful wedlock. Luckily for me she threw me over for a neighbouring pork butcher, but at the time I took it hardly, and it made me sex-shy. I was a very poor man in those days. One feels one's griefs more keenly then, one hasn't the wherewithal to buy distraction. Besides, ladies snubbed me rather, on the rare occasions I met them. Later I fell in for a legacy, the forerunner of several; indeed, I may say I am beastly rich. My tastes are simple too, and I haven't any poor relations. I believe they are of great assistance in getting rid of superfluous capital, wish I had some! It was after the legacy that women discovered my attractions. They found that there was something superb in my plainness (before, they said ugliness), something after the style of the late Victor Emanuel, something infinitely more striking than mere ordinary beauty. At least so Harding told me his sister said, and she had the reputation of being a clever girl. Being an only child, I never had the opportunity other fellows had of

studying the undress side of women through familiar intercourse, say with sisters. Their most ordinary belongings were
sacred to me. I had, I used to be told, ridiculous high-flown
notions about them (by the way I modified those considerably on
closer acquaintance). I ought to study them, nothing like a woman
for developing a fellow. So I laid in a stock of books in different
languages, mostly novels, in which women played title roles, in
order to get up some definite data before venturing amongst
them. I can't say I derived much benefit from this course. There
seemed to be as great a diversity of opinion about the female
species as, let us say, about the salmonidae.

My friend Ponsonby Smith, who is one of the oldest fly-fishers
in the three kingdoms, said to me once: 'Take my word for it,
there are only four true salmo; the salar, the trutta, the fario, the
ferox; all the rest are just varieties, subgenuses of the above;
stick to that. Some writing fellow divided all the women into
good-uns and bad-uns. But as a conscientious stickler for truth, I
must say that both in trout as in women, I have found myself
faced with most puzzling varieties, that were a tantalizing blend-
ing of several qualities.' I then resolved to study them on my own
account. I pursued the Eternal Feminine in a spirit of purely
scientific investigation. I knew you'd laugh sceptically at that,
but it's a fact. I was impartial in my selection of subjects for
observation – French, German, Spanish, as well as the home
product. Nothing in petticoats escaped me. I devoted myself to
the freshest *ingenue* as well as the experienced widow of three
departed; and I may as well confess that the more I saw of her,
the less I understood her. But I think they understood me. They
refused to take me *au sérieux*. When they weren't fleecing me,
they were interested in the state of my soul (I preferred the
former), but all humbugged me equally, so I gave them up. I took
to rod and gun instead, *pro salute animae*; it's decidedly safer. I
have scoured every country in the globe; indeed I can say that I
have shot and fished in woods and waters where no other white
man, perhaps ever dropped a beast or played a fish before. There
is no life like the life of a free wanderer, and no lore like the lore
one gleans in the great book of nature. But one must have freed
one's spirit from the taint of the town before one can even read
the alphabet of its mystic meaning.

What has this to do with the glove? True, not much, and yet it has a connection – it accounts for me.

Well, for twelve years I have followed the impulses of the wandering spirit that dwells in me. I have seen the sun rise in Finland and gild the Devil's Knuckles as he sank behind the Drachensberg. I have caught the barba and the gamer yellow fish in the Vaal river, taken muskelunge and black-bass in Canada, thrown a fly over *guapote* and *cavallo* in Central American lakes, and choked the monster eels of the Mauritius with a cunningly faked-up duckling. But I have been shy as a chub at the shadow of a woman.

Well, it happened last year I came back on business – another confounded legacy; end of June too, just as I was off to Finland. But Messrs. Thimble and Rigg, the highly respectable firm who look after my affairs, represented that I owed it to others, whom I kept out of their share of the legacy, to stay near town till affairs were wound up. They told me, with a view to reconcile me perhaps, of a trout stream with a decent inn near it; an unknown stream in Kent. It seems a junior member of the firm is an angler, at least he sometimes catches pike or perch in the Medway some way from the stream where the trout rise in audacious security from artificial lures. I stipulated for a clerk to come down with any papers to be signed, and started at once for Victoria. I decline to tell the name of my find, firstly because the trout are the gamest little fish that ever rose to fly and run to a good two pounds. Secondly, I have paid for all the rooms in the inn for the next year, and I want it to myself. The glove is lying on the table next me as I write. If it isn't in my breast-pocket or under my pillow, it is in some place where I can see it. It has a delicate grey body (suède, I think they call it) with a whipping of silver round the top, and a darker grey silk tag to fasten it. It is marked 5¾ inside, and has a delicious scent about it, to keep off moths, I suppose; naphthaline is better. It reminds me of a 'silver-sedge' tied on a ten hook. I startled the good landlady of the little inn (there is no village fortunately) when I arrived with the only porter of the tiny station laden with traps. She hesitated about a private sitting-room, but eventually we compromised matters, as I was willing to share it with the other visitor. I got into knickerbockers at once, collared a boy to get me worms and minnow for the morrow, and as I felt too lazy to unpack tackle, just sat in the shiny armchair (made comfortable by the successive sitting of former occupants) at the open window and looked out. The river, not the trout stream, winds to the right, and the trees cast trembling shadows into its clear depths. The red tiles of a farm roof show between the beeches, and break the monotony of blue sky background. A dusty waggoner is slaking his thirst with a tankard of ale. I am conscious of the strange lonely feeling that a visit to England always gives me. Away in strange lands, even in solitary places, one doesn't feel it somehow. One is filled with the hunter's lust, bent on a 'kill', but at home in the quiet country, with the smoke curling up from some fireside, the mowers busy laying the hay in swaths, the children tumbling under the trees in the orchards, and a girl singing as she spreads the clothes on the sweetbriar hedge, amidst a scene quick with home sights and sounds, a strange lack creeps in and makes itself felt in a dull, aching way. Oddly enough, too, I had a sense of uneasiness, a 'something going to happen'. I had often experienced it when out alone in a great forest, or on an unknown lake, and it always meant 'ware danger' of some kind. But why should I feel it here? Yet I did, and I couldn't shake it off. I took to examining the room. It was a commonplace one of the usual type. But there was a work-basket on the table, a dainty thing, lined with blue satin. There was a bit of lace stretched over shiny blue linen, with the needle sticking in it; such fairy work, like cobwebs seen from below, spun from a branch against a background of sky. A gold thimble, too, with initials, not the landlady's, I know. What pretty things, too, in the basket! A scissors, a capital shape for fly-making; a little file, and some floss silk and tinsel, the identical colour I want for a new fly I have in my head, one that will be a demon to kill. The northern devil I mean to call him. Some one looks in behind me, and a light step passes upstairs. I drop the basket, I don't know why. There are some reviews near it. I take up one, and am soon buried in an article on Tasmanian fauna. It is strange, but whenever I do know anything about a subject, I always find these writing fellows either entirely ignorant or damned wrong.

After supper, I took a stroll to see the river. It was a silver grey evening, with just the last lemon and pink streaks of the sunset staining the sky. There had been a shower, and somehow the smell

of the dust after rain mingled with the mignonette in the garden
brought back vanished scenes of small-boyhood, when I caught
minnows in a bottle, and dreamt of a shilling rod as happiness
unattainable. I turned aside from the road in accordance with
directions, and walked towards the stream. Holloa! someone
before me, what a bore! The angler is hidden by an elder-bush, but
I can see the fly drop delicately, artistically on the water. Fishing
upstream, too! There is a bit of broken water there, and the
midges dance in myriads; a silver gleam, and the line spins out,
and the fly falls just in the right place. It is growing dusk, but the
fellow is an adept at quick, fine casting – I wonder what fly he has
on – why, he's going to try downstream now? I hurry forward,
and as I near him, I swerve to the left out of the way. S-s-s-s! a
sudden sting in the lobe of my ear. Hey! I cry as I find I am caught;
the tail fly is fast in it. A slight, grey-clad woman holding the rod
lays it carefully down and comes towards me through the
gathering dusk. My first impulse is to snap the gut and take to my
heels, but I am held by something less tangible but far more
powerful than the grip of the Limerick hook in my ear.

'I am very sorry!' she says in a voice that matched the evening, it
was so quiet and soft; 'but it was exceedingly stupid of you to
come behind like that.'

'I didn't think you threw such a long line; I thought I was safe,' I
stammered.

'Hold this!' she says, giving me a diminutive fly-book, out of
which she has taken a scissors. I obey meekly. She snips the gut.

'Have you a sharp knife? If I strip the hook you can push it
through; it is lucky it isn't in the cartilage.'

I suppose I am an awful idiot, but I only handed her the knife,
and she proceeded as calmly as if stripping a hook in a man's ear
were an everyday occurrence. Her gown is of some soft grey stuff,
and her grey leather belt is silver clasped. Her hands are soft and
cool and steady, but there is a rarely disturbing thrill in their
gentle touch. The thought flashed through my mind that I had just
missed that, a woman's voluntary tender touch, not a paid caress,
all my life.

'Now you can push it through yourself. I hope it won't hurt
much.' Taking the hook, I push it through, and a drop of blood
follows it. 'Oh!' she cries, but I assure her it is nothing, and stick

the hook surreptitiously in my coat sleeve. Then we both laugh, and I look at her for the first time. She has a very white forehead, with little tendrils of hair blowing round it under her grey cap, her eyes are grey. I didn't see that then, I only saw they were steady, smiling eyes that matched her mouth. Such a mouth, the most maddening mouth a man ever longed to kiss, above a too-pointed chin, soft as a child's; indeed, the whole face looks soft in the misty light.

'I am sorry I spoilt your sport!' I say.

'Oh, that don't matter, it's time to stop. I got two brace, one a beauty.'

She is winding in her line, and I look in her basket; they *are* beauties, one two-pounder, the rest running from a half to a pound.

'What fly?'

'Yellow dun took that one, but your assailant was a partridge spider.' I sling her basket over my shoulder; she takes it as a matter of course, and we retrace our steps. I feel curiously happy as we walk towards the road; there is a novel delight in her nearness; the feel of woman works subtly and strangely in me; the rustle of her skirt as it brushes the black-heads in the meadow-grass, and the delicate perfume, partly violets, partly herself, that comes to me with each of her movements is a rare pleasure. I am hardly surprised when she turns into the garden of the inn, I think I knew from the first that she would.

'Better bathe that ear of yours, and put a few drops of carbolic in the water.' She takes the basket as she says it, and goes into the kitchen. I hurry over this, and go into the little sitting-room. There is a tray with a glass of milk and some oaten cakes upon the table. I am too disturbed to sit down; I stand at the window and watch the bats flitter in the gathering moonlight, and listen with quivering nerves for her step – perhaps she will send for the tray, and not come after all. What a fool I am to be disturbed by a grey-clad witch with a tantalizing mouth! That comes of loafing about doing nothing. I mentally darn the old fool who saved her money instead of spending it. Why the devil should I be bothered? I don't want it anyhow. She comes in as I fume, and I forget everything at her entrance. I push the armchair towards the table, and she sinks quietly into it, pulling the tray nearer. She has a wedding ring on, but somehow it never strikes me to wonder if she is married or a widow or who she may be. I am content to watch her break her biscuits. She has the prettiest hands, and a trick of separating her last fingers when she takes hold of anything. They remind me of white orchids I saw somewhere. She led me to talk; about Africa, I think. I liked to watch her eyes glow deeply in the shadow and then catch light as she bent forward to say something in her quick responsive way.

'Long ago when I was a girl,' she said once.

'Long ago?' I echo incredulously, 'surely not?'

'Ah, but yes, you haven't seen me in the daylight,' with a soft little laugh. 'Do you know what the gipsies say? "Never judge a woman or a ribbon by candle-light." They might have said moonlight equally well.'

She rises as she speaks, and I feel an overpowering wish to have her put out her hand. But she does not, she only takes the work-basket and a book, and says good night with an inclination of her little head.

I go over and stand next to her chair; I don't like to sit in it, but I like to put my hand where her head leant, and fancy, if she were there, how she would look up.

I woke next morning with a curious sense of pleasurable excitement. I whistled from very lightness of heart as I dressed. When I got down I found the landlady clearing away her breakfast things. I felt disappointed and resolved to be down earlier in future. I didn't feel inclined to try the minnow. I put them in a tub in the yard and tried to read and listen for her step. I dined alone. The day dragged terribly. I did not like to ask about her, I had a notion she might not like it. I spent the evening on the river. I might have filled a good basket, but I let the beggars rest. After all, I had caught fish enough to stock all the rivers in Great Britain. There are other things than trout in the world. I sit and smoke a pipe where she caught me last night. If I half close my eyes I can see hers, and her mouth in the smoke. That is one of the curious charms of baccy, it helps to reproduce brain pictures. After a bit, I think 'perhaps she has left'. I get quite feverish at the thought and hasten back. I must ask. I look up at the window as I pass; there is surely a gleam of white. I throw down my traps and hasten up. She is leaning with her arms on the window-ledge staring out into the gloom. I could swear I caught a suppressed sob as I entered. I cough, and she turns quickly and bows slightly. A bonnet and gloves and lace affair and a lot of papers are lying on the table. I am awfully afraid she is going. I say –

'Please don't let me drive you away, it is so early yet. I half expected to see you on the river.'

'Nothing so pleasant; I have been up in town (the tears have certainly got into her voice) all day; it was so hot and dusty, I am tired out.'

The little servant brings in the lamp and a tray with a bottle of lemonade.

'Mistress hasn't any lemons, 'm, will this do?'

'Yes,' she says wearily, she is shading her eyes with her hand; 'anything; I am fearfully thirsty.'

'Let me concoct you a drink instead. I have lemons and ice and things. My man sent me down supplies today; I leave him in town. I am rather a dab at drinks; I learnt it from the Yankees; about the only thing I did learn from them I care to remember. Susan!' The little maid helps me to get the materials, and *she* watches me quietly. When I give it to her she takes it with a smile (she *has* been crying). That is an ample thank you. She looks quite old. Something more than tiredness called up those lines in her face.

*

Well, ten days passed, sometimes we met at breakfast, sometimes at supper, sometimes we fished together or sat in the straggling orchard and talked; she neither avoided me nor sought me. She is the most charming mixture of child and woman I ever met. She is a dual creature. Now I never met that in a man. When she is here without getting a letter in the morning or going to town, she seems like a girl. She runs about in her grey gown and little cap and laughs, and seems to throw off all thought like an irresponsible child. She is eager to fish, or pick gooseberries and eat them daintily, or sit under the trees and talk. But when she goes to town – I notice she always goes when she gets a lawyer's letter, there is no mistaking the envelope – she comes home tired and haggard-looking, an old woman of thirty-five. I wonder why. It takes her, even with her elasticity of temperament, nearly a day to get young again. I hate her to go to town; it is extraordinary how I miss her; I can't recall, when she is absent, her saying anything very wonderful, but she converses all the time. She has a gracious way of filling the place with herself, there is an entertaining quality in her very presence. We had one rainy afternoon; she tied me some flies (I shan't use any of them); I watched the lights in her hair as she moved, it is quite golden in some places, and she has a tiny mole near her left ear and another on her left wrist. On the eleventh day she got a letter but she didn't go to town, she stayed up in her room all day; twenty times I felt inclined to send her a line, but I had no excuse. I heard the landlady say as I passed the kitchen window: 'Poor dear! I'm sorry to lose her!' Lose her? I should think not. It has come to this with me that I don't care to face any future without her; and yet I know nothing about her, not even if she is a free woman. I shall find that out the next time I see her. In the evening I catch a glimpse of her gown in the orchard, and I follow her. We sit down near the river. Her left hand is lying gloveless next to me in the grass.

'Do you think from what you have seen of me, that I would ask a question out of any mere impertinent curiosity?'

She starts. 'No, I do not!'

I take up her hand and touch the ring. 'Tell me, does this bind you to any one?'

I am conscious of a buzzing in my ears and a dancing blurr of water and sky and trees, as I wait (it seems to me an hour) for her reply. I felt the same sensation once before, when I got drawn into some rapids and had an awfully narrow shave, but of that another time.

The voice is shaking.

'I am not legally bound to anyone, at least; but why do you ask?' she looks me square in the face as she speaks, with a touch of haughtiness I never saw in her before.

Perhaps the great relief I feel, the sense of joy at knowing she is free, speaks out of my face, for hers flushes and she drops her eyes, her lips tremble. I don't look at her again, but I can see her all the same. After a while she says —

'I half intended to tell you something about myself this evening, now I *must*. Let us go in. I shall come down to the sitting-room after your supper.' She takes a long look at the river and the inn, as if fixing the place in her memory; it strikes me with a chill that there is a goodbye in her gaze. Her eyes rest on me a moment as they come back, there is a sad look in their grey clearness. She swings her little grey gloves in her hand as we walk back. I can hear her walking up and down overhead; how tired she will be, and how slowly the time goes. I am standing at one side of the window when she enters; she stands at the other, leaning her head against the shutter with her hands clasped before her. I can hear my own heart beating, and, I fancy, hers through the stillness. The suspense is fearful. At length she says –

'You have been a long time out of England; you don't read the papers?'

'No.' A pause. I believe my heart is beating inside my head.

'You asked me if I was a free woman. I don't pretend to misunderstand why you asked me. I am not a beautiful woman, I never was. But there must be something about me, there is in some women, "essential femininity" perhaps, that appeals to all men. What I read in your eyes I have seen in many men's before, but before God I never tried to rouse it. Today (with a sob), I can say I am free, yesterday morning I could not. Yesterday my husband gained his case and divorced me!' she closes her eyes and draws in her under-lip to stop its quivering. I want to take her in my arms, but I am afraid to.

'I did not ask you any more than if you were free!'

'No, but I am afraid you don't quite take in the meaning. I did not divorce my husband, he divorced *me*, he got a decree *nisi*; do you understand now? (she is speaking with difficulty), do you know what that implies?'

I can't stand her face any longer. I take her hands, they are icy cold, and hold them tightly.

'Yes, I know what it implies, that is, I know the legal and social conclusion to be drawn from it – if that is what you mean. But I never asked you for that information. I have nothing to do with your past. You did not exist for me before the day we met on the river. I take you from that day and I ask you to marry me.'

I feel her tremble and her hands get suddenly warm. She turns her head and looks at me long and searchingly, then she says –

'Sit down, I want to say something!'

I obey, and she comes and stands next the chair. I can't help it, I reach up my arm, but she puts it gently down.

'No, you must listen without touching me, I shall go back to the window. I don't want to influence you a bit by any personal magnetism I possess. I want you to listen – I have told you he divorced me, the co-respondent was an old friend, a friend of my childhood, of my girlhood. He died just after the first application was made, luckily for me. He would have considered my honour before my happiness. *I* did not defend the case, it wasn't likely – ah, if you knew all? He proved his case; given clever counsel, willing witnesses to whom you make it worth while, and no defence, divorce is always attainable even in England. But remember: I figure as an adulteress in every English-speaking paper. If you buy last week's evening papers – do you remember the day I was in town?' – I nod – 'you will see a sketch of me in that day's; someone, perhaps he, must have given it; it was from an old photograph. I bought one at Victoria as I came out; it is funny (with an hysterical laugh) to buy a caricature of one's own poor face at a news-stall. Yet in spite of that I have felt glad. The point for you is that I made no defence to the world, and (with a lifting of her head) I will make no apology, no explanation, no denial to you, now nor ever. I am very desolate and your attention came very warm to me, but I don't love you. Perhaps I could learn to (with a rush of colour), for what you have said tonight, and it is because of that I tell you to weigh what this means. Later, when your care for me will grow into habit, you may chafe at my past. It is from that I would save you.'

I hold out my hands and she comes and puts them aside and takes me by the beard and turns up my face and scans it earnestly. She must have been deceived a good deal. I let her do as she pleases, it is the wisest way with women, and it is good to have her touch me in that way. She seems satisfied. She stands leaning against the arm of the chair and says –

'I must learn first to think of myself as a free woman again, it almost seems wrong today to talk like this; can you understand that feeling?'

I nod assent.

'Next time I must be sure, and you must be sure,' she lays her fingers on my mouth as I am about to protest, 'S-sh! You shall have a year to think. If you repeat then what you have said today, I shall give you your answer. You must not try to find me. I have money. If I am living, I will come here to you. If I am dead, you will be told of it. In the year between I shall look upon myself as belonging to you, and render an account if you wish of every hour. You will not be influenced by me in any way, and you will be able to reason it out calmly. If you think better of it, don't come.'

I feel there would be no use trying to move her, I simply kiss her hands and say:

'As you will, dear woman, I shall be here.'

We don't say any more; she sits down on a footstool with her head against my knee, and I just smooth it. When the clocks strike ten through the house, she rises and I stand up. I see that she has been crying quietly, poor lonely little soul. I lift her off her feet and kiss her, and stammer out my sorrow at losing her, and she is gone. Next morning the little maid brought me an envelope from the lady, who left by the first train. It held a little grey glove; that is why I carry it always, and why I haunt the inn and never leave it for longer than a week; why I sit and dream in the old chair that has a ghost of her presence always; dream of the spring to come with the May-fly on the wing, and the young summer when midges dance, and the trout are growing fastidious; when she will come to me across the meadow grass, through the silver haze, as she did before; come with her grey eyes shining to exchange herself for her little grey glove.

Israel Zangwill

THE WOMAN BEATER

(*The Grey Wig/Stories and Novelettes*, New York: The Macmillan
Company, 1903)

I

She came 'to meet John Lefolle', but John Lefolle did not know he
was to meet Winifred Glamorys. He did not even know he was
himself the meeting-point of all the brilliant and beautiful
persons, assembled in the publisher's Saturday Salon, for although a youthful minor poet, he was modest and lovable.
Perhaps his Oxford tutorship was sobering. At any rate his head
remained unturned by his precocious fame, and to meet these
other young men and women – his reverend seniors on the slopes
of Parnassus – gave him more pleasure than the receipt of
'royalties'. Not that his publisher afforded him much opportunity
of contrasting the two pleasures. The profits of the Muse went to
provide this room of old furniture and roses, this beautiful garden
a-twinkle with Japanese lanterns, like gorgeous fire-flowers
blossoming under the white crescent-moon of early June.

Winifred Glamorys was not literary herself. She was better than
a poetess, she was a poem. The publisher always threw in a few
realities, and some beautiful brainless creature would generally be
found the nucleus of a crowd, while Clio in spectacles languished
in a corner. Winifred Glamorys, however, was reputed to have a
tongue that matched her eye; paralleling with whimsies and
epigrams its freakish fires and witcheries, and, assuredly, flitting
in her white gown through the dark balmy garden, she seemed the
very spirit of moonlight, the subtle incarnation of night and roses.

When John Lefolle met her, Cecilia was with her, and the first
conversation was triangular. Cecilia fired most of the shots; she
was a bouncing, rattling beauty, chockful of confidence and high
spirits, except when asked to do the one thing she could do – sing!

Then she became — quite genuinely — a nervous, hesitant, pale little thing. However, the suppliant hostess bore her off, and presently her rich contralto notes passed through the garden, adding to its passion and mystery, and through the open French windows, John could see her standing against the wall near the piano, her head thrown back, her eyes half-closed, her creamy throat swelling in the very abandonment of artistic ecstasy.

'What a charming creature!' he exclaimed involuntarily.

'That is what everybody thinks, except her husband,' Winifred laughed.

'Is he blind then?' asked John with his cloistral *naïveté*.

'Blind? No, love is blind. Marriage is never blind.'

The bitterness in her tone pierced John. He felt vaguely the passing of some icy current from unknown seas of experience. Cecilia's voice soared out enchantingly.

'Then, marriage must be deaf,' he said, 'or such music as that would charm it.'

She smiled sadly. Her smile was the tricksy play of moonlight among clouds of faëry.

'You have never been married,' she said simply.

'Do you mean that you, too, are neglected?' something impelled him to exclaim.

'Worse,' she murmured.

'It is incredible!' he cried. 'You!'

'Hush! My husband will hear you.'

Her warning whisper brought him into a delicious conspiracy with her. 'Which is your husband?' he whispered back.

'There! Near the casement, standing gazing open-mouthed at Cecilia. He always opens his mouth when she sings. It is like two toys moved by the same wire.'

He looked at the tall, stalwart, ruddy-haired Anglo-Saxon. 'Do you mean to say he —?'

'I mean to say nothing.'

'But you said —'

'I said "worse".'

'Why, what can be worse?'

She put her hand over her face. 'I am ashamed to tell you.' How adorable was that half-divined blush!

'But you must tell me everything.' He scarcely knew how he had leapt into this role of confessor. He only felt they were 'moved by the same wire'.

Her head drooped on her breast. 'He – beats – me.'

'What!' John forgot to whisper. It was the greatest shock his recluse life had known, compact as it was of horror at the revelation, shamed confusion at her candour, and delicious pleasure in her confidence.

This fragile, exquisite creature under the rod of a brutal bully!

Once he had gone to a wedding reception, and among the serious presents some grinning Philistine drew his attention to an uncouth club – 'a wife-beater' he called it. The flippancy had jarred upon John terribly: this intrusive reminder of the customs of the slums. It grated like Billingsgate in a boudoir. Now that savage weapon recurred to him – for a lurid instant he saw Winifred's husband wielding it. Oh, abomination of his sex! And did he stand there, in his immaculate evening dress, posing as an English gentleman? Even so might some gentleman burglar bear through a salon his imperturbable swallow-tail.

Beat a woman! Beat that essence of charm and purity, God's best gift to man, redeeming him from his own grossness! Could such things be? John Lefolle would as soon have credited the French legend that English wives are sold in Smithfield. No! it could not be real that this flower-like figure was thrashed.

'Do you mean to say –?' he cried. The rapidity of her confidence alone made him feel it all of a dreamlike unreality.

'Hush! Cecilia's singing!' she admonished him with an unexpected smile, as her fingers fell from her face.

'Oh, you have been making fun of me.' He was vastly relieved. 'He beats you – at chess – or at lawn-tennis?'

'Does one wear a high-necked dress to conceal the traces of chess, or lawn-tennis?'

He had not noticed her dress before, save for its spiritual whiteness. Susceptible though he was to beautiful shoulders, Winifred's enchanting face had been sufficiently distracting. Now the thought of physical bruises gave him a second spasm of righteous horror. That delicate rose-leaf flesh abraded and lacerated!

'The ruffian! Does he use a stick or a fist?'

'Both! But as a rule he just takes me by the arms and shakes me like a terrier a rat. I'm all black and blue now.'

'Poor butterfly!' he murmured poetically.

'Why did I tell you?' she murmured back with subtler poetry.

The poet thrilled in every vein. 'Love at first sight', of which he had often read and often written, was then a reality! It could be as mutual, too, as Romeo's and Juliet's. But how awkward that Juliet should be married and her husband a Bill Sykes in broad-cloth!

II

Mrs Glamorys herself gave 'At Homes', every Sunday afternoon, and so, on the morrow, after a sleepless night mitigated by perpended sonnets, the love-sick young tutor presented himself by invitation at the beautiful old house in Hampstead. He was enchanted to find his heart's mistress set in an eighteenth-century frame of small-paned windows and of high oak-panelling, and at once began to image her dancing minuets and playing on virginals. Her husband was absent, but a broad band of velvet round Winifred's neck was a painful reminder of his possibilities. Winifred, however, said it was only a touch of sore throat caught in the garden. Her eyes added that there was nothing in the pathological dictionary which she would not willingly have caught for the sake of those divine, if draughty moments; but that, alas! it was more than a mere bodily ailment she had caught there.

There were a great many visitors in the two delightfully quaint rooms, among whom he wandered disconsolate and admired, jealous of her scattered smiles, but presently he found himself seated by her side on a 'cosy corner' near the open folding-doors, with all the other guests huddled round a violinist in the inner room. How Winifred had managed it he did not know but she sat plausibly in the outer room, awaiting newcomers, and this particular niche was invisible, save to a determined eye. He took her unresisting hand – that dear, warm hand, with its begemmed artistic fingers, and held it in uneasy beatitude. How wonderful! She – the beautiful and adored hostess, of whose sweetness and charm he heard even her own guests murmur to one another – it was her actual flesh-and-blood hand that lay in his – thrillingly tangible. Oh, adventure beyond all merit, beyond all hoping!

But every now and then, the outer door facing them would open on some newcomer, and John had hastily to release her soft magnetic fingers and sit demure, and jealously overhear her effusive welcome to those innocent intruders, nor did his brow clear till she had shepherded them within the inner fold. Fortunately, the refreshments were in this section, so that once therein, few of the sheep strayed back, and the jiggling wail of the violin was succeeded by a shrill babble of tongues and the clatter of cups and spoons. 'Get me an ice, please — strawberry,' she ordered John during one of these forced intervals in manual flirtation; and when he had steered laboriously to and fro, he found a young actor beside her in his cosy corner, and his jealous fancy almost saw *their* hands dispart. He stood over them with a sickly smile, while Winifred ate her ice. When he returned from depositing the empty saucer, the player-fellow was gone, and in remorse for his mad suspicion he stooped and reverently lifted her fragrant finger-tips to his lips. The door behind his back opened abruptly.

'Goodbye,' she said, rising in a flash. The words had the calm conventional cadence, and instantly extorted from him — amid all his dazedness — the corresponding 'Goodbye'. When he turned and saw it was Mr Glamorys who had come in, his heart leapt wildly at the nearness of his escape. As he passed this masked ruffian, he nodded perfunctorily and received a cordial smile. Yes, he was handsome and fascinating enough externally, this blonde savage.

'A man may smile and smile and be a villain,' John thought. 'I wonder how he'd feel, if he knew I knew he beats women.'

Already John had generalized the charge. 'I hope Cecilia will keep him at arm's length,' he had said to Winifred, 'if only that she may not smart for it some day.'

He lingered purposely in the hall to get an impression of the brute, who had begun talking loudly to a friend with irritating bursts of laughter, speciously frank-ringing. Golf, fishing, comic operas — ah, the Boeotian! These were the men who monopolized the ethereal divinities.

But this brusque separation from his particular divinity was disconcerting. How to see her again? He must go up to Oxford in the morning, he wrote her that night, but if she could possibly let him call during the week he would manage to run down again.

*

'Oh, my dear, dreaming poet,' she wrote to Oxford, 'how could you possibly send me a letter to be laid on the breakfast-table beside *The Times*! With a poem in it, too. Fortunately my husband was in a hurry to get down to the City, and he neglected to read my correspondence. ('The unchivalrous blackguard,' John commented. 'But what can be expected of a woman beater?') Never, never write to me again at the house. A letter, care of Mrs Best, 8A Foley Street, W.C., will always find me. She is my maid's mother. And you must not come here either, my dear handsome head-in-the-clouds, except to my 'At Homes', and then only at judicious intervals. I shall be walking round the pond in Kensington Gardens at four next Wednesday, unless Mrs Best brings me a letter to the contrary. And now thank you for your delicious poem; I do not recognize my humble self in the dainty lines, but I shall always be proud to think I inspired them. Will it be in the new volume? I have never been in print before; it will be a novel sensation. I cannot pay you song for song, only feeling for feeling. Oh, John Lefolle, why did we not meet when I had still my girlish dreams? Now, I have grown to distrust all men – to fear the brute beneath the cavalier. . . .'

*

Mrs Best did bring her a letter, but it was not to cancel the appointment, only to say he was not surprised at her horror of the male sex, but that she must beware of false generalizations. Life was still a wonderful and beautiful thing – *vide* poem enclosed. He was counting the minutes till Wednesday afternoon. It was surely a popular mistake that only sixty went to the hour.

This chronometrical reflection recurred to him even more poignantly in the hour that he circumambulated the pond in Kensington Gardens. Had she forgotten – had her husband locked her up? What could have happened? It seemed six hundred minutes, ere, at ten past five she came tripping daintily towards him. His brain had been reduced to insanely devising problems for his pupils – if a man walks two strides of one and a half feet a second round a lake fifty acres in area, in how many turns will he overtake a lady who walks half as fast and isn't there? – but the moment her pink parasol loomed on the horizon, all his long misery vanished in an ineffable peace and uplifting. He hurried, bare-headed, to clasp her little gloved hand. He had forgotten her unpunctuality, nor did she remind him of it.

'How sweet of you to come all that way,' was all she said, and it was a sufficient reward for the hours in the train and the six hundred minutes among the nursemaids and perambulators. The elms were in their glory, the birds were singing briskly, the water sparkled, the sunlit sward stretched fresh and green – it was the loveliest, coolest moment of the afternoon. John instinctively turned down a leafy avenue. Nature and Love! What more could poet ask?

'No, we can't have tea by the Kiosk,' Mrs Glamorys protested. 'Of course I love anything that savours of Paris, but it's become so fashionable. There will be heaps of people who know me. I suppose you've forgotten it's the height of the season. I know a quiet little place in the High Street.' She led him, unresisting but bemused, towards the gate, and into a confectioner's. Conversation languished on the way.

'Tea,' he was about to instruct the pretty attendant.

'Strawberry ices,' Mrs Glamorys remarked gently. 'And some of those nice French cakes.'

The ice restored his spirits, it was really delicious, and he had got so hot and tired, pacing round the pond. Decidedly Winifred was a practical person and he was a dreamer. The pastry he dared not touch – being a genius – but he was charmed at the gaiety with which Winifred crammed cake after cake into her rosebud of a mouth. What an enchanting creature! how bravely she covered up her life's tragedy!

The thought made him glance at her velvet band – it was broader than ever.

'He has beaten you again!' he murmured furiously. Her joyous eyes saddened, she hung her head, and her fingers crumbled the cake. 'What is his pretext?' he asked, his blood burning.

'Jealousy,' she whispered.

His blood lost its glow, ran cold. He felt the bully's blows on his own skin, his romance turning suddenly sordid. But he recovered his courage. He, too, had muscles. 'But I thought he just missed seeing me kiss your hand.'

She opened her eyes wide. 'It wasn't you, you darling old dreamer.'

He was relieved and disturbed in one.

'Somebody else?' he murmured. Somehow the vision of the player-fellow came up.

She nodded. 'Isn't it lucky he has himself drawn a red-herring across the track? I didn't mind his blows – *you* were safe!' Then, with one of her adorable transitions, 'I am dreaming of another ice,' she cried with roguish wistfulness.

'I was afraid to confess my own greediness,' he said, laughing. He beckoned the waitress. 'Two more.'

'We haven't got any more strawberries,' was her unexpected reply. 'There's been such a run on them today.'

Winifred's face grew overcast. 'Oh, nonsense!' she pouted. To John the moment seemed tragic.

'Won't you have another kind?' he queried. He himself liked any kind, but he could scarcely eat a second ice without her.

Winifred meditated. 'Coffee?' she queried.

The waitress went away and returned with a face as gloomy as Winifred's. 'It's been such a hot day,' she said deprecatingly. 'There is only one ice in the place and that's Neapolitan.'

'Well, bring two Neapolitans,' John ventured.

'I mean there is only one Neapolitan ice left.'

'Well, bring that. I don't really want one.'

He watched Mrs Glamorys daintily devouring the solitary ice, and felt a certain pathos about the parti-coloured oblong, a something of the haunting sadness of 'The Last Rose of Summer'. It would make a graceful, serio-comic triolet, he was thinking. But at the last spoonful, his beautiful companion dislocated his rhymes by her sudden upspringing.

'Goodness gracious,' she cried, 'how late it is!'

'Oh, you're not leaving me yet!' he said. A world of things sprang to his brain, things that he was going to say – to arrange. They had said nothing – not a word of their love even; nothing but cakes and ices.

'Poet!' she laughed. 'Have you forgotten I live at Hampstead?' She picked up her parasol.

'Put me into a hansom, or my husband will be raving at his lonely dinner-table.'

He was so dazed as to be surprised when the waitress blocked his departure with a bill. When Winifred was spirited away, he remembered she might, without much risk, have given him a lift to Paddington. He hailed another hansom and caught the next train to Oxford. But he was too late for his own dinner in Hall.

III

He was kept very busy for the next few days, and could only exchange a passionate letter or two with her. For some time the examination fever had been raging, and in every college poor patients sat with wet towels round their heads. Some, who had neglected their tutor all the term, now strove to absorb his omniscience in a sitting.

On the Monday, John Lefolle was good-naturedly giving a special audience to a muscular dunce, trying to explain to him the political effects of the Crusades, when there was a knock at the sitting-room door, and the scout ushered in Mrs Glamorys. She was bewitchingly dressed in white, and stood in the open doorway, smiling – an embodiment of the summer he was neglecting. He rose, but his tongue was paralysed. The dunce became suddenly important – a symbol of the decorum he had been outraging. His soul, torn so abruptly from history to romance, could not get up the right emotion. Why this imprudence of Winifred's? She had been so careful heretofore.

'What a lot of boots there are on your staircase!' she said gaily.

He laughed. The spell was broken. 'Yes, the heap to be cleaned is rather obtrusive,' he said, 'but I suppose it is a sort of tradition.'

'I think I've got hold of the thing pretty well now, sir.' The dunce rose and smiled, and his tutor realized how little the dunce had to learn in some things. He felt quite grateful to him.

'Oh, well, you'll come and see me again after lunch, won't you, if one or two points occur to you for elucidation,' he said, feeling vaguely a liar, and generally guilty. But when, on the departure of the dunce, Winifred held out her arms, everything fell from him but the sense of the exquisite moment. Their lips met for the first time, but only for an instant. He had scarcely time to realize that this wonderful thing had happened before the mobile creature had darted to his book-shelves and was examining a Thucydides upside down.

'How clever to know Greek!' she exclaimed. 'And do you really talk it with the other dons?'

'No, we never talk shop,' he laughed. 'But, Winifred, what made you come here?'

'I had never seen Oxford. Isn't it beautiful?'

'There's nothing beautiful *here*,' he said, looking round his sober study.

'No,' she admitted; 'there's nothing I care for here,' and had left another celestial kiss on his lips before he knew it. 'And now you must take me to lunch and on the river.'

He stammered, 'I have – work.'

She pouted. 'But I can't stay beyond tomorrow morning, and I want so much to see all your celebrated oarsmen practising.'

'You are not staying over the night?' he gasped.

'Yes, I am,' and she threw him a dazzling glance.

His heart went pit-a-pat. 'Where?' he murmured.

'Oh, some poky little hotel near the station. The swell hotels are full.'

He was glad to hear she was not conspicuously quartered.

'So many people have come down already for Commem,' he said. 'I suppose they are anxious to see the Generals get their degrees. But hadn't we better go somewhere and lunch?'

They went down the stone staircase, past the battalion of boots, and across the quad. He felt that all the windows were alive with eyes, but she insisted on standing still and admiring their ivied picturesqueness. After lunch he shamefacedly borrowed the dunce's punt. The necessities of punting, which kept him far from her, and demanded much adroit labour, gradually restored his self-respect, and he was able to look the uncelebrated oarsmen they met in the eyes, except when they were accompanied by their parents and sisters, which subtly made him feel uncomfortable again. But Winifred, piquant under her pink parasol, was singularly at ease, enraptured with the changing beauty of the river, applauding with childish glee the wild flowers on the banks, or the rippling reflections in the water.

'Look, look!' she cried once, pointing skyward. He stared

upwards, expecting a balloon at least. But it was only 'Keats' little rosy cloud', she explained. It was not her fault if he did not find the excursion unreservedly idyllic.

'How stupid,' she reflected, 'to keep all those nice boys cooped up reading dead languages in a spot made for life and love.'

'I'm afraid they don't disturb the dead languages so much as you think,' he reassured her, smiling. 'And there will be plenty of love-making during Commem.'

'I am so glad. I suppose there are lots of engagements that week.'

'Oh, yes – but not one per cent come to anything.'

'Really? Oh, how fickle men are!'

That seemed rather question-begging, but he was so thrilled by the implicit revelation that she could not even imagine feminine inconstancy, that he forebore to draw her attention to her inadequate logic.

So childish and thoughtless indeed was she that day that nothing would content her but attending a 'Viva', which he had incautiously informed her was public.

'Nobody will notice us,' she urged with strange unconsciousness of her loveliness. 'Besides, they don't know I'm not your sister.'

'The Oxford intellect is sceptical,' he said, laughing. 'It cultivates philosophical doubt.'

But, putting a bold face on the matter, and assuming a fraternal air, he took her to the torture-chamber, in which candidates sat dolefully on a row of chairs against the wall, waiting their turn to come before the three grand inquisitors at the table. Fortunately, Winifred and he were the only spectators; but unfortunately they blundered in at the very moment when the poor owner of the punt was on the rack. The central inquisitor was trying to extract from him information about à Becket, almost prompting him with the very words, but without penetrating through the duncical denseness. John Lefolle breathed more freely when the Crusades were broached; but, alas, it very soon became evident that the dunce had by no means 'got hold of the thing'. As the dunce passed out sadly, obviously ploughed, John Lefolle suffered more than he. So conscience-stricken was he that, when he had accompanied Winifred as far as her hotel, he refused her invitation to come in, pleading the compulsoriness of duty and dinner in Hall. But he could not get away without promising to call in during the evening.

The prospect of this visit was with him all through dinner, at once tempting and terrifying. Assuredly there was a skeleton at his feast, as he sat at the high table, facing the Master. The venerable portraits round the Hall seemed to rebuke his romantic wayward-ness. In the common-room, he sipped his port uneasily, listening as in a daze to the discussion on Free Will, which an eminent stranger had stirred up. How academic it seemed, compared with the passionate realities of life. But somehow he found himself lingering on at the academic discussion, postponing the realities of life. Every now and again, he was impelled to glance at his watch; but suddenly murmuring, 'It is very late,' he pulled himself together, and took leave of his learned brethren. But in the street the sight of a telegraph office drew his steps to it, and almost mechanically he wrote out the message: 'Regret detained. Will call early in morning.'

When he did call in the morning, he was told she had gone back to London the night before on receipt of a telegram. He turned away with a bitter pang of disappointment and regret.

IV

Their subsequent correspondence was only the more amorous. The reason she had fled from the hotel, she explained, was that she could not endure the night in those stuffy quarters. He consoled himself with the hope of seeing much of her during the Long Vacation. He did see her once at her own reception, but this time her husband wandered about the two rooms. The cosy corner was impossible, and they could only manage to gasp out a few mutual endearments amid the buzz and movement, and to arrange a *rendezvous* for the end of July. When the day came, he received a heart-broken letter, stating that her husband had borne her away to Goodwood. In a postscript she informed him that 'Quicksilver was a sure thing'. Much correspondence passed without another meeting being effected, and he lent her five pounds to pay a debt of honour incurred through her husband's 'absurd confidence in Quicksilver'. A week later this horsey husband of hers brought her on to Brighton for the races there, and hither John Lefolle flew. But her husband shadowed her, and he could only lift his hat to her as they passed each other on the Lawns. Sometimes he saw her sitting pensively on a chair while her lord and thrasher perused a pink sporting-paper. Such tantalizing proximity raised their correspondence through the Hove Post Office to fever heat. Life apart, they felt, was impossible, and, removed from the sobering influences of his cap and gown, John Lefolle dreamed of throwing everything to the winds. His literary reputation had opened out a new career. The Winifred lyrics alone had brought in a tidy sum, and though he had expended that and more on despatches of flowers and trifles to her, yet he felt this extravagance would become extinguished under daily companionship, and the poems provoked by her charms would go far towards their daily maintenance. Yes, he could throw up the University. He would rescue her from this bully, this gentleman bruiser. They would live openly and nobly in the world's eye. A poet was not even expected to be conventional.

She, on her side, was no less ardent for the great step. She raged against the world's law, the injustice by which a husband's cruelty was not sufficient ground for divorce. 'But we finer souls must take the law into our own hands,' she wrote. 'We must teach society that the ethics of a barbarous age are unfitted for our century of enlightenment.' But somehow the actual time and place of the elopement could never get itself fixed. In September her husband dragged her to Scotland, in October after the pheasants. When the dramatic day was actually fixed, Winifred wrote by the next post deferring it for a week. Even the few actual preliminary meetings they planned for Kensington Gardens or Hampstead Heath rarely came off. He lived in a whirling atmosphere of express letters of excuse, and telegrams that transformed the situation from hour to hour. Not that her passion in any way abated, or her romantic resolution really altered: it was only that her conception of time and place and ways and means was dizzily mutable.

But after nigh six months of palpitating negotiations with the adorable Mrs Glamorys, the poet, in a moment of dejection, penned the prose apophthegm, 'It is of no use trying to change a changeable person.'

V

But at last she astonished him by a sketch plan of the elopement, so detailed, even to band-boxes and the Paris night route *via* Dieppe, that no further room for doubt was left in his intoxicated soul, and he was actually further astonished when, just as he was putting his hand-bag into the hansom, a telegram was handed to him saying: 'Gone to Homburg. Letter follows.'

He stood still for a moment on the pavement in utter distraction. What did it mean? Had she failed him again? Or was it simply that she had changed the city of refuge from Paris to Homburg? He was about to name the new station to the cabman, but then, 'letter follows'. Surely that meant that he was to wait for it. Perplexed and miserable, he stood with the telegram crumpled up in his fist. What a ridiculous situation! He had wrought himself up to the point of breaking with the world and his past, and now – it only remained to satisfy the cabman!

He tossed feverishly all night, seeking to soothe himself, but really exciting himself the more by a hundred plausible explanations. He was now strung up to such a pitch of uncertainty that he was astonished for the third time when the 'letter' did duly 'follow'.

*

'Dearest,' it ran, 'as I explained in my telegram, my husband became suddenly ill' – ('if she *had* only put that in the telegram,' he groaned) – 'and was ordered to Homburg. Of course it was impossible to leave him in this crisis, both for practical and sentimental reasons. You yourself, darling, would not like me to have aggravated his illness by my flight just at this moment, and thus possibly have his death on my conscience.' ('Darling, you are always right,' he said, kissing the letter.) 'Let us possess our souls in patience a little longer. I need not tell you how vexatious it will be to find myself nursing him in Homburg – out of the season even – instead of the prospect to which I had looked forward with my whole heart and soul. But what can one do? How true is the French proverb, 'Nothing happens but the unexpected'! Write to me immediately *Poste Restante*, that I may at least console myself with your dear words.'

*

The unexpected did indeed happen. Despite draughts of Elizabeth-brunnen and promenades on the Kurhaus terrace, the stalwart woman beater succumbed to his malady. The curt telegram from Winifred gave no indication of her emotions. He sent a reply-telegram of sympathy with her trouble. Although he could not pretend to grieve at this sudden providential solution of their life-problem, still he did sincerely sympathize with the distress inevitable in connection with a death, especially on foreign soil.

He was not able to see her till her husband's body had been brought across the North Sea and committed to the green repose of the old Hampstead churchyard. He found her pathetically altered – her face wan and spiritualized, and all in subtle harmony with the exquisite black gown. In the first interview, he did not dare speak of their love at all. They discussed the immortality of the soul, and she quoted George Herbert. But with the weeks the question of their future began to force its way back to his lips.

'We could not decently marry before six months,' she said, when definitely confronted with the problem.

'Six months!' he gasped.

'Well, surely you don't want to outrage everybody,' she said, pouting.

At first he was outraged himself. What! She who had been ready to flutter the world with a fantastic dance was now measuring her footsteps. But on reflection he saw that Mrs Glamorys was right once more. Since Providence had been good enough to rescue them, why should they fly in its face? A little patience, and a blameless happiness lay before them. Let him not blind himself to the immense relief he really felt at being spared social obloquy. After all, a poet could be unconventional in his *work* – he had no need of the practical outlet demanded for the less gifted.

VI

They scarcely met at all during the next six months – it had, naturally, in this grateful reaction against their recklessness, become a sacred period, even more charged with tremulous emotion than the engagement periods of those who have not so nearly scorched themselves. Even in her presence he found a certain pleasure in combining distant adoration with the confident expectation of proximity, and thus she was restored to the sanctity which she had risked by her former easiness. And so all was for the best in the best of all possible worlds.

When the six months had gone by, he came to claim her hand. She was quite astonished. 'You promised to marry me at the end of six months,' he reminded her.

'Surely it isn't six months already,' she said.

He referred her to the calendar, recalled the date of her husband's death.

'You are strangely literal for a poet,' she said. 'Of course I *said* six months, but six months doesn't mean twenty-six weeks by the clock. All I meant was that a decent period must intervene. But even to myself it seems only yesterday that poor Harold was walking beside me in the Kurhaus Park.' She burst into tears, and in the face of them he could not pursue the argument.

Gradually, after several interviews and letters, it was agreed that they should wait another six months.

'She *is* right,' he reflected again. 'We have waited so long, we may as well wait a little longer and leave malice no handle.

The second six months seemed to him much longer than the first. The charm of respectful adoration had lost its novelty, and once again his breast was racked by fitful fevers which could scarcely calm themselves even by conversion into sonnets. The one point of repose was that shining fixed star of marriage. Still smarting under Winifred's reproach of his unpoetic literality, he did not intend to force her to marry him exactly at the end of the twelve-month. But he was determined that she should have no later than this exact date for at least 'naming the day'. Not the most punctilious stickler for convention, he felt, could deny that Mrs Grundy's claim had been paid to the last minute.

The publication of his new volume – containing the Winifred lyrics – had served to colour these months of intolerable delay. Even the reaction of the critics against his poetry, that conventional revolt against every second volume, that parrot cry of over-praise from the very throats that had praised him, though it pained and perplexed him, was perhaps really helpful. At any rate, the long waiting was over at last. He felt like Jacob after his years of service for Rachel.

The fateful morning dawned bright and blue, and, as the towers of Oxford were left behind him he recalled that distant Saturday when he had first gone down to meet the literary lights of London in his publisher's salon. How much older he was now than then – and yet how much younger! The nebulous melancholy of youth, the clouds of philosophy, had vanished before this beautiful creature of sunshine whose radiance cut out a clear line for his future through the confusion of life.

At a florist's in the High Street of Hampstead he bought a costly bouquet of white flowers, and walked airily to the house and rang the bell jubilantly. He could scarcely believe his ears when the maid told him her mistress was not at home. How dared the girl stare at him so impassively? Did she not know by what appointment – on what errand – he had come? Had he not written to her mistress a week ago that he would present himself that afternoon?

'Not at home!' he gasped. 'But when will she be home?'

'I fancy she won't be long. She went out an hour ago, and she has an appointment with her dressmaker at five.'

'Do you know in what direction she'd have gone?'

'Oh, she generally walks on the Heath before tea.'

The world suddenly grew rosy again. 'I will come back again,' he said. Yes, a walk in this glorious air – heathward – would do him good.

As the door shut he remembered he might have left the flowers, but he would not ring again, and besides, it was, perhaps, better he should present them with his own hand, than let her find them on the hall table. Still, it seemed rather awkward to walk about the streets with a bouquet, and he was glad, accidentally to strike the old Hampstead Church, and to seek a momentary seclusion in passing through its avenue of quiet gravestones on his heathward way.

Mounting the few steps, he paused idly a moment on the verge of this green 'God's-acre' to read a perpendicular slab on a wall, and his face broadened into a smile as he followed the absurdly elaborate biography of a rich, self-made merchant who had taught himself to read, 'Reader, go thou and do likewise,' was the delicious bull at the end. As he turned away, the smile still lingering about his lips, he saw a dainty figure tripping down the stony graveyard path, and though he was somehow startled to find her still in black, there was no mistaking Mrs Glamorys. She ran to meet him with a glad cry, which filled his eyes with happy tears.

'How good of you to remember!' she said, as she took the bouquet from his unresisting hand, and turned again on her footsteps. He followed her wonderingly across the uneven road towards a narrow aisle of graves on the left. In another instant she has stooped before a shining white stone, and laid his bouquet reverently upon it. As he reached her side, he saw that his flowers were almost lost in the vast mass of floral offerings with which the grave of the woman beater was bestrewn.

'How good of you to remember the anniversary,' she murmured again.

'How could I forget it?' he stammered, astonished. 'Is not this the end of the terrible twelve-month?'

The soft gratitude died out of her face. 'Oh, is *that* what you were thinking of?'

'What else?' he murmured, pale with conflicting emotions.

'What else! I think decency demanded that this day, at least, should be sacred to his memory. Oh, what brutes men are!' And she burst into tears.

His patient breast revolted at last. 'You said *he* was the brute!' he retorted, outraged.

'Is that your chivalry to the dead? Oh, my poor Harold, my poor Harold!'

For once her tears could not extinguish the flame of his anger. 'But you told me he beat you,' he cried.

'And if he did, I dare say I deserved it. Oh, my darling, my darling!' She laid her face on the stone and sobbed.

John Lefolle stood by in silent torture. As he helplessly watched her white throat swell and fall with the sobs, he was suddenly struck by the absence of the black velvet band – the truer mourning she had worn in the lifetime of the so lamented. A faint scar, only perceptible to his conscious eye, added to his painful bewilderment.

At last she rose and walked unsteadily forward. He followed her in mute misery. In a moment or two they found themselves on the outskirts of the deserted heath. How beautiful stretched the gorsy rolling country! The sun was setting in great burning furrows of gold and green — a panorama to take one's breath away. The beauty and peace of Nature passed into the poet's soul.

'Forgive me, dearest,' he begged, taking her hand.

She drew it away sharply. 'I cannot forgive you. You have shown yourself in your true colours.'

Her unreasonableness angered him again. 'What do you mean? I only came in accordance with our long-standing arrangement. You have put me off long enough.'

'It is fortunate I did put you off long enough to discover what you are.'

He gasped. He thought of all the weary months of waiting, all the long comedy of telegrams and express letters, the far-off flirtations of the cosy corner, the baffled elopement to Paris. 'Then you won't marry me?'

'I cannot marry a man I neither love nor respect.'

'You don't love me!' Her spontaneous kiss in his sober Oxford study seemed to burn on his angry lips.

'No, I never loved you.'

He took her by the arms and turned her round roughly. 'Look me in the face and dare to say you have never loved me.'

His memory was buzzing with passionate phrases from her endless letters. They stung like a swarm of bees. The sunset was like blood-red mist before his eyes.

'I have never loved you,' she said obstinately.

'You —!' His grasp on her arms tightened. He shook her.

'You are bruising me,' she cried.

His grasp fell from her arms as though they were red-hot. He had become a woman beater.

STORIES OF TROUBLED
MARRIAGES

Rudyard Kipling

THE BRONCKHORST DIVORCE-CASE

(*Civil and Military Gazette*, 26 September 1884)

In the daytime, when she moved about me,
  In the night, when she was sleeping at my side,–
I was wearied, I was wearied of her presence,
Day by day and night by night I grew to hate her –
  Would God that she or I had died!
                                    CONFESSIONS

There was a man called Bronckhorst – a three-cornered, middle-aged man in the Army – grey as a badger, and, some people said, with a touch of country-blood in him. That, however, cannot be proved. Mrs Bronckhorst was not exactly young, though fifteen years younger than her husband. She was a large, pale, quiet woman, with heavy eyelids over weak eyes, and hair that turned red or yellow as the lights fell on it.

Bronckhorst was not nice in any way. He had no respect for the pretty public and private lies that make life a little less nasty than it is. His manner towards his wife was coarse. There are many things – including actual assault with the clenched fist – that a wife will endure; but seldom a wife can bear – as Mrs Bronckhorst bore – with a long course of brutal, hard chaff, making light of her weaknesses, her headaches, her small fits of gaiety, her dresses, her queer little attempts to make herself attractive to her husband when she knows that she is not what she has been, and – worst of all – the love that she spends on her children. That particular sort of heavy-handed jest was specially dear to Bronckhorst. I suppose that he had first slipped into it, meaning no harm, in the honeymoon, when folk find their ordinary stock of endearments run short, and so go to the other extreme to express their feelings. A similar impulse makes a man say, '*Hutt*, you old beast!' when a favourite horse nuzzles his coat-front. Unluckily, when the reaction of marriage sets in, the form of speech remains, and, the tenderness having died out, hurts the wife more than she cares to say. But Mrs Bronckhorst was devoted to her 'Teddy' as she called him. Perhaps that was why he objected to her. Perhaps – this is only a theory to account for his infamous behaviour later on – he gave way to the queer, savage feeling that sometimes takes by the throat a husband twenty years married, when he sees, across the table, the same, same face of his wedded wife, and knows that, as he has sat facing it, so must he continue to sit until the day of its death or his own. Most men and all women know the spasm. It only lasts for three breaths as a rule, must be a 'throw-back' to times when men and women were rather worse than they are now, and is too unpleasant to be discussed.

Dinner at the Bronckhorsts' was an infliction few men cared to undergo. Bronckhorst took a pleasure in saying things that made his wife wince. When their little boy came in at dessert Bronckhorst used to give him half a glass of wine, and, naturally enough, the poor little mite got first riotous, next miserable, and was removed screaming. Bronckhorst asked if that was the way Teddy usually behaved, and whether Mrs Bronckhorst could not spare some of her time 'to teach the little beggar decency'. Mrs Bronckhorst, who loved the boy more than her own life, tried not to cry – her spirit seemed to have been broken by her marriage. Lastly, Bronckhorst used to say, 'There! That'll do, that'll do. For God's sake try to behave like a rational woman. Go into the drawing-room.' Mrs Bronckhorst would go, trying to carry it all off with a smile; and the guest of the evening would feel angry and uncomfortable.

After three years of this cheerful life – for Mrs Bronckhorst had no women-friends to talk to – the station was startled by the news that Bronckhorst had instituted proceedings *on the criminal count*, against a man called Biel, who certainly had been rather attentive to Mrs Bronckhorst whenever she had appeared in public. The utter want of reserve with which Bronckhorst treated his own dishonour helped us to know that the evidence against Biel would be entirely circumstantial and native. There were no letters; but Bronckhorst said openly that he would rack Heaven and Earth until he saw Biel superintending the manufacture of carpets in the Central Jail. Mrs Bronckhorst kept entirely to her house, and let charitable folks say what they pleased. Opinions were divided. Some two-thirds of the station jumped at once to the conclusion that Biel was guilty; but a dozen men who knew and liked him held by him. Biel was furious and surprised. He denied the whole thing, and vowed that he would thrash Bronckhorst within an inch of his life. No jury, we knew, would convict a man on the criminal count on native evidence in a land where you can buy a murder-charge, including the corpse, all complete for fifty-four rupees; but Biel did not care to scrape through by the benefit of a doubt. He wanted the whole thing cleared; but, as he said one night, 'He can prove anything with servants' evidence, and I've only my bare word.' This was almost a month before the case came on; and beyond agreeing with Biel, we could do little. All that we could be sure of was that the native evidence would be bad enough to blast Biel's character for the rest of his service; for when a native begins perjury he perjures himself thoroughly. He does not boggle over details.

Some genius at the end of the table whereat the affair was being talked over, said, 'Look here! I don't believe lawyers are any good. Get a man to wire to Strickland, and beg him to come down and pull us through.'

Strickland was about a hundred and eighty miles up the line. He had not long been married to Miss Youghal, but he scented in the telegram a chance of return to the old detective work that his soul lusted after, and next time he came in and heard our story. He finished his pipe and said oracularly, 'We must get at the evidence. Oorya bearer, Mussulman *khit* and sweeper *ayah*, I suppose, are the pillars of the charge. I am on in this piece; but I'm afraid I'm getting rusty in my talk.'

He rose and went into Biel's bedroom, where his trunk had been put, and shut the door. An hour later, we heard him say, 'I hadn't the heart to part with my old make-ups when I married. Will this do?' There was a loathly *fakir* salaaming in the doorway.

'Now lend me fifty rupees,' said Strickland, 'and give me your Words of Honour that you won't tell my wife.'

He got all that he asked for, and left the house while the table drank his health. What he did only he himself knows. A *fakir* hung about Bronckhorst's compound for twelve days. Then a sweeper appeared, and when Biel heard of *him*, he said that Strickland was an angel full-fledged. Whether the sweeper made love to Janki, Mrs Bronckhorst's *ayah*, is a question which concerns Strickland exclusively.

He came back at the end of three weeks, and said quietly, 'You spoke the truth, Biel. The whole business is put up from beginning to end.' Jove! It almost astonishes *me*! That Bronckhorst beast isn't fit to live.'

There was uproar and shouting, and Biel said, 'How are you going to prove it? You can't say that you've been trespassing on Bronckhorst's compound in disguise!'

'No,' said Strickland. 'Tell your lawyer-fool, whoever he is, to get up something strong about "inherent improbabilities" and "discrepancies of evidence". He won't have to speak, but it will make him happy. *I*'m going to run this business.'

Biel held his tongue, and the other men waited to see what would happen. They trusted Strickland as men trust quiet men. When the case came off the Court was crowded. Strickland hung about in the veranda of the Court, till he met the Mohammedan *khitmutgar*. Then he murmured a *fakir*'s blessing in his ear, and asked him how his second wife did. The man spun round, and, as he looked into the eyes of 'Estreekin Sahib', his jaw dropped. You must remember that before Strickland was married, he was, as I have told you already, a power among natives. Strickland whispered a rather coarse vernacular proverb to the effect that he was abreast of all that was going on, and went into the Court armed with a gut trainer's-whip.

The Mohammedan was the first witness, and Strickland beamed upon him from the back of the Court. The man moistened his lips with his tongue and, in his abject fear of 'Estreekin Sahib', the *fakir* went back on every detail of his evidence – said he was a poor man, and God was his witness that he had forgotten everything that Bronckhorst Sahib had told him to say. Between his terror of Strickland, the Judge, and Bronckhorst he collapsed weeping.

Then began the panic among the witnesses. Janki, the *ayah*, leering chastely behind her veil, turned grey, and the bearer left the Court. He said that his Mamma was dying, and that it was not wholesome for any man to lie unthriftily in the presence of 'Estreekin Sahib'.

Biel said politely to Bronckhorst, 'Your witnesses don't seem to work. Haven't you any forged letters to produce?' But Bronckhorst was swaying to and fro in his chair, and there was a dead pause after Biel had been called to order.

Bronckhorst's Counsel saw the look on his client's face, and without more ado pitched his papers on the little green-baize table, and mumbled something about having been misinformed. The whole Court applauded wildly, like soldiers at a theatre, and the Judge began to say what he thought.

*

Biel came out of the Court, and Strickland dropped a gut trainer's-whip in the veranda. Ten minutes later, Biel was cutting Bronckhorst into ribbons behind the old Court cells, quietly and without scandal. What was left of Bronckhorst was sent home in a carriage; and his wife wept over it and nursed it into a man again.

Later on, after Biel had managed to hush up the counter-charge against Bronckhorst of fabricating false evidence, Mrs Bronckhorst, with her faint, watery smile, said that there had been a mistake, but it wasn't her Teddy's fault altogether. She would wait till her Teddy came back to her. Perhaps he had grown tired of her, or she had tried his patience, and perhaps we wouldn't cut her any more, and perhaps the mothers would let their children play with 'little Teddy' again. He was so lonely. Then the station invited Mrs Bronckhorst everywhere, until Bronckhorst was fit to appear in public, when he went Home and took his wife with him. According to latest advices, her Teddy did come back to her, and they are moderately happy. Though, of course, he can never forgive her the thrashing that she was the indirect means of getting for him.

*

What Biel wants to know is, 'Why didn't I press home the charge against the Bronckhorst brute, and have him run in?'

What Mrs Strickland wants to know is, 'How *did* my husband bring such a lovely, lovely Waler from your station? I know *all* his money affairs; and I'm *certain* he didn't *buy* it.'

What I want to know is, 'How do women like Mrs Bronckhorst come to marry men like Bronckhorst?'

And my conundrum is the most unanswerable of the three.

Ella D'Arcy

IRREMEDIABLE

(*Monochromes*, London: John Lane, 1893)

A young man strolled along a country road one August evening after a long delicious day – a day of that blessed idleness the man of leisure never knows: one must be a bank clerk forty-nine weeks out of the fifty-two before one can really appreciate the exquisite enjoyment of doing nothing for twelve hours at a stretch. Willoughby had spent the morning lounging about a sunny rickyard; then, when the heat grew unbearable, he had retreated to an orchard, where, lying on his back in the long cool grass, he had traced the pattern of the apple-leaves diapered above him upon the summer sky; now that the heat of the day was over he had come to roam whither sweet fancy led him, to lean over gates, view the prospect, and meditate upon the pleasures of a well-spent day. Five such days had already passed over his head, fifteen more remained to him. Then farewell to freedom and clean country air! Back again to London and another year's toil.

He came to a gate on the right of the road. Behind it a footpath meandered up over a grassy slope. The sheep nibbling on its summit cast long shadows down the hill almost to his feet. Road and fieldpath were equally new to him, but the latter offered greener attractions; he vaulted lightly over the gate and had so little idea he was taking thus the first step towards ruin that he began to whistle 'White Wings' from pure joy of life.

The sheep stopped feeding and raised their heads to stare at him from pale-lashed eyes; first one and then another broke into a startled run, until there was a sudden woolly stampede of the entire flock. When Willoughby gained the ridge from which they had just scattered, he came in sight of a woman sitting on a stile at the further end of the field. As he advanced towards her he saw that she was young, and that she was not what is called 'a lady' – of which he was glad: an earlier episode in his career having indissolubly associated in his mind ideas of feminine refinement with those of feminine treachery.

He thought it probable this girl would be willing to dispense with the formalities of an introduction, and that he might venture with her on some pleasant foolish chat.

As she made no movement to let him pass he stood still, and, looking at her, began to smile.

She returned his gaze from unabashed dark eyes, and then laughed, showing teeth white, sound, and smooth as split hazel-nuts.

'Do you wanter get over?' she remarked familiarly.

'I'm afraid I can't without disturbing you.'

'Dontcher think you're much better where you are?' said the girl, on which Willoughby hazarded:

'You mean to say looking at you? Well, perhaps I am!'

The girl at this laughed again, but nevertheless dropped herself down into the further field; then, leaning her arms upon the cross-bar, she informed the young man: 'No, I don't wanter spoil your walk. You were goin' p'raps ter Beacon Point? It's very pretty that wye.'

'I was going nowhere in particular,' he replied; 'just exploring, so to speak. I'm a stranger in these parts.'

'How funny! Imer stranger here too. I only come down larse Friday to stye with a Naunter mine in Horton. Are you stying in Horton?'

Willoughby told her he was not in Orton, but at Povey Cross Farm out in the other direction.

'Oh, Mrs Payne's, ain't it? I've heard aunt speak ovver. She takes summer boarders, don't chee? I egspeck you come from London, heh?'

'And I expect you come from London too?' said Willoughby, recognizing the familiar accent.

'You're as sharp as a needle,' cried the girl with her unrestrained laugh; 'so I do. I'm here for a hollerday 'cos I was so done up with the work and the hot weather. I don't look as though I'd bin ill, do I? But I was, though: for it was just stiflin' hot up in our workrooms all larse month, an' tailorin's awful hard work at the bester times.'

Willoughby felt a sudden accession of interest in her. Like many intelligent young men, he had dabbled a little in Socialism, and at one time had wandered among the dispossessed; but since then, had caught up and held loosely the new doctrine – it is a good and fitting thing that Woman also should earn her bread by the sweat of her brow. Always in reference to the woman who, fifteen months before, had treated him ill; he had said to himself that even the breaking of stones in the road should be considered a more feminine employment than the breaking of hearts.

He gave way therefore to a movement of friendliness for this working daughter of the people, and joined her on the other side of the stile in token of his approval. She, twisting round to face him, leaned now with her back against the bar, and the sunset fires lent a fleeting glory to her face. Perhaps she guessed how becoming the light was, for she took off her hat and let it touch to gold the ends and fringes of her rough abundant hair. Thus and at this moment she made an agreeable picture, to which stood as background all the beautiful, wooded Southshire view.

'You don't really mean to say you are a tailoress?' said Willoughby, with a sort of eager compassion.

'I do, though! An' I've bin one ever since I was fourteen. Look at my fingers if you don't b'lieve me.'

She put out her right hand, and he took hold of it, as he was expected to do. The finger-ends were frayed and blackened by needle-pricks, but the hand itself was plump, moist, and not unshapely. She meanwhile examined Willoughby's fingers enclosing hers.

'It's easy ter see you've never done no work!' she said, half admiring, half envious. 'I s'pose you're a tip-top swell, ain't you?'

'Oh, yes! I'm a tremendous swell indeed!' said Willoughby, ironically. He thought of his hundred and thirty pounds' salary; and he mentioned his position in the British and Colonial Banking house, without shedding much illumination on her mind, for she insisted:

'Well, anyhow, you're a gentleman. I've often wished I was a lady. It must be so nice ter wear fine clo'es an' never have ter do any work all day long.'

Willoughby thought it innocent of the girl to say this; it reminded him of his own notion as a child – that kings and queens put on their crowns the first thing on rising in the morning. His cordiality rose another degree.

'If being a gentleman means having nothing to do,' said he, smiling, 'I can certainly lay no claim to the title. Life isn't all beer and skittles with me, any more than it is with you. Which is the better reason for enjoying the present moment, don't you think? Suppose, now, like a kind little girl, you were to show me the way to Beacon Point, which you say is so pretty?'

She required no further persuasion. As he walked beside her through the upland fields where the dusk was beginning to fall, and the white evening moths to emerge from their daytime hiding-places, she asked him many personal questions, most of which he thought fit to parry. Taking no offence thereat, she told him, instead, much concerning herself and her family. Thus he learned her name was Esther Stables, that she and her people lived Whitechapel way; that her father was seldom sober, and her mother always ill; and that the aunt with whom she was staying kept the post-office and general shop in Orton village. He learned, too, that Esther was discontented with life in general; that, though she hated being at home, she found the country dreadfully dull; and that, consequently, she was extremely glad to have made his acquaintance. But what he chiefly realized when they parted was that he had spent a couple of pleasant hours talking nonsense with a girl who was natural, simple-minded, and entirely free from that repellently protective atmosphere with which a woman of the 'classes' so carefully surrounds herself. He and Esther had 'made friends' with the ease and rapidity of children before they have learned the dread meaning of 'etiquette', and they said good night, not without some talk of meeting each other again.

Obliged to breakfast at a quarter to eight in town, Willoughby was always luxuriously late when in the country, where he took his meals also in leisurely fashion, often reading from a book propped up on the table before him. But the morning after his meeting with Esther Stables found him less disposed to read than usual. Her image obtruded itself upon the printed page, and at length grew so importunate he came to the conclusion the only way to lay it was to confront it with the girl herself.

Wanting some tobacco, he saw a good reason for going into Orton. Esther had told him he could get tobacco and everything else at her aunt's. He found the post-office to be one of the first houses in the widely spaced village street. In front of the cottage was a small garden ablaze with old-fashioned flowers; and in a large garden at one side were apple-trees, raspberry and currant bushes, and six thatched beehives on a bench. The bowed windows of the little shop were partly screened by sunblinds; nevertheless the lower panes still displayed a heterogeneous collection of goods – lemons, hanks of yarn, white linen buttons upon blue cards, sugar cones, churchwarden pipes, and tobacco jars. A letter-box opened its narrow mouth low down in one wall, and over the door swung the sign, 'Stamps and money-order office', in black letters on white enamelled iron.

The interior of the shop was cool and dark. A second glass-door at the back permitted Willoughby to see into a small sitting-room, and out again through a low and square-paned window to the sunny landscape beyond. Silhouetted against the light were the heads of two women; the rough young head of yesterday's Esther, the lean outline and bugled cap of Esther's aunt.

It was the latter who at the jingling of the doorbell rose from her work and came forward to serve the customer; but the girl, with much mute meaning in her eyes, and a finger laid upon her smiling mouth, followed behind. Her aunt heard her footfall. 'What do you want here, Esther?' she said with thin disapproval; 'get back to your sewing.'

Esther gave the young man a signal seen only by him and slipped out into the side-garden, where he found her when his purchases were made. She leaned over the privet-hedge to intercept him as he passed.

'Aunt's an awful ole maid,' she remarked apologetically; 'I b'lieve she'd never let me say a word to enny one if she could help it.'

'So you got home all right last night?' Willoughby inquired; 'what did your aunt say to you?'

'Oh, she arst me where I'd been, and I tolder a lotter lies.' Then, with a woman's intuition, perceiving that this speech jarred, Esther made haste to add, 'She's so dreadful hard on me. I dursn't tell her I'd been with a gentleman or she'd never have let me out alone again.'

'And at present I suppose you'll be found somewhere about that same stile every evening?' said Willoughby foolishly, for he really did not much care whether he met her again or not. Now he was actually in her company, he was surprised at himself for having given her a whole morning's thought; yet the eagerness of her answer flattered him, too.

'Tonight I can't come, worse luck! It's Thursday, and the shops here close of a Thursday at five. I'll havter keep aunt company. But tomorrer? I can be there tomorrer. You'll come, say?'

'Esther!' cried a vexed voice, and the precise, right-minded aunt emerged through a row of raspberry-bushes; 'whatever are you thinking about, delayin' the gentleman in this fashion?' She was full of rustic and official civility for 'the gentleman', but indignant with her niece. 'I don't want none of your London manners down here,' Willoughby heard her say as she marched the girl off.

He himself was not sorry to be released from Esther's too friendly eyes, and he spent an agreeable evening over a book, and this time managed to forget her completely.

Though he remembered her first thing next morning, it was to smile wisely and determine he would not meet her again. Yet by dinner-time the day seemed long; why, after all, should he not meet her? By tea-time prudence triumphed anew – no, he would not go. Then he drank his tea hastily and set off for the stile.

Esther was waiting for him. Expectation had given an additional colour to her cheeks, and her red-brown hair showed here and there a beautiful glint of gold. He could not help admiring the vigorous way in which it waved and twisted, or the little curls which grew at the nape of her neck, tight and close as those of a young lamb's fleece. Her neck here was admirable, too, in its smooth creaminess; and when her eyes lighted up with such evident pleasure at his coming, how avoid the conviction she was a good and nice girl after all?

He proposed they should go down into the little copse on the right, where they would be less disturbed by the occasional passer-by. Here, seated on a felled tree-trunk, Willoughby began that bantering, silly, meaningless form of conversation known among the 'classes' as flirting. He had but the wish to make himself agreeable, and to while away the time. Esther, however, misunderstood him.

Willoughby's hand lay palm downwards on his knee, and she, noticing a ring which he wore on his little finger, took hold of it.

'What a funny ring!' she said; 'let's look?'

To disembarrass himself of her touch, he pulled the ring off and gave it her to examine.

'What's that ugly dark green stone?' she asked.

'It's called a sardonyx.'

'What's it for?' she said, turning it about.

'It's a signet ring, to seal letters with.'

'An' there's a sorter king's head scratched on it, an' some writin' too, only I carnt make it out?'

'It isn't the head of a king, although it wears a crown,' Willoughby explained, 'but the head and bust of a Saracen against whom my ancestor of many hundred years ago went to fight in the Holy Land. And the words cut round it are our motto, "Vertue vauncet", which means virtue prevails.'

Willoughby may have displayed some accession of dignity in giving this bit of family history, for Esther fell into uncontrolled laughter, at which he was much displeased. And when the girl made as though she would put the ring on her own finger, asking, 'Shall I keep it?' he coloured up with sudden annoyance.

'It was only my fun!' said Esther hastily, and gave him the ring back, but his cordiality was gone. He felt no inclination to renew the idle-word pastime, said it was time to go, and, swinging his cane vexedly, struck off the heads of the flowers and the weeds as he went. Esther walked by his side in complete silence, a phenomenon of which he presently became conscious. He felt rather ashamed of having shown temper.

'Well, here's your way home,' said he with an effort at friendliness. 'Goodbye; we've had a nice evening anyhow. It was pleasant down there in the woods, eh?'

He was astonished to see her eyes soften with tears, and to hear the real emotion in her voice as she answered, 'It was just heaven down there with you until you turned so funny-like. What had I done to make you cross? Say you forgive me, do!'

'Silly child!' said Willoughby, completely mollified, 'I'm not the least angry. There, goodbye!' and like a fool he kissed her.

He anathematized his folly in the white light of next morning, and, remembering the kiss he had given her, repented it very sincerely. He had an uncomfortable suspicion she had not received it in the same spirit in which it had been bestowed, but, attaching more serious meaning to it, would build expectations thereon which must be left unfulfilled. It was best indeed not to meet her again; for he acknowledged to himself that, though he only half liked, and even slightly feared her, there was a certain attraction about her – was it in her dark unflinching eyes or in her very red lips? – which might lead him into greater follies still.

Thus it came about that for two successive evenings Esther waited for him in vain, and on the third evening he said to himself, with a grudging relief, that by this time she had probably transferred her affections to someone else.

It was Saturday, the second Saturday since he left town. He spent the day about the farm, contemplated the pigs, inspected the feeding of the stock, and assisted at the afternoon milking. Then at evening, with a refilled pipe, he went for a long lean over the west gate, while he traced fantastic pictures and wove romances in the glories of the sunset clouds.

He watched the colours glow from gold to scarlet, change to crimson, sink at last to sad purple reefs and isles, when the sudden consciousness of someone being near him made him turn round. There stood Esther, and her eyes were full of eagerness and anger.

'Why have you never been to the stile again?' she asked him. 'You promised to come faithful, and you never came. Why have you not kep' your promise? Why? Why?' she persisted, stamping her foot because Willoughby remained silent.

What could he say? Tell her she had no business to follow him like this; or own, what was, unfortunately, the truth, he was just a little glad to see her?

'Praps you don't care for me any more?' she said. 'Well, why did you kiss me, then?'

Why, indeed! thought Willoughby, marvelling at his own idiocy, and yet – such is the inconsistency of man – not wholly without the desire to kiss her again. And while he looked at her she suddenly flung herself down on the hedge-bank at his feet and burst into tears. She did not cover up her face, but simply pressed one cheek down upon the grass while the water poured from her eyes with astonishing abundance. Willoughby saw the dry earth turn dark and moist as it drank the tears in. This, his first experience of Esther's powers of weeping, distressed him horribly; never in his life before had he seen anyone weep like that, he should not have believed such a thing possible; he was alarmed, too, lest she should be noticed from the house. He opened the gate; 'Esther!' he begged, 'don't cry. Come out here, like a dear girl, and let us talk sensibly.'

Because she stumbled, unable to see her way through wet eyes, he gave her his hand, and they found themselves in a field of corn, walking along the narrow grass-path that skirted it, in the shadow of the hedgerow.

'What is there to cry about because you have not seen me for two days?' he began; 'why, Esther, we are only strangers, after all. When we have been at home a week or two we shall scarcely remember each other's names.'

Esther sobbed at intervals, but her tears had ceased. 'It's fine for you to talk of home,' she said to this. 'You've got something that is a home, I s'pose? But me! my home's like hell, with nothing but quarrellin' and cursin', and a father who beats us whether sober or drunk. Yes!' she repeated shrewdly, seeing the lively disgust on Willoughby's face, 'he beat me, all ill as I was, jus' before I come away. I could show you the bruises on my arms still. And now to go back there after knowin' you! It'll be worse than ever. I can't endure it, and I won't! I'll put an end to it or myself somehow, I swear!'

'But my poor Esther, how can I help it? what can I do?' said Willoughby. He was greatly moved, full of wrath with her father, with all the world which makes women suffer. He had suffered himself at the hands of a woman and severely, but this, instead of hardening his heart, had only rendered it the more supple. And yet he had a vivid perception of the peril in which he stood. An interior voice urged him to break away, to seek safety in flight even at the cost of appearing cruel or ridiculous; so, coming to a point in the field where an elm-bole jutted out across the path, he saw with relief he could now withdraw his hand from the girl's, since they must walk singly to skirt round it.

Esther took a step in advance, stopped and suddenly turned to face him; she held out her two hands and her face was very near his own.

'Don't you care for me one little bit?' she said wistfully, and surely sudden madness fell upon him. For he kissed her again, he kissed her many times, he took her in his arms, and pushed all thoughts of the consequences far from him.

*

But when, an hour later, he and Esther stood by the last gate on the road to Orton, some of these consequences were already calling loudly to him.

'You know I have only £130 a year?' he told her; 'it's no very brilliant prospect for you to marry me on that.'

For he had actually offered her marriage, although to the mediocre man such a proceeding must appear incredible, uncalled for. But to Willoughby, overwhelmed with sadness and remorse, it seemed the only atonement possible.

Sudden exultation leaped at Esther's heart.

'Oh! I'm used to managin',' she told him confidently, and mentally resolved to buy herself, so soon as she was married, a black feather boa, such as she had coveted last winter.

Willoughby spent the remaining days of his holiday in thinking out and planning with Esther the details of his return to London and her own, the secrecy to be observed, the necessary legal steps to be taken, and the quiet suburb in which they would set up housekeeping. And, so successfully did he carry out his arrangements, that within five weeks from the day on which he had first met Esther Stables, he and she came out one morning from a church in Highbury, husband and wife. It was a mellow September day, the streets were filled with sunshine, and Willoughby, in reckless high spirits, imagined he saw a reflection of his own gaiety on the indifferent faces of the passersby. There being no one else to perform the office, he congratulated himself very warmly, and Esther's frequent laughter filled in the pauses of the day.

*

Three months later Willoughby was dining with a friend, and the hour-hand of the clock nearing ten, the host no longer resisted the guest's growing anxiety to be gone. He arose and exchanged with him good wishes and goodbyes.

'Marriage is evidently a most successful institution,' said he, half-jesting, half-sincere; 'you almost make me inclined to go and get married myself. Confess now your thoughts have been at home the whole evening.'

Willoughby thus addressed turned red to the roots of his hair, but did not deny it.

The other laughed. 'And very commendable they should be,' he continued, 'since you are scarcely, so to speak, out of your honeymoon.'

With a social smile on his lips, Willoughby calculated a moment before replying, 'I have been married exactly three months and three days.' Then, after a few words respecting their next meeting, the two shook hands and parted – the young host to finish the evening with books and pipe, the young husband to set out on a twenty minutes' walk to his home.

It was a cold, clear December night following a day of rain. A touch of frost in the air had dried the pavements, and Willoughby's footfall ringing upon the stones re-echoed down the empty suburban street. Above his head was a dark, remote sky thickly powdered with stars, and as he turned westward Alpherat hung for a moment 'comme le point sur un *i*', over the slender spire of St John's. But he was insensible to the worlds about him; he was absorbed in his own thoughts, and these, as his friend had surmised, were entirely with his wife. For Esther's face was always before his eyes, her voice was always in his ears, she filled the universe for him; yet only four months ago he had never seen her, had never heard her name. This was the curious part of it – here in December he found himself the husband of a girl who was completely dependent upon him not only for food, clothes, and lodging, but for her present happiness, her whole future life; and last July he had been scarcely more than a boy himself, with no greater care on his mind than the pleasant difficulty of deciding where he should spend his annual three weeks' holiday.

But it is events, not months or years, which age. Willoughby, who was only twenty-six, remembered his youth as a sometime companion irrevocably lost to him; its vague, delightful hopes were now crystallized into definite ties, and its happy irresponsibilities displaced by a sense of care, inseparable perhaps from the most fortunate of marriages.

As he reached the street in which he lodged his pace involuntarily slackened. While still some distance off, his eye sought out and distinguished the windows of the room in which Esther awaited him. Through the broken slats of the Venetian blinds he could see the yellow gaslight within. The parlour beneath was in darkness; his landlady had evidently gone to bed, there being no light over the hall-door either. In some apprehension he consulted his watch under the last street-lamp he passed, to find comfort in assuring himself it was only ten minutes after ten. He let himself in with his latch-key, hung up his hat and overcoat by the sense of touch, and, groping his way upstairs, opened the door of the first floor sitting-room.

At the table in the centre of the room sat his wife, leaning upon her elbows, her two hands thrust up into her ruffled hair; spread out before her was a crumpled yesterday's newspaper, and so interested was she to all appearance in its contents that she neither spoke nor looked up as Willoughby entered. Around her were the still uncleared tokens of her last meal: tea-slops, bread-crumbs, and an egg-shell crushed to fragments upon a plate, which was one of those trifles that set Willoughby's teeth on edge – whenever his wife ate an egg she persisted in turning the egg-cup upside down upon the tablecloth, and pounding the shell to pieces in her plate with her spoon.

The room was repulsive in its disorder. The one lighted burner of the gaselier, turned too high, hissed up into a long tongue of flame. The fire smoked feebly under a newly administered shovelful of 'slack', and a heap of ashes and cinders littered the grate. A pair of walking boots, caked in dry mud, lay on the hearthrug just where they had been thrown off. On the mantel-piece, amidst a dozen other articles which had no business there, was a bedroom-candlestick; and every single article of furniture stood crookedly out of its place.

Willoughby took in the whole intolerable picture, and yet spoke with kindliness. 'Well, Esther! I'm not so late, after all. I hope you did not find the time dull by yourself?' Then he explained the reason of his absence. He had met a friend he had not seen for a couple of years, who had insisted on taking him home to dine.

His wife gave no sign of having heard him; she kept her eyes riveted on the paper before her.

'You received my wire, of course,' Willoughby went on, 'and did not wait?'

Now she crushed the newspaper up with a passionate movement, and threw it from her. She raised her head, showing cheeks blazing with anger, and dark, sullen, unflinching eyes.

'I did wyte then!' she cried 'I wyted till near eight before I got your old telegraph! I s'pose that's what you call the manners of a "gentleman", to keep your wife mewed up here, while you go gallivantin' off with your fine friends?'

Whenever Esther was angry, which was often, she taunted Willoughby with being 'a gentleman', although this was the precise point about him which at other times found most favour in her eyes. But tonight she was envenomed by the idea he had been enjoying himself without her, stung by fear lest he should have been in company with some other woman.

Willoughby, hearing the taunt, resigned himself to the inevitable. Nothing that he could do might now avert the breaking storm; all his words would only be twisted into fresh griefs. But sad experience had taught him that to take refuge in silence was more fatal still. When Esther was in such a mood as this it was best to supply the fire with fuel, that, through the very violence of the conflagration, it might the sooner burn itself out.

So he said what soothing things he could, and Esther caught them up, disfigured them, and flung them back at him with scorn. She reproached him with no longer caring for her; she vituperated the conduct of his family in never taking the smallest notice of her marriage; and she detailed the insolence of the landlady who had told her that morning she pitied 'poor Mr Willoughby', and had refused to go out and buy herrings for Esther's early dinner.

Every affront or grievance, real or imaginary, since the day she and Willoughby had first met, she poured forth with a fluency due to frequent repetition, for, with the exception of today's added injuries, Willoughby had heard the whole litany many times before.

While she raged and he looked at her, he remembered he had once thought her pretty. He had seen beauty in her rough brown hair, her strong colouring, her full red mouth. He fell into musing . . . a woman may lack beauty, he told himself, and yet be loved . . .

Meanwhile Esther reached white heats of passion, and the strain could no longer be sustained. She broke into sobs and began to shed tears with the facility peculiar to her. In a moment her face was all wet with the big drops which rolled down her cheeks faster and faster, and fell with audible splashes on to the table, on to her lap, on to the floor. To this tearful abundance, formerly a surprising spectacle, Willoughby was now acclimatized; but the remnant of chivalrous feeling not yet extinguished in his bosom forbade him to sit stolidly by while a woman wept, without seeking to console her. As on previous occasions, his peace-overtures were eventually accepted. Esther's tears gradually ceased to flow, she began to exhibit a sort of compunction, she wished to be forgiven, and, with the kiss of reconciliation, passed into a phase of demonstrative affection perhaps more trying to Willoughby's patience than all that had preceded it. 'You don't love me?' she questioned, 'I'm sure you don't love me?' she reiterated; and he asseverated that he loved her until he despised himself. Then at last, only half satisfied, but wearied out with vexation – possibly, too, with a movement of pity at the sight of his haggard face – she consented to leave him. Only, what was he going to do? she asked suspiciously; write those rubbishing stories of his? Well, he must promise not to stay up more than half-an-hour at the latest – only until he had smoked one pipe.

Willoughby promised, as he would have promised anything on earth to secure to himself a half-hour's peace and solitude. Esther groped for her slippers, which were kicked off under the table; scratched four or five matches along the box and threw them away before she succeeded in lighting her candle; set it down again to contemplate her tear-swollen reflection in the chimney-glass, and burst out laughing.

'What a fright I do look, to be sure!' she remarked complacently, and again thrust her two hands up through her disordered curls. Then, holding the candle at such an angle that the grease ran over on to the carpet, she gave Willoughby another vehement kiss and trailed out of the room with an ineffectual attempt to close the door behind her.

Willoughby got up to shut it himself, and wondered why it was that Esther never did any one mortal thing efficiently or well. Good God! how irritable he felt. It was impossible to write. He must find an outlet for his impatience, rend or mend something. He began to straighten the room, but a wave of disgust came over him before the task was fairly commenced. What was the use?

Tomorrow all would be bad as before. What was the use of doing anything? He sat down by the table and leaned his head upon his hands.

*

The past came back to him in pictures: his boyhood's past first of all. He saw again the old home, every inch of which was familiar to him as his own name; he reconstructed in his thought all the old well-known furniture, and replaced it precisely as it had stood long ago. He passed again a childish finger over the rough surface of the faded Utrecht velvet chairs, and smelled again the strong fragrance of the white lilac tree, blowing in through the open parlour-window. He savoured anew the pleasant mental atmosphere produced by the dainty neatness of cultured women, the companionship of a few good pictures, of a few good books. Yet this home had been broken up years ago, the dear familiar things had been scattered far and wide, never to find themselves under the same roof again; and from those near relatives who still remained to him he lived now hopelessly estranged.

Then came the past of his first love-dream, when he worshipped at the feet of Nora Beresford, and, with the whole-heartedness of the true fanatic, clothed his idol with every imaginable attribute of virtue and tenderness. To this day there remained a secret shrine in his heart wherein the Lady of his young ideal was still enthroned, although it was long since he had come to perceive she had nothing whatever in common with the Nora of reality. For the real Nora he had no longer any sentiment, she had passed altogether out of his life and thoughts; and yet, so permanent is all influence, whether good or evil, that the effect she wrought upon his character remained. He recognized tonight that her treatment of him in the past did not count for nothing among the various factors which had determined his fate.

Now, the past of only last year returned, and, strangely enough, this seemed farther removed from him than all the rest. He had been particularly strong, well, and happy this time last year. Nora was dismissed from his mind, and he had thrown all his energies into his work. His tastes were sane and simple, and his dingy, furnished rooms had become through habit very pleasant to him. In being his own, they were invested with a greater charm than another man's castle. Here he had smoked and studied, here he had made many a glorious voyage into the land of books. Many a homecoming, too, rose up before him out of the dark ungenial streets, to a clear blazing fire, a neatly laid cloth, an evening of ideal enjoyment; many a summer twilight when he mused at the open window, plunging his gaze deep into the recesses of his neighbour's lime-tree, where the unseen sparrows chattered with such unflagging gaiety.

He had always been given to much daydreaming, and it was in the silence of his rooms of an evening that he turned his phantasmal adventures into stories for the magazines; here had come to him many an editorial refusal, but here, too, he had received the news of his first unexpected success. All his happiest memories were embalmed in those shabby, badly-furnished rooms.

Now all was changed. Now might there be no longer any soft indulgence of the hour's mood. His rooms and everything he owned belonged now to Esther, too. She had objected to most of his photographs, and had removed them. She hated books, and were he ever so ill-advised as to open one in her presence, she immediately began to talk, no matter how silent or how sullen her previous mood had been. If he read aloud to her she either yawned despairingly, or was tickled into laughter where there was no reasonable cause. At first Willoughby had tried to educate her, and had gone hopefully to the task. It is so natural to think you may make what you will of the woman who loves you. But Esther had no wish to improve. She evinced all the self-satisfaction of an illiterate mind. To her husband's gentle admonitions she replied with brevity that she thought her way quite as good as his; or, if he didn't approve of her pronunciation, he might do the other thing, she was too old to go to school again. He gave up the attempt, and, with humiliation at his previous fatuity, perceived that it was folly to expect that a few weeks of his companionship could alter or pull up the impressions of years, or rather of generations.

Yet here he paused to admit a curious thing: it was not only Esther's bad habits which vexed him, but habits quite unblameworthy in themselves which he never would have noticed in another, irritated him in her. He disliked her manner of standing, of walking, of sitting in a chair, of folding her hands. Like a lover, he was conscious of her proximity without seeing her. Like a lover, too, his eyes followed her every movement, his ear noted every change in her voice. But then, instead of being charmed by everything as the lover is, everything jarred upon him.

What was the meaning of this? Tonight the anomaly pressed upon him: he reviewed his position. Here was he, quite a young man, just twenty-six years of age, married to Esther, and bound to live with her so long as life should last – twenty, forty, perhaps fifty years more. Every day of those years to be spent in her society; he and she face to face, soul to soul; they two alone amid all the whirling, busy, indifferent world. So near together in semblance; in truth, so far apart as regards all that makes life dear.

Willoughby groaned. From the woman he did not love, whom he had never loved, he might not again go free; so much he recognized. The feeling he had once entertained for Esther, strange compound of mistaken chivalry and flattered vanity, was long since extinct; but what, then, was the sentiment with which she inspired him? For he was not indifferent to her – no, never for one instant could he persuade himself he was indifferent, never for one instant could he banish her from his thoughts. His mind's eye followed her during his hours of absence as pertinaciously as his bodily eye dwelt upon her actual presence. She was the principal object of the universe to him, the centre around which his wheel of life revolved with an appalling fidelity.

What did it mean? What could it mean? he asked himself with anguish.

And the sweat broke out upon his forehead and his hands grew cold, for on a sudden the truth lay there like a written word upon the tablecloth before him. This woman, whom he had taken to himself for better, for worse, inspired him with a passion, intense indeed, all-masterful, soul-subduing as Love itself . . . But when he understood the terror of his Hatred, he laid his head upon his arms and wept, not facile tears like Esther's, but tears wrung out from his agonizing, unavailing regret.

'A POOR STICK'

(*Tales of Mean Streets*, London: Methuen and Co., 1894)
Published by permission of Methuen and Co.

Mrs Jennings (or Jinnins, as the neighbours would have it) ruled absolutely at home, when she took so much trouble as to do anything at all there – which was less often than might have been. As for Robert her husband, he was a poor stick, said the neighbours. And yet he was a man with enough of hardihood to remain a non-unionist in the erectors' shop at Maidment's all the years of his service; no mean test of a man's fortitude and resolution, as many a sufferer for independent opinion might testify. The truth was that Bob never grew out of his courtship-blindness. Mrs Jennings governed as she pleased, stayed out or came home as she chose, and cooked a dinner or didn't, as her inclination stood. Thus it was for ten years, during which time there were no children, and Bob bore all things uncomplaining: cooking his own dinner when he found none cooked, and sewing on his own buttons. Then of a sudden came children, till in three years there were three; and Bob Jennings had to nurse and to wash them as often as not.

Mrs Jennings at this time was what is called rather a fine woman: a woman of large scale and full development; whose slatternly habit left her coarse black hair to tumble in snake-locks about her face and shoulders half the day; who, clad in half-hooked clothes, bore herself notoriously and unabashed in her fullness; and of whom ill things were said regarding the lodger. The gossips had their excuse. The lodger was an irregular young cabinet-maker, who lost quarters and halves and whole days; who had been seen abroad with his landlady, what time Bob Jennings was putting the children to bed at home; who on his frequent holidays brought in much beer, which he and the woman shared, while Bob was at work. To carry the tale to Bob would have been a thankless errand, for he would have none of anybody's sympathy, even in regard to miseries plain to his eye. But the thing got about in the workshop, and there his days were made bitter.

At home things grew worse. To return at half-past five, and find the children still undressed, screaming, hungry and dirty, was a matter of habit: to get them food, to wash them, to tend the cuts and bumps sustained through the day of neglect, before lighting a fire and getting tea for himself, were matters of daily duty. 'Ah,' he said to his sister, who came at intervals to say plain things about Mrs Jennings, 'you shouldn't go for to set a man agin 'is wife, Jin. Melier do'n' like work, I know, but that's nach'ral to 'er. She ought to married a swell 'stead o' me; she might 'a' done easy if she liked, bein' sich a fine gal; but she's good-'arted, is Melier; an' she can't 'elp bein' a bit thoughtless.' Whereat his sister called him a fool (it was her customary goodbye at such times), and took herself off.

Bob Jennings's intelligence was sufficient for his common needs, but it was never a vast intelligence. Now, under a daily burden of dull misery, it clouded and stooped. The base wit of the workshop he comprehended less, and realized more slowly, than before; and the gaffer cursed him for a sleepy dolt.

Mrs Jennings ceased from any pretence of housewifery, and would sometimes sit – perchance not quite sober – while Bob washed the children in the evening, opening her mouth only to express her contempt for him and his establishment, and to make him understand that she was sick of both. Once, exasperated by his quietness, she struck at him, and for a moment he was another man. 'Don't do that, Melier,' he said, 'else I might forget myself.' His manner surprised his wife: and it was such that she never did do that again.

So was Bob Jennings: without a friend in the world, except his sister, who chid him, and the children, who squalled at him: when his wife vanished with the lodger, the clock, a shade of wax flowers, Bob's best boots (which fitted the lodger), and his silver watch. Bob had returned, as usual, to the dirt and the children, and it was only when he struck a light that he found the clock was gone.

'Mummy tooked ve t'ock,' said Milly, the eldest child, who had followed him in from the door, and now gravely observed his movements. 'She tooked ve t'ock an' went ta-ta. An' she tooked ve fyowers.'

Bob lit the paraffin lamp with the green glass reservoir, and carried it and its evil smell about the house. Some things had been turned over and others had gone, plainly. All Melier's clothes were gone. The lodger was not in, and under his bedroom window, where his box had stood, there was naught but an oblong patch of conspicuously clean wallpaper. In a muddle of doubt and perplexity, Bob found himself at the front door, staring up and down the street. Divers women-neighbours stood at their doors, and eyed him curiously; for Mrs Webster, moralist, opposite, had not watched the day's proceedings (nor those of many other days) for nothing, nor had she kept her story to herself.

He turned back into the house, a vague notion of what had befallen percolating feebly through his bewilderment. 'I dunno – I dunno,' he faltered, rubbing his ear. His mouth was dry, and he moved his lips uneasily, as he gazed with aimless looks about the walls and ceiling. Presently his eyes rested on the child, and 'Milly,' he said decisively, 'come an 'ave yer face washed.'

He put the children to bed early, and went out. In the morning, when his sister came, because she had heard the news in common with everybody else, he had not returned. Bob Jennings had never lost more than two quarters in his life, but he was not seen at the workshop all this day. His sister stayed in the house, and in the evening, at his regular homing-time, he appeared, haggard and dusty, and began his preparations for washing the children. When he was made to understand that they had been already attended to, he looked doubtful and troubled for a moment. Presently he said: 'I ain't found 'er yet, Jin; I was in 'opes she might 'a' bin back by this. I – I don't expect she'll be very long. She was alwis a bit larky, was Melier; but very good-'arted.'

His sister had prepared a strenuous lecture on the theme of 'I told you so'; but the man was so broken, so meek, and so plainly unhinged in his faculties, that she suppressed it. Instead, she gave him comfortable talk, and made him promise in the end to sleep that night, and take up his customary work in the morning.

He did these things, and could have worked placidly enough had he but been alone; but the tale had reached the workshop, and there was no lack of brutish chaff to disorder him. This the decenter men would have no part in, and even protested against.

But the ill-conditioned kept their way, till, at the cry of 'Bell O!' when all were starting for dinner, one of the worst shouted the cruellest gibe of all. Bob Jennings turned on him and knocked him over a scrap-heap.

A shout went up from the hurrying workmen, with a chorus of 'Serve ye right,' and the fallen joker found himself awkwardly confronted by the shop bruiser. But Bob had turned to a corner, and buried his eyes in the bend of his arm, while his shoulders heaved and shook.

He slunk away home, and stayed there: walking restlessly to and fro, and often peeping down the street from the window. When, at twilight, his sister came again, he had become almost cheerful, and said with some briskness: 'I'm agoin' to meet 'er, Jin, at seven. I know where she'll be waitin'.'

He went upstairs, and after a little while came down again in his best black coat, carefully smoothing a tall hat of obsolete shape with his pocket-handkerchief. 'I ain't wore it for years,' he said. 'I ought to 'a' wore it – it might 'a' pleased 'er. She used to say she wouldn't walk with me in no other – when I used to meet 'er in the evenin', at seven o'clock.' He brushed assiduously, and put the hat on. 'I'd better 'ave a shave round the corner as I go along,' he added, fingering his stubbly chin.

He received as one not comprehending his sister's persuasion to remain at home; but when he went she followed at a little distance. After his penny shave he made for the main road, where company-keeping couples walked up and down all evening. He stopped at a church, and began pacing slowly to and fro before it, eagerly looking out each way as he went.

His sister watched him for nearly half an hour, and then went home. In two hours more she came back with her husband. Bob was still there, walking to and fro.

''Ullo, Bob,' said his brother-in-law; 'come along 'ome an' get to bed, there's a good chap. You'll be awright in the mornin'.'

'She ain't turned up,' Bob complained, 'or else I've missed 'er. This is the reg'lar place – where I alwis used to meet 'er. But she'll come tomorrer. She used to leave me in the lurch sometimes, bein' nach'rally larky. But very good-'arted, mindjer; very good-'arted.'

She did not come the next evening, nor the next, nor the evening after, nor the one after that. But Bob Jennings, howbeit depressed and anxious, was always confident. 'Somethink's prevented 'er tonight,' he would say, 'but she'll come tomorrer. . . . I'll buy a blue tie tomorrer – she used to like me in a blue tie. I won't miss 'er tomorrer. I'll come a little earlier.'

So it went. The black coat grew ragged in the service, and hobbledehoys, finding him safe sport, smashed the tall hat over his eyes time after time. He wept over the hat, and straightened it as best he might. Was she coming? Night after night, and night and night. But tomorrow. . . .

Arthur Conan Doyle

THE ADVENTURE OF THE ABBEY GRANGE

(*The Strand Magazine*, 23 January 1897)

It was on a bitterly cold night and frosty morning, towards the end of the winter of '97, that I was awakened by a tugging at my shoulder. It was Holmes. The candle in his hand shone upon his eager, stooping face, and told me at a glance that something was amiss.

'Come, Watson, come!' he cried. 'The game is afoot. Not a word! Into your clothes and come!'

Ten minutes later we were both in a cab, and rattling through the silent streets on our way to Charing Cross Station. The first faint winter's dawn was beginning to appear, and we could dimly see the occasional figure of an early workman as he passed us, blurred and indistinct in the opalescent London reek. Holmes nestled in silence into his heavy coat, and I was glad to do the same, for the air was most bitter, and neither of us had broken our fast.

It was not until we had consumed some hot tea at the station and taken our places in the Kentish train that we were sufficiently thawed, he to speak and I to listen. Holmes drew a note from his pocket, and read aloud:

> Abbey Grange, Marsham, Kent
> 3:30 A.M.
>
> My Dear Mr Holmes:
> I should be very glad of your immediate assistance in what promises to be a most remarkable case. It is something quite in your line. Except for releasing the lady I will see that everything is kept exactly as I have found it, but I beg you not to lose an instant, as it is difficult to leave Sir Eustace there.
> Yours faithfully,
> STANLEY HOPKINS

'Hopkins has called me in seven times, and on each occasion his summons has been entirely justified,' said Holmes. 'I fancy that every one of his cases has found its way into your collection, and I must admit, Watson, that you have some power of selection, which atones for much which I deplore in your narratives. Your fatal habit of looking at everything from the point of view of a story instead of as a scientific exercise has ruined what might have been an instructive and even classical series of demonstrations. You slur over work of the utmost finesse and delicacy, in order to dwell upon sensational details which may excite, but cannot possibly instruct, the reader.'

'Why do you not write them yourself?' I said, with some bitterness.

'I will, my deat Watson, I will. At present I am, as you know, fairly busy, but I propose to devote my declining years to the composition of a textbook, which shall focus the whole art of detection into one volume. Our present research appears to be a case of murder.'

'You think this Sir Eustace is dead, then?'

'I should say so. Hopkins's writing shows considerable agitation, and he is not an emotional man. Yes, I gather there has been violence, and that the body is left for our inspection. A mere suicide would not have caused him to send for me. As to the release of the lady, it would appear that she has been locked in her room during the tragedy. We are moving in high life, Watson, crackling paper, 'E. B.' monogram, coat-of-arms, picturesque address. I think that friend Hopkins will live up to his reputation, and that we shall have an interesting morning. The crime was committed before twelve last night.'

'How can you possibly tell?'

'By an inspection of the trains, and by reckoning the time. The local police had to be called in, they had to communicate with Scotland Yard, Hopkins had to go out, and he in turn had to send for me. All that makes a fair night's work. Well, here we are at Chislehurst Station, and we shall soon set our doubts at rest.'

A drive of a couple of miles through narrow country lanes brought us to a park gate, which was opened for us by an old lodge-keeper, whose haggard face bore the reflection of some great disaster. The avenue ran through a noble park, between lines of ancient elms, and ended in a low, widespread house, pillared in front after the fashion of Palladio. The central part was evidently of a great age and shrouded in ivy, but the large windows showed that modern changes had been carried out, and one wing of the house appeared to be entirely new. The youthful figure and alert, eager face of Inspector Stanley Hopkins confronted us in the open doorway.

'I'm very glad you have come, Mr Holmes. And you, too, Dr Watson. But, indeed, if I had my time over again, I should not have troubled you, for since the lady has come to herself, she has given so clear an account of the affair that there is not much left for us to do. You remember that Lewisham gang of burglars?'

'What, the three Randalls?'

'Exactly; the father and two sons. It's their work. I have not a doubt of it. They did a job at Sydenham a fortnight ago and were seen and described. Rather cool to do another so soon and so near, but it is they, beyond all doubt. It's a hanging matter this time.'

'Sir Eustace is dead, then?'

'Yes, his head was knocked in with his own poker.'

'Sir Eustace Brackenstall, the driver tells me.'

'Exactly — one of the richest men in Kent — Lady Brackenstall is in the morning-room. Poor lady, she has had a most dreadful experience. She seemed half dead when I saw her first. I think you had best see her and hear her account of the facts. Then we will examine the dining-room together.'

Lady Brackenstall was no ordinary person. Seldom have I seen so graceful a figure, so womanly a presence, and so beautiful a face. She was a blonde, golden-haired, blue-eyed, and would no doubt have had the perfect complexion which goes with such colouring, had not her recent experience left her drawn and haggard. Her sufferings were physical as well as mental, for over one eye rose a hideous, plum-coloured swelling, which her maid, a tall, austere woman, was bathing assiduously with vinegar and water. The lady lay back exhausted upon a couch, but her quick, observant gaze, as we entered the room, and the alert expression of her beautiful features, showed that neither her wits nor her courage had been shaken by her terrible experience. She was enveloped in a loose dressing-gown of blue and silver, but a black sequin-covered dinner-dress lay upon the couch beside her.

'I have told you all that happened, Mr Hopkins,' she said, wearily. 'Could you not repeat it for me? Well, if you think it necessary, I will tell these gentlemen what occurred. Have they been in the dining-room yet?'

'I thought they had better hear your ladyship's story first.'

'I shall be glad when you can arrange matters. It is horrible to me to think of him still lying there.' She shuddered and buried her face in her hands. As she did so, the loose gown fell back from her forearms. Holmes uttered an exclamation.

'You have other injuries, madam! What is this?' Two vivid red spots stood out on one of the white, round limbs. She hastily covered it.

'It is nothing. It has no connection with this hideous business tonight. If you and your friend will sit down, I will tell you all I can.

'I am the wife of Sir Eustace Brackenstall. I have been married about a year. I suppose that it is no use my attempting to conceal that our marriage has not been a happy one. I fear that all our neighbours would tell you that, even if I were to attempt to deny it. Perhaps the fault may be partly mine. I was brought up in the freer, less conventional atmosphere of South Australia, and this English life, with its proprieties and its primness, is not congenial to me. But the main reason lies in the one fact, which is notorious to everyone, and that is that Sir Eustace was a confirmed drunkard. To be with such a man for an hour is unpleasant. Can you imagine what it means for a sensitive and high-spirited woman to be tied to him for day and night? It is a sacrilege, a crime, a villany to hold that such a marriage is binding. I say that these monstrous laws of yours will bring a curse upon the land – God will not let such wickedness endure.' For an instant she sat up, her cheeks flushed, and her eyes blazing from under the terrible mark upon her brow. Then the strong, soothing hand of the austere maid drew her head down on to the cushion, and the wild anger died away into passionate sobbing. At last she continued:

'I will tell you about last night. You are aware, perhaps, that in this house all the servants sleep in the modern wing. This central block is made up of the dwelling-rooms, with the kitchen behind and our bedroom above. My maid, Theresa, sleeps above my room. There is no one else, and no sound could alarm those who are in the farther wing. This must have been well known to the robbers, or they would not have acted as they did.

'Sir Eustace retired about half-past ten. The servants had already gone to their quarters. Only my maid was up, and she had remained in her room at the top of the house until I needed her services. I sat until after eleven in this room, absorbed in a book. Then I walked round to see that all was right before I went upstairs. It was my custom to do this myself, for, as I have explained, Sir Eustace was not always to be trusted. I went into the kitchen, the butler's pantry, the gun-room, the billiard-room, the drawing-room, and finally the dining-room. As I approached the window, which is covered with thick curtains, I suddenly felt the wind blow upon my face and realized that it was open. I flung the curtain aside and found myself face to face with a broad shouldered elderly man, who had just stepped into the room. The window is a long French one, which really forms a door leading to the lawn. I held my bedroom candle lit in my hand, and, by its light, behind the first man I saw two others, who were in the act of entering. I stepped back, but the fellow was on me in an instant. He caught me first by the wrist and then by the throat. I opened my mouth to scream, but he struck me a savage blow with his fist over the eye, and felled me to the ground. I must have been unconscious for a few minutes, for when I came to myself, I found that they had torn down the bell-rope, and had secured me tightly to the oaken chair which stands at the head of the dining-table. I was so firmly bound that I could not move, and a handkerchief round my mouth prevented me from uttering a sound. It was at this instant that my unfortunate husband entered the room. He had evidently heard some suspicious sounds, and he came prepared for such a scene as he found. He was dressed in nightshirt and trousers, with his favourite blackthorn cudgel in his hand. He rushed at the burglars, but another – it was an elderly man – stooped, picked the poker out of the grate and struck him a horrible blow as he passed. He fell with a groan and never moved again. I fainted once more, but again it could only have been for a very few minutes during which I was insensible. When I opened my eyes I found that they had collected the silver from the sideboard, and they had drawn a bottle of wine which stood there.

Each of them had a glass in his hand. I have already told you, have I not, that one was elderly, with a beard, and the others young, hairless lads. They might have been a father and his two sons. They talked together in whispers. Then they came over and made sure that I was securely bound. Finally they withdrew, closing the window after them. It was quite a quarter of an hour before I got my mouth free. When I did so, my screams brought the maid to my assistance. The other servants were soon alarmed, and we sent for the local police, who instantly communicated with London. That is really all that I can tell you, gentlemen, and I trust that it will not be necessary for me to go over so painful a story again.'

'Any questions, Mr Holmes?' asked Hopkins.

'I will not impose any further tax upon Lady Brackenstall's patience and time,' said Holmes. 'Before I go into the dining-room, I should like to hear your experience.' He looked at the maid.

'I saw the men before ever they came into the house,' said she. 'As I sat by my bedroom window I saw three men in the moonlight down by the lodge gate yonder, but I thought nothing of it at the time. It was more than an hour after that I heard my mistress scream, and down I ran, to find her, poor lamb, just as she says, and him on the floor, with his blood and brains over the room. It was enough to drive a woman out of her wits, tied there, and her very dress spotted with him, but she never wanted courage, did Miss Mary Fraser of Adelaide and Lady Brackenstall of Abbey Grange hasn't learned new ways. You've questioned her long enough, you gentlemen, and now she is coming to her own room, just with her old Theresa, to get the rest that she badly needs.'

With a motherly tenderness the gaunt woman put her arm round her mistress and led her from the room.

'She had been with her all her life,' said Hopkins. 'Nursed her as a baby, and came with her to England when they first left Australia, eighteen months ago. Theresa Wright is her name, and the kind of maid you don't pick up nowadays. This way, Mr Holmes, if you please!'

The keen interest had passed out of Holmes's expressive face, and I knew that with the mystery all the charm of the case had departed. There still remained an arrest to be effected, but what were these commonplace rogues that he should soil his hands with them? An abstruse and learned specialist who finds that he has been called in for a case of measles would experience something of the annoyance which I read in my friend's eyes. Yet the scene in the dining-room of the Abbey Grange was sufficiently strange to arrest his attention and to recall his waning interest.

It was a very large and high chamber, with carved oak ceiling, oaken panelling, and a fine array of deer's heads and ancient weapons around the walls. At the further end from the door was the high French window of which we had heard. Three smaller windows on the right-hand side filled the apartment with cold winter sunshine. On the left was a large, deep fireplace, with a massive, overhanging oak mantelpiece. Beside the fireplace was a heavy oaken chair with arms and crossbars at the bottom. In and out through the open woodwork was woven a crimson cord, which was secured at each side to the crosspiece below. In releasing the lady, the cord had been slipped off her, but the knots with which it had been secured still remained. These details only struck our attention afterwards, for our thoughts were entirely absorbed by the terrible object which lay upon the tiger-skin heathrug in front of the fire.

It was the body of a tall, well-made man, about forty years of age. He lay upon his back, his face upturned, with his white teeth grinning through his short, black beard. His two clenched hands were raised above his head, and a heavy, blackthorn stick lay across them. His dark, handsome, aquiline features were convulsed into a spasm of vindictive hatred, which had set his dead face in a terribly fiendish expression. He had evidently been in his bed when the alarm had broken out, for he wore a foppish, embroidered nightshirt, and his bare feet projected from his trousers. His head was horribly injured, and the whole room bore witness to the savage ferocity of the blow which had struck him down. Beside him lay the heavy poker, bent into a curve by the concussion. Holmes examined both it and the indescribable wreck which it had wrought.

'He must be a powerful man, this elder Randall,' he remarked.

'Yes,' said Hopkins. 'I have some record of the fellow, and he is a rough customer.'

'You should have no difficulty in getting him.'

'Not the slightest. We have been on the look-out for him, and there was some idea that he had got away to America. Now that we know that the gang are here, I don't see how they can escape. We have the news at every seaport already, and a reward will be offered before evening. What beats me is how they could have done so mad a thing, knowing that the lady could describe them and that we could not fail to recognize the description.'

'Exactly. One would have expected that they would silence Lady Brackenstall as well.'

'They may not have realized,' I suggested, 'that she had recovered from her faint.'

'That is likely enough. If she seemed to be senseless, they would not take her life. What about this poor fellow, Hopkins? I seem to have heard some queer stories about him.'

'He was a good-hearted man when he was sober, but a perfect fiend when he was drunk, or rather when he was half drunk, for he seldom really went the whole way. The devil seemed to be in him at such times, and he was capable of anything. From what I hear, in spite of all his wealth and his title, he very nearly came our way once or twice. There was a scandal about his drenching a dog with petroleum and setting it on fire – her ladyship's dog, to make the matter worse – and that was only hushed up with difficulty. Then he threw a decanter at that maid, Theresa Wright – there was trouble about that. On the whole, and between ourselves, it will be a brighter house without him. What are you looking at now?'

Holmes was down on his knees, examining with great attention the knots upon the red cord with which the lady had been secured. Then he carefully scrutinized the broken and frayed end where it had snapped off when the burglar had dragged it down.

'When this was pulled down, the bell in the kitchen must have rung loudly,' he remarked.

'No one could hear it. The kitchen stands right at the back of the house.'

'How did the burglar know no one would hear it? How dared he pull at a bell-rope in that reckless fashion?'

'Exactly, Mr Holmes, exactly. You put the very question which I have asked myself again and again. There can be no doubt that this fellow must have known the house and its habits. He must have perfectly understood that the servants would all be in bed at that comparatively early hour, and that no one could possibly hear a bell ring in the kitchen. Therefore, he must have been in close league with one of the servants. Surely that is evident. But there are eight servants, and all of good character.'

'Other things being equal,' said Holmes, 'one would suspect the one at whose head the master threw a decanter. And yet that would involve treachery towards the mistress to whom this woman seems devoted. Well, well, the point is a minor one, and when you have Randall you will probably find no difficulty in securing his accomplice. The lady's story certainly seems to be corroborated, if it needed corroboration, by every detail which we see before us.' He walked to the French window and threw it open. 'There are no signs here, but the ground is iron hard, and one would not expect them. I see that these candles in the mantelpiece have been lighted.'

'Yes, it was by their light, and that of the lady's bedroom candle, that the burglars saw their way about.'

'And what did they take?'

'Well, they did not take much – only half a dozen articles of plate off the sideboard. Lady Brackenstall thinks that they were themselves so disturbed by the death of Sir Eustace that they did not ransack the house, as they would otherwise have done.'

'No doubt that is true, and yet they drank some wine, I understand.'

'To steady their nerves.'

'Exactly. These three glasses upon the sideboard have been untouched, I suppose?'

'Yes, and the bottle stands as they left it.'

'Let us look at it. Halloa, halloa! What is this?'

The three glasses were grouped together, all of them tinged with wine, and one of them containing some dregs of beeswing. The bottle stood near them, two-thirds full, and beside it lay a long, deeply stained cork. Its appearance and the dust upon the bottle showed that it was no common vintage which the murderers had enjoyed.

A change had come over Holmes's manner. He had lost his listless expression, and again I saw an alert light of interest in his keen, deepset eyes. He raised the cork and examined it minutely.

'How did they draw it?' he asked.

Hopkins pointed to a half-opened drawer. In it lay some table linen and a large corkscrew.

'Did Lady Brackenstall say that screw was used?'

'No, you remember that she was senseless at the moment when the bottle was opened.'

'Quite so. As a matter of fact, that screw was *not* used. This bottle was opened by a pocket screw, probably contained in a knife, and not more than an inch and a half long. If you will examine the top of the cork, you will observe that the screw was driven in three times before the cork was extracted. It has never been transfixed. This long screw would have transfixed it and drawn it up with a single pull. When you catch this fellow, you will find that he has one of these multiplex knives in his possession.'

'Excellent!' said Hopkins.

'But these glasses do puzzle me, I confess. Lady Brackenstall actually *saw* the three men drinking, did she not?'

'Yes; she was clear about that.'

'Then there is an end of it. What more is to be said? And yet, you must admit, that the three glasses are very remarkable, Hopkins. What? You see nothing remarkable? Well, well, let it pass. Perhaps, when a man has special knowledge and special powers like my own, it rather encourages him to seek a complex explanation when a simpler one is at hand. Of course, it must be a mere chance about the glasses. Well, good-morning, Hopkins. I don't see that I can be of any use to you, and you appear to have your case very clear. You will let me know when Randall is arrested, and any further developments which may occur. I trust that I shall soon have to congratulate you upon a successful conclusion. Come, Watson, I fancy that we may employ ourselves more profitably at home.'

During our return journey, I could see by Holmes's face that he was much puzzled by something which he had observed. Every now and then, by an effort, he would throw off the impression, and talk as if the matter were clear, but then his doubts would settle down upon him again, and his knitted brows and abstracted eyes would show that his thoughts had gone back once more to the great dining-room of the Abbey Grange, in which this midnight tragedy had been enacted. At last, by a sudden impulse, just as our train was crawling out of a suburban station, he sprang on to the platform and pulled me out after him.

'Excuse me, my dear fellow,' said he, as we watched the rear carriages of our train disappearing round a curve, 'I am sorry to make you the victim of what may seem a mere whim, but on my life, Watson, I simply *can't* leave that case in this condition. Every instinct that I possess cries out against it. It's wrong – it's all wrong – I'll swear that it's wrong. And yet the lady's story was complete, the maid's corroboration was sufficient, the detail was fairly exact. What have I to put up against that? Three wine-glasses, that is all. But if I had not taken things for granted, if I had examined everything with care which I should have shown had we approached the case *de novo* and had no cut-and-dried story to warp my mind, should I not then have found something more definite to go upon? Of course I should. Sit down on this bench, Watson, until a train for Chislehurst arrives, and allow me to lay the evidence before you, imploring you in the first instance to dismiss from your mind the idea that anything which the maid or her mistress may have said must necessarily be true. The lady's charming personality must not be permitted to warp our judgment.

'Surely there are details in her story which, if we looked at in cold blood, would excite our suspicion. These burglars made a considerable haul at Sydenham a fortnight ago. Some account of them and of their appearance was in the papers, and would naturally occur to anyone who wished to invent a story in which imaginary robbers should play a part. As a matter of fact, burglars who have done a good stroke of business are, as a rule, only too glad to enjoy the proceeds in peace and quiet without embarking on another perilous undertaking. Again, it is unusual for burglars to operate at so early an hour, it is unusual for burglars to strike a lady to prevent her screaming, since one would imagine that was the sure way to make her scream, it is unusual for them to commit murder when their numbers are sufficient to overpower one man, it is unusual for them to be content with a limited plunder when there was much more within their reach, and finally, I should say, that it was very unusual for such men to leave a bottle half empty. How do all these unusuals strike you, Watson?'

'Their cumulative effect is certainly considerable, and yet each of them is quite possible in itself. The most unusual thing of all, as it seems to me, is that the lady should be tied to the chair.'

'Well, I am not so clear about that, Watson, for it is evident that they must either kill her or else secure her in such a way that she could not give immediate notice of their escape. But at any rate I have shown, have I not, that there is a certain element of improbability about the lady's story? And now, on the top of this, comes the incident of the wineglasses.'

'What about the wineglasses?'

'Can you see them in your mind's eye?'

'I see them clearly.'

'We are told that three men drank from them. Does that strike you as likely?'

'Why not? There was wine in each glass.'

'Exactly, but there was beeswing only in one glass. You must have noticed that fact. What does that suggest to your mind?'

'The last glass filled would be most likely to contain beeswing.'

'Not at all. The bottle was full of it, and it is inconceivable that the first two glasses were clear and the third heavily charged with it. There are two possible explanations, and only two. One is that after the second glass was filled the bottle was violently agitated, and so the third glass received the beeswing. That does not appear probable. No, no, I am sure that I am right.'

'What, then, do you suppose?'

'That only two glasses were used, and that the dregs of both were poured into a third glass, so as to give the false impression that three people had been here. In that way all the beeswing would be in the last glass, would it not? Yes, I am convinced that this is so. But if I have hit upon the true explanation of this one small phenomenon, then in an instant the case rises from the commonplace to the exceedingly remarkable, for it can only mean that Lady Brackenstall and her maid have deliberately lied to us, that not one word of their story is to be believed, that they have some very strong reason for covering the real criminal, and that we must construct our case for ourselves without any help from them. That is the mission which now lies before us, and here, Watson, is the Sydenham train.'

The household at the Abbey Grange were much surprised at our return, but Sherlock Holmes, finding that Stanley Hopkins had gone off to report to headquarters, took possession of the dining-room, locked the door upon the inside, and devoted himself for two hours to one of those minute and laborious investigations which form the solid basis on which his brilliant edifices of deduction were reared. Seated in a corner like an interested student who observes the demonstration of his professor, I followed every step of that remarkable research. The window, the curtains, the carpet, the chair, the rope – each in turn was minutely examined and duly pondered. The body of the unfortunate baronet had been removed, and all else remained as we had seen it in the morning. Finally, to my astonishment, Holmes climbed up on to the massive mantelpiece. Far above his head hung the few inches of red cord which were still attached to the wire. For a long time he gazed upward at it, and then in an attempt to get nearer to it he rested his knee upon a wooden bracket on the wall. This brought his hand within a few inches of the broken end of the rope, but it was not this so much as the bracket itself which seemed to engage his attention. Finally, he sprang down with an ejaculation of satisfaction.

'It's all right, Watson,' said he. 'We have got our case – one of the most remarkable in our collection. But, dear me, how slow-witted I have been, and how nearly I have committed the blunder of my lifetime! Now, I think that, with a few missing links, my chain is almost complete.'

'You have got your men?'

'Man, Watson, man. Only one, but a very formidable person. Strong as a lion – witness the blow that bent that poker! Six foot three in height, active as a squirrel, dexterous with his fingers, finally, remarkably quick-witted, for this whole ingenious story is of his concoction. Yes, Watson, we have come upon the handiwork of a very remarkable individual. And yet, in that bell-rope, he has given us a clue which should not have left us a doubt.'

'Where was the clue?'

'Well, if you were to pull down a bell-rope, Watson, where would you expect it to break? Surely at the spot where it is attached to the wire. Why should it break three inches from the top, as this one has done?'

'Because it is frayed there?'

'Exactly. This end, which we can examine, is frayed. He was cunning enough to do that with his knife. But the other end is not frayed. You could not observe that from here, but if you were on the mantelpiece you would see that it is cut clean off without any mark of fraying whatever. You can reconstruct what occurred. The man needed the rope. He would not tear it down for fear of giving the alarm by ringing the bell. What did he do? He sprang up on the mantelpiece, could not quite reach it, put his knee on the bracket – you will see the impression in the dust – and so got his knife to bear upon the cord. I could not reach the place by at least three inches – from which I infer that he is at least three inches a bigger man than I. Look at that mark upon the seat of the oaken chair! What is it?'

'Blood.'

'Undoubtedly it is blood. This alone puts the lady's story out of court. If she were seated on the chair when the crime was done, how comes that mark? No, no, she was placed in the chair *after* the death of her husband. I'll wager that the black dress shows a corresponding mark to this. We have not yet met our Waterloo, Watson, but this is our Marengo, for it begins in defeat and ends in victory. I should like now to have a few words with the nurse, Theresa. We must be wary for a while, if we are to get the information which we want.'

She was an interesting person, this stern Australian nurse – taciturn, suspicious, ungracious, it took some time before Holmes's pleasant manner and frank acceptance of all that she said thawed her into a corresponding amiability. She did not attempt to conceal her hatred for her late employer.

'Yes, sir, it is true that he threw the decanter at me. I heard him call my mistress a name, and I told him that he would not dare to speak so if her brother had been there. Then it was that he threw it at me. He might have thrown a dozen if he had but left my bonny bird alone. He was forever ill-treating her, and she too proud to complain. She will not even tell me all that he has done to her. She never told me of those marks on her arm that you saw this morning, but I know very well that they come from a stab with a hatpin. The sly devil – God forgive me that I should speak of him so, now that he is dead! But a devil he was, if ever one walked the earth. He was all honey when first we met him – only eighteen months ago, and we both feel as if it were eighteen years. She had only just arrived in London. Yes, it was her first voyage – she had never been from home before. He won her with his title and his money and his false London ways. If she made a mistake she has paid for it, if ever a woman did. What month did we meet him? Well, I tell you it was just after we arrived. We arrived in June, and it was July. They were married in January of last year. Yes, she is down in the morning-room again, and I have no doubt she will see you, but you must not ask too much of her, for she has gone through all that flesh and blood will stand.'

Lady Brackenstall was reclining on the same couch, but looked brighter than before. The maid had entered with us, and began once more to foment the bruise upon her mistress's brow.

'I hope,' said the lady, 'that you have not come to cross-examine me again?'

'No,' Holmes answered, in his gentlest voice. 'I will not cause you any unnecessary trouble, Lady Brackenstall, and my whole desire is to make things easy for you, for I am convinced that you are a much-tried woman. If you will treat me as a friend and trust me, you may find that I will justify your trust.'

'What do you want me to do?'

'To tell me the truth.'

'Mr Holmes!'

'No, no, Lady Brackenstall – it is no use. You may have heard of any little reputation which I possess. I will stake it all on the fact that your story is an absolute fabrication.'

Mistress and maid were both staring at Holmes with pale faces and frightened eyes.

'You are an impudent fellow!' cried Theresa. 'Do you mean to say that my mistress has told a lie?'

Holmes rose from his chair.

'Have you nothing to tell me?'

'I have told you everything.'

'Think once more, Lady Brackenstall. Would it not be better to be frank?'

For an instant there was hesitation in her beautiful face. Then some new strong thought caused it to set like a mask.

'I have told you all I know.'

Holmes took his hat and shrugged his shoulders. 'I am sorry,' he said, and without another word we left the room and the house. There was a pond in the park, and to this my friend led the way. It was frozen over, but a single hole was left for the convenience of a solitary swan. Holmes gazed at it, and then passed on to the lodge gate. There he scribbled a short note for Stanley Hopkins, and left it with the lodge-keeper.

'It may be a hit, or it may be a miss, but we are bound to do something for friend Hopkins, just to justify this second visit,' said he. 'I will not quite take him into my confidence yet. I think our next scene of operations must be the shipping office of the Adelaide–Southampton line, which stands at the end of Pall Mall, if I remember right. There is a second line of steamers which connect South Australia with England, but we will draw the larger cover first.'

Holmes's card sent in to the manager ensured instant attention, and he was not long in acquiring all the information he needed. In June of '95, only one of their line had reached a home port. It was the *Rock of Gibraltar*, their largest and best boat. A reference to the passenger list showed that Miss Fraser, of Adelaide, with her maid had made the voyage in her. The boat was now somewhere south of the Suez Canal on her way to Australia. Her officers were the same as in '95, with one exception. The first officer, Mr Jack Crocker, had been made a captain and was to take charge of their new ship, the *Bass Rock*, sailing in two days' time from Southampton. He lived at Sydenham, but he was likely to be in that morning for instructions, if we cared to wait for him.

No, Mr Holmes had no desire to see him, but would be glad to know more about his record and character.

His record was magnificent. There was not an officer in the fleet to touch him. As to his character, he was reliable on duty, but a wild, desperate fellow off the deck of his ship – hot-headed, excitable, but loyal, honest, and kind-hearted. That was the pith of the information with which Holmes left the office of the Adelaide–Southampton company. Thence he drove to Scotland Yard, but, instead of entering, he sat in his cab with his brows drawn down, lost in profound thought. Finally he drove round to the Charing Cross telegraph office, sent off a message, and then, at last, we made for Baker Street once more.

'No, I couldn't do it, Watson,' said he, as we re-entered our room. 'Once that warrant was made out, nothing on earth would save him. Once or twice in my career I feel that I have done more real harm by my discovery of the criminal than ever he had done by his crime. I have learned caution now, and I had rather play tricks with the law of England than with my own conscience. Let us know a little more before we act.'

Before evening, we had a visit from Inspector Stanley Hopkins. Things were not going very well with him.

'I believe that you are a wizard, Mr Holmes. I really do sometimes think that you have powers that are not human. Now, how on earth could you know that the stolen silver was at the bottom of that pond?'

'I didn't know it.'

'But you told me to examine it.'

'You got it, then?'

'Yes, I got it.'

'I am very glad if I have helped you.'

'But you haven't helped me. You have made the affair far more difficult. What sort of burglars are they who steal silver and then throw it into the nearest pond?'

'It was certainly rather eccentric behaviour. I was merely going on the idea that if the silver had been taken by persons who did not want it – who merely took it for a blind, as it were – then they would naturally be anxious to get rid of it.'

'But why should such an idea cross your mind?'

'Well, I thought it was possible. When they came out through the French window, there was the pond with one tempting little hole in the ice, right in front of their noses. Could there be a better hiding-place?'

'Ah, a hiding-place – that is better!' cried Stanley Hopkins. 'Yes, yes, I see it all now! It was early, there were folk upon the roads, they were afraid of being seen with the silver, so they sank it in the pond, intending to return for it when the coast was clear. Excellent, Mr Holmes – that is better than your idea of a blind.'

'Quite so, you have got an admirable theory. I have no doubt that my own ideas were quite wild, but you must admit that they have ended in discovering the silver.'

'Yes, sir – yes. It was all your doing. But I have had a bad set-back.'

'A setback?'

'Yes, Mr Holmes. The Randall gang were arrested in New York this morning.'

'Dear me, Hopkins! That is certainly rather against your theory that they committed a murder in Kent last night.'

'It is fatal, Mr Holmes – absolutely fatal. Still, there are other gangs of three besides the Randalls, or it may be some new gang of which the police have never heard.'

'Quite so, it is perfectly possible. What, are you off?'

'Yes, Mr Holmes, there is no rest for me until I have got to the bottom of the business. I suppose you have no hint to give me?'

'I have given you one.'

'Which?'

'Well, I suggested a blind.'

'But why, Mr Holmes, why?'

'Ah, that's the question, of course. But I commend the idea to your mind. You might possibly find that there was something in it. You won't stop for dinner? Well, goodbye, and let us know how you get on.'

Dinner was over, and the table cleared before Holmes alluded to the matter again. He had lit his pipe and held his slippered feet to the cheerful blaze of the fire. Suddenly he looked at his watch.

'I expect developments, Watson.'

'When?'

'Now – within a few minutes. I dare say you thought I acted rather badly to Stanley Hopkins just now.'

'I trust your judgment.'

'A very sensible reply, Watson. You must look at it this way: what I know is unofficial, what he knows is official. I have the right to private judgment, but he has none. He must disclose all, or he is a traitor to his service. In a doubtful case I would not put him in so painful a position, and so I reserve my information until my own mind is clear upon the matter.'

'But when will that be?'

'The time has come. You will now be present at the last scene of a remarkable little drama.'

There was a sound upon the stairs, and our door was opened to admit as fine a specimen of manhood as ever passed through it. He was a very tall young man, golden-moustached, blue-eyed, with a skin which had been burned by tropical suns, and a springy step, which showed that the huge frame was as active as it was strong. He closed the door behind him, and then he stood with clenched hands and heaving breast, choking down some overmastering emotion.

'Sit down, Captain Crocker. You got my telegram?'

Our visitor sank into an armchair and looked from one to the other of us with questioning eyes.

'I got your telegram, and I came at the hour you said. I heard that you had been down to the office. There was no getting away from you. Let's hear the worst. What are you going to do with me? Arrest me? Speak out, man! You can't sit there and play with me like a cat with a mouse.'

'Give him a cigar,' said Holmes. 'Bite on that, Captain Crocker, and don't let your nerves run away with you. I should not sit here smoking with you if I thought that you were a common criminal, you may be sure of that. Be frank with me and we may do some good. Play tricks with me, and I'll crush you.'

'What do you wish me to do?'

'To give me a true account of all that happened at the Abbey Grange last night – a *true* account, mind you, with nothing added and nothing taken off. I know so much already that if you go one inch off the straight, I'll blow this police whistle from my window and the affair goes out of my hands forever.'

The sailor thought for a little. Then he struck his leg with his great sunburned hand.

'I'll chance it,' he cried. 'I believe you are a man of your word, and a white man, and I'll tell you the whole story. But one thing I will say first. So far as I am concerned, I regret nothing and I fear nothing, and I would do it all again and be proud of the job. Damn the beast, if he had as many lives as a cat, he would owe them all to me! But it's the lady, Mary – Mary Fraser – for never will I call her by that accursed name. When I think of getting her into trouble, I who would give my life just to bring one smile to her dear face, it's that that turns my soul into water. And yet – and yet – what less could I do? I'll tell you my story gentlemen, and then I'll ask you, as man to man, what less could I do?

'I must go back a bit. You seem to know everything, so I expect that you know that I met her when she was a passenger and I was first officer of the *Rock of Gibraltar*. From the first day I met her, she was the only woman to me. Every day of that voyage I loved her more, and many a time since have I kneeled down in the darkness of the night watch and kissed the deck of that ship because I knew her dear feet had trod it. She was never engaged to me. She treated me as fairly as ever a woman treated a man. I have no complaint to make. It was all love on my side, and all good comradeship and friendship on hers. When we parted she was a free woman, but I could never again be a free man.

'Next time I came back from sea, I heard of her marriage. Well, why shouldn't she marry whom she liked? Title and money – who could carry them better than she? She was born for all that is beautiful and dainty. I didn't grieve over her marriage. I was not such a selfish hound as that. I just rejoiced that good luck had come her way, and that she had not thrown herself away on a penniless sailor. That's how I loved Mary Fraser.

'Well, I never thought to see her again, but last voyage I was promoted, and the new boat was not yet launched, so I had to wait for a couple of months with my people at Sydenham. One day out in a country lane I met Theresa Wright, her old maid. She told me all about her, about him, about everything. I tell you, gentlemen, it nearly drove me mad. This drunken hound, that he should dare to raise his hand to her, whose boots he was not worthy to lick! I met Theresa again. Then I met Mary herself – and met her again. Then she would meet me no more. But the other day I had a notice that I was to start on my voyage within a week, and I determined that I would see her once before I left. Theresa was always my friend, for she loved Mary and hated this villain almost as much as I did. From her I learned the ways of the house. Mary used to sit up reading in her own little room downstairs. I crept round there last night and scratched at the window. At first she would not open to me, but in her heart I know that now she loves me, and she could not leave me in the frosty night. She whispered to me to come round to the big front window, and I found it open before me, so as to let me into the dining-room. Again I heard from her own lips things that made my blood boil, and again I cursed this brute who mishandled the woman I loved. Well, gentlemen, I was standing with her just inside the window, in all innocence, as God is my judge, when he rushed like a madman into the room, called her the vilest name that a man could use to a woman, and welted her across the face with the stick he had in his hand. I had sprung for the poker, and it was a fair fight between us. See here, on my arm, where his first blow fell. Then it was my turn, and I went through him as if he had been a rotten pumpkin. Do you think I was sorry? Not I! It was his life or mine, but far more than that, it was his life or hers, for how could I leave her in the power of this madman? That was how I killed him. Was I wrong? well, then, what would either of you gentlemen have done, if you had been in my position?

'She had screamed when he struck her, and that brought old Theresa down from the room above. There was a bottle of wine on the sideboard, and I opened it and poured a little between Mary's lips, for she was half dead with shock. Then I took a drop myself. Theresa was as cool as ice, and it was her plot as much as mine. We must make it appear that burglars had done the thing. Theresa kept on repeating our story to her mistress, while I swarmed up and cut the rope of the bell. Then I lashed her in her chair, and frayed out the end of the rope to make it look natural, else they would wonder how in the world a burglar could have got up there to cut it. Then I gathered up a few plates and pots of silver, to carry out the idea of the robbery, and there I left them, with orders to give the alarm when I had a quarter of an hour's start. I dropped the silver into the pond, and made off for Sydenham, feeling that for once in my life I had done a real good night's work. And that's the truth and the whole truth, Mr Holmes, if it costs me my neck.'

Holmes smoked for some time in silence. Then he crossed the room, and shook our visitor by the hand.

'That's what I think,' said he. 'I know that every word is true, for you have hardly said a word which I did not know. No one but an acrobat or a sailor could have got up to that bell-rope from the bracket, and no one but a sailor could have made the knots with which the cord was fastened to the chair. Only once had this lady been brought into contact with sailors, and that was on her voyage, and it was someone of her own class of life, since she was trying hard to shield him, and so showing that she loved him. You see how easy it was for me to lay my hands upon you when once I started upon the right trail.'

'I thought the police never could have seen through our dodge.'

'And the police haven't, nor will they, to the best of my belief. Now, look here, Captain Crocker, this is a very serious matter, though I am willing to admit that you acted under the most extreme provocation to which any man could be subjected. I am not sure that in defence of your own life your action will not be pronounced legitimate. However, that is for a British jury to decide. Meanwhile I have so much sympathy for you that, if you choose to disappear in the next twenty-four hours, I will promise you that no one will hinder you.'

'And then it will all come out?'

'Certainly it will come out.'

The sailor flushed with anger.

'What sort of proposal is that to make a man? I know enough of law to understand that Mary would be held as accomplice. Do you think I would leave her alone to face the music while I slunk away? No, sir, let them do their worst upon me, but for heaven's sake, Mr Holmes, find some way of keeping my poor Mary out of the courts.'

Holmes for a second time held out his hand to the sailor.

'I was only testing you, and you ring true every time. Well, it is a great responsibility that I take upon myself, but I have given Hopkins an excellent hint, and if he can't avail himself of it I can do no more. See here, Captain Crocker, we'll do this in due form of law. You are the prisoner. Watson, you are a British jury, and I never met a man who was more eminently fitted to represent one. I am the judge. Now, gentleman of the jury, you have heard the evidence. Do you find the prisoner guilty or not guilty?'

'Not guilty, my lord,' said I.

'*Vox populi, vox Dei*. You are acquitted, Captain Crocker. So long as the law does not find some other victim you are safe from me. Come back to this lady in a year, and may her future and yours justify us in the judgment which we have pronounced this night!'

George Gissing

THE PRIZE LODGER

(*Human Odds and Ends/Stories and Sketches*, London: Lawrence and Bullen Ltd, 1898)

The ordinary West-End Londoner – who is a citizen of no city at all, but dwells amid a mere conglomerate of houses at a certain distance from Charing Cross – has known a fleeting surprise when, by rare chance, his eye fell upon the name of some such newspaper as the *Battersea Times*, the *Camberwell Mercury*, or the *Islington Gazette*. To him, these and the like districts are nothing more than compass points of the huge metropolis. He may be in practice acquainted with them; if historically inclined, he may think of them as old-time villages swallowed up by insatiable London; but he has never grasped the fact that in Battersea, Camberwell, Islington, there are people living who name these places as their home; who are born, subsist, and die there as though in a distinct town, and practically without consciousness of its obliteration in the map of a world capital.

The stable element of this population consists of more or less old-fashioned people. Round about them is the ceaseless coming and going of nomads who keep abreast with the time, who take their lodgings by the week, their houses by the month; who camp indifferently in regions old and new, learning their geography in train and tram-car. Abiding parishioners are wont to be either very poor or established in a moderate prosperity; they lack enterprise, either for good or ill: if comfortably off, they owe it, as a rule, to some predecessor's exertion. And for the most part, though little enough endowed with the civic spirit, they abundantly pride themselves on their local permanence.

Representative of this class was Mr Archibald Jordan, a native of Islington, and, at the age of five-and-forty, still faithful to the streets which he had trodden as a child. His father started a small grocery business in Upper Street; Archibald succeeded to the shop, advanced soberly, and at length admitted a partner, by whose capital and energy the business was much increased. After his thirtieth year Mr Jordan ceased to stand behind the counter. Of no very active disposition, and but moderately set on gain, he found it pleasant to spend a few hours daily over the books and the correspondence, and for the rest of his time to enjoy a gossipy leisure, straying among the acquaintances of a lifetime, or making new in the decorous bar-parlours, billiard-rooms, and other such retreats which allured his bachelor liberty. His dress and bearing were unpretentious, but impressively respectable; he never allowed his garments (made by an Islington tailor, an old schoolfellow) to exhibit the least sign of wear, but fashion affected their style as little as possible. Of middle height, and tending to portliness, he walked at an unvarying pace, as a man who had never known undignified hurry; in his familiar thoroughfares he glanced about him with a good-humoured air of proprietorship, or with a look of thoughtful criticism for any changes that might be going forward. No one had ever spoken flatteringly of his visage; he knew himself a very homely-featured man, and accepted the fact, as something that had neither favoured nor hindered him in life. But it was his conviction that no man's eye had a greater power of solemn and overwhelming rebuke, and this gift he took a pleasure in exercising, however trivial the occasion.

For five-and-twenty years he had lived in lodgings; always within the narrow range of Islington respectability, yet never for more than a twelvemonth under the same roof. This peculiar feature of Mr Jordan's life had made him a subject of continual interest to local landladies, among whom were several lifelong residents, on friendly terms of old time with the Jordan family. To them it seemed an astonishing thing that a man in such circumstances had not yet married; granting this eccentricity, they could not imagine what made him change his abode so often. Not a landlady in Islington but would welcome Mr Jordan in her rooms, and, having got him, do her utmost to prolong the connection. He had been known to quit a house on the paltriest excuse, removing to another in which he could not expect equally good treatment. There was no accounting for it: it must be taken as an ultimate mystery of life, and made the most of as a perennial topic of neighbourly conversation.

As to the desirability of having Mr Jordan for a lodger there could be no difference of opinion among rational womankind. Mrs Wiggins, indeed, had taken his sudden departure from her house, so ill that she always spoke of him abusively; but who heeded Mrs Wiggins? Even in the sadness of hope deferred, those ladies who had entertained him once, and speculated on his possible return, declared Mr Jordan a 'thorough gentleman'. Lodgers, as a class, do not recommend themselves in Islington; Mr Jordan shone against the dusky background with almost dazzling splendour. To speak of lodgers as of cattle, he was a prize creature. A certain degree of comfort he firmly exacted; he might be a trifle fastidious about cooking; he stood upon his dignity; but no one could say that he grudged reward for service rendered. It was his practice to pay more than the landlady asked. 'Twenty-five shillings a week, you say? I shall give you twenty-eight. *But* —' and with raised forefinger he went through the catalogue of his demands. Everything must be done precisely as he directed; even in the laying of his table he insisted upon certain minute peculiarities, and to forget one of them was to earn that gaze of awful reprimand which Mr Jordan found (or thought) more efficacious than any spoken word. Against this precision might be set his strange indulgence in the matter of bills; he merely regarded the total, was never known to dispute an item. Only twice in his long experience had he quitted a lodging because of exorbitant charges, and on these occasions he sternly refused to discuss the matter. 'Mrs Hawker, I am paying your account with the addition of one week's rent. Your rooms will be vacant at eleven o'clock tomorrow morning.' And until the hour of departure no entreaty, no prostration, could induce him to utter a syllable.

It was on the 1st of June, 1889, his forty-fifth birthday, that Mr Jordan removed from quarters he had occupied for ten months, and became a lodger in the house of Mrs Elderfield.

Mrs Elderfield, a widow, aged three-and-thirty, with one little girl, was but a casual resident in Islington; she knew nothing of Mr Jordan, and made no inquiries about him. Strongly impressed, as every woman must needs be, by his air and tone of mild authority, she congratulated herself on the arrival of such an inmate; but no subservience appeared in her demeanour; she behaved with studious civility, nothing more. Her words were few and well chosen. Always neatly dressed, yet always busy, she moved about the house with quick, silent step, and cleanliness marked her path. The meals were well cooked, well served. Mr Jordan being her only lodger, she could devote to him an undivided attention. At the end of his first week the critical gentleman felt greater satisfaction than he had ever known.

The bill lay upon his table at breakfast-time. He perused the items, and, much against his habit, reflected upon them. Having breakfasted, he rang the bell.

'Mrs Elderfield —'

He paused, and looked gravely at the widow. She had a plain, honest, healthy face, with resolute lips, and an eye that brightened when she spoke; her well-knit figure, motionless in its respectful attitude, declared a thoroughly sound condition of the nerves.

'Mrs Elderfield, your bill is so very moderate that I think you must have forgotten something.'

'Have you looked it over, sir?'

'I never trouble with the details. Please examine it.'

'There is no need, sir. I never make a mistake.'

'I said, Mrs Elderfield, please *examine* it.'

She seemed to hesitate, but obeyed.

'The bill is quite correct, sir.'

'Thank you.'

He paid it at once and said no more.

The weeks went on. To Mr Jordan's surprise, his landlady's zeal and efficiency showed no diminution, a thing unprecedented in his long and varied experience. After the first day or two he had found nothing to correct; every smallest instruction was faithfully carried out. Moreover, he knew for the first time in his life the comfort of absolutely clean rooms. The best of his landladies hitherto had not risen above that conception of cleanliness which is relative to London soot and fog. His palate, too, was receiving an education. Probably he had never eaten of a joint rightly cooked, or tasted a potato boiled as it should be; more often than not, the food set before him had undergone a process which left it masticable indeed, but void of savour and nourishment. Many little attentions of which he had never dreamed kept him in a wondering cheerfulness. And at length he said to himself: 'Here I shall stay.'

Not that his constant removals had been solely due to discomfort and a hope of better things. The secret – perhaps not entirely revealed even to himself – lay in Mr Jordan's sense of his own importance, and his uneasiness whenever he felt that, in the eyes of a landlady, he was becoming a mere everyday person – an ordinary lodger. No sooner did he detect a sign of this than he made up his mind to move. It gave him the keenest pleasure of which he was capable when, on abruptly announcing his immediate departure, he perceived the landlady's profound mortification. To make the blow heavier he had even resorted to artifice, seeming to express a most lively contentment during the very days when he had decided to leave and was asking himself where he should next abide. One of his delights was to return to a house which he had quitted years ago, to behold the excitement and bustle occasioned by his appearance, and play the good-natured autocrat over grovelling dependents. In every case, save the two already mentioned, he had parted with his landlady on terms of friendliness, never vouchsafing a reason for his going away, genially eluding every attempt to obtain an explanation, and at the last abounding in graceful recognition of all that had been done for him. Mr Jordan shrank from dispute, hated every sort of contention; this characteristic gave a certain refinement to his otherwise commonplace existence. Vulgar vanity would have displayed itself in precisely the acts and words from which his self-esteem nervously shrank. And of late he had been thinking over the list of landladies, with a half-formed desire to settle down, to make himself a permanent home. Doubtless as a result of this state of mind, he betook himself to a strange house, where, as from neutral ground, he might reflect upon the lodgings he knew, and judge between their merits. He could not foresee what awaited him under Mrs Elderfield's roof; the event impressed him as providential; he felt, with singular emotion, that choice was taken out of his hands. Lodgings could not be more than perfect, and such he had found.

It was not his habit to chat with landladies. At times he held forth to them on some topic of interest, suavely, instructively; if he gave in to their ordinary talk, it was with a half-absent smile of condescension. Mrs Elderfield seeming as little disposed to gossip as himself, a month elapsed before he knew anything of her history; but one evening the reserve on both sides was broken. His landlady modestly inquired whether she was giving satisfaction, and Mr Jordan replied with altogether unwonted fervour. In the dialogue that ensued, they exchanged personal confidences. The widow had lost her husband four years ago; she came from the Midlands, but had long dwelt in London. Then fell from her lips a casual remark which made the hearer uneasy.

'I don't think I shall always stay here. The neighbourhood is too crowded. I should like to have a house somewhere further out.'

Mr Jordan did not comment on this, but it kept a place in his daily thoughts, and became at length so much of an anxiety that he invited a renewal of the subject.

'You have no intention of moving just yet, Mrs Elderfield?'

'I was going to tell you, sir,' replied the landlady, with her respectful calm, 'that I have decided to make a change next spring. Some friends of mine have gone to live at Wood Green, and I shall look for a house in the same neighbourhood.'

Mr Jordan was, in private, gravely disturbed. He who had flitted from house to house for many years, distressing the souls of landladies, now lamented the prospect of a forced removal. It was open to him to accompany Mrs Elderfield, but he shrank from the thought of living in so remote a district. Wood Green! The very name appalled him, for he had never been able to endure the country. He betook himself one dreary autumn afternoon to that northern suburb, and what he saw did not at all reassure him. On his way back he began once more to review the list of old lodgings.

But from that day his conversations with Mrs Elderfield grew more frequent, more intimate. In the evening he occasionally made an excuse for knocking at her parlour door, and lingered for a talk which ended only at supper time. He spoke of his own affairs, and grew more ready to do so as his hearer manifested a genuine interest, without impertinent curiosity. Little by little he imparted to Mrs Elderfield a complete knowledge of his commercial history, of his pecuniary standing – matters of which he had never before spoken to a mere acquaintance. A change was coming over him; the foundations of habit crumbled beneath his feet; he lost his look of complacence, his self-confident and superior tone. Bar-parlours and billiard-rooms saw him but rarely and flittingly. He seemed to have lost his pleasure in the streets of

Islington, and spent all his spare time by the fireside, perpetually musing.

On a day in March one of his old landladies, Mrs Higdon, sped to the house of another, Mrs Evans, panting under a burden of strange news. Could it be believed! Mr Jordan was going to marry – to marry that woman in whose house he was living! Mrs Higdon had it on the very best authority – that of Mr Jordan's partner, who spoke of the affair without reserve. A new house had already been taken – at Wood Green. Well! After all these years, after so many excellent opportunities, to marry a mere stranger and forsake Islington! In a moment Mr Jordan's character was gone; had he figured in the police-court under some disgraceful charge, these landladies could hardly have felt more shocked and professed themselves more disgusted. The intelligence spread. Women went out of their way to have a sight of Mrs Elderfield's house; they hung about for a glimpse of that sinister person herself. She had robbed them, every one, of a possible share in Islington's prize lodger. Had it been one of themselves they could have borne the chagrin; but a woman whom not one of them knew, an alien! What base arts had she practised? Ah, it was better not to inquire too closely into the secrets of that lodging-house.

Though every effort was made to learn the time and place of the ceremony, Mr Jordan's landladies had the mortification to hear of his wedding only when it was over. Of course, this showed that he felt the disgracefulness of his behaviour; he was not utterly lost to shame. It could only be hoped that he would not know the bitterness of repentance.

Not till he found himself actually living in the house at Wood Green did Mr Jordan realize how little his own will had had to do with the recent course of events. Certainly, he had made love to the widow, and had asked her to marry him; but from that point onward he seemed to have put himself entirely in Mrs Elderfield's hands, granting every request, meeting half-way every suggestion she offered, becoming, in short, quite a different kind of man from his former self. He had not been sensible of a moment's reluctance; he enjoyed the novel sense of yielding himself to affectionate guidance. His wits had gone wool-gathering; they returned to him only after the short honeymoon at Brighton, when he stood upon his own hearth-rug, and looked round at the new furniture and ornaments which symbolized a new beginning of life.

The admirable landlady had shown herself energetic, clear-headed, and full of resource; it was she who chose the house, and transacted all the business in connection with it; Mr Jordan had merely run about in her company from place to place, smiling approval and signing cheques. No one could have gone to work more prudently, or obtained what she wanted at smaller outlay; for all that, Mr Jordan, having recovered something like his normal frame of mind, viewed the results with consternation. Left to himself, he would have taken a very small house, and furnished it much in the style of Islington lodgings; as it was, he occupied a ten-roomed 'villa', with appointments which seemed to him luxurious, aristocratic. True, the expenditure was of no moment to a man in his position, and there was no fear that Mrs Jordan would involve him in dangerous extravagance; but he had always lived with such excessive economy that the sudden change to a life correspondent with his income could not but make him uncomfortable.

Mrs Jordan had, of course, seen to it that her personal appearance harmonized with the new surroundings. She dressed herself and her young daughter with careful appropriateness. There was no display, no purchase of gewgaws – merely garments of good quality, such as became people in easy circumstances. She impressed upon her husband that this was nothing more than a return to the habits of her earlier life. Her first marriage had been a sad mistake; it had brought her down in the world. Now she felt restored to her natural position.

After a week of restlessness, Mr Jordan resumed his daily visits to the shop in Upper Street, where he sat as usual among the books and the correspondence, and tried to assure himself that all would henceforth be well with him. No more changing from house to house; a really comfortable home in which to spend the rest of his days; a kind and most capable wife to look after all his needs, to humour all his little habits. He could not have taken a wiser step.

For all that, he had lost something, though he did not yet understand what it was. The first perception of a change not for the better flashed upon him one evening in the second week, when he came home an hour later than his wont. Mrs Jordan, who always stood waiting for him at the window, had no smile as he entered.

'Why are you late?' she asked, in her clear, restrained voice.

'Oh – something or other kept me.'

This would not do. Mrs Jordan quietly insisted on a full explanation of the delay, and it seemed to her unsatisfactory.

'I hope you won't be irregular in your habits, Archibald,' said his wife, with gentle admonition. 'What I always liked in you was your methodical way of living. I shall be very uncomfortable if I never know when to expect you.'

'Yes, my dear, but – business, you see —'

'But you have explained that you *could* have been back at the usual time.'

'Yes – that's true – but —'

'Well, well, you won't let it happen again. Oh really, Archibald!' she suddenly exclaimed. 'The idea of you coming into the room with muddy boots! Why, look! There's a patch of mud on the carpet —'

'It was my hurry to speak to you,' murmured Mr Jordan, in confusion.

'Please go at once and take your boots off. And you left your slippers in the bedroom this morning. You must always bring them down, and put them in the dining-room cupboard; then they're ready for you when you come into the house.'

Mr Jordan had but a moderate appetite for his dinner, and he did not talk so pleasantly as usual. This was but the beginning of troubles such as he had not for a moment foreseen. His wife, having since their engagement taken the upper hand, began to show her determination to keep it, and day by day her rule grew more galling to the ex-bachelor. He himself, in the old days, had plagued his landladies by insisting upon method and routine, by his faddish attention to domestic minutiae; he now learnt what it was to be subjected to the same kind of despotism, exercised with much more exasperating persistence. Whereas Mrs Elderfield had scrupulously obeyed every direction given by her lodger, Mrs Jordan was evidently resolved that her husband should live, move, and have his being in the strictest accordance with her own ideal. Not in any spirit of nagging, or ill-tempered unreasonableness; it was merely that she had her favourite way of doing every conceivable thing, and felt so sure it was the best of all possible ways that she could not endure any other. The first serious disagreement between them had reference to conduct at the breakfast-table. After a broken night, feeling headachy and worried, Mr Jordan took up his newspaper, folded it conveniently, and set it against the bread so that he could read while eating. Without a word, his wife gently removed it, and laid it aside on a chair.

'What are you doing?' he asked gruffly.

'You musn't read at meals, Archibald. It's bad manners, and bad for your digestion.'

'I've read the news at breakfast all my life, and I shall do so still,' exclaimed the husband, starting up and recovering his paper.

'Then you will have breakfast by yourself. Nelly, we must go into the other room till papa has finished.'

Mr Jordan ate mechanically, and stared at the newspaper with just as little consciousness. Prompted by the underlying weakness of his character to yield for the sake of peace, wrath made him dogged, and the more steadily he regarded his position, the more was he appalled by the outlook. Why, this meant downright slavery! He had married a woman so horribly like himself in several points that his only hope lay in overcoming her by sheer violence. A thoroughly good and well-meaning woman, an excellent housekeeper, the kind of wife to do him credit and improve his social position; but self-willed, pertinacious, and probably thinking herself his superior in every respect. He had nothing to fear but subjection – the one thing he had never anticipated, the one thing he could never endure.

He went off to business without seeing his wife again, and passed a lamentable day. At his ordinary hour of return, instead of setting off homeward, he strayed about the by-streets of Islington and Pentonville. Not till this moment had he felt how dear they were to him, the familiar streets; their very odours fell sweet upon his nostrils. Never again could he go hither and thither, among the old friends, the old places, to his heart's content. What had possessed him to abandon this precious liberty! The thought of Wood Green revolted him; live there as long as he might, he would never be at home. He thought of his wife (now waiting for him) with fear, and then with a reaction of rage. Let her wait! He – Archibald Jordan – before whom women had bowed and trembled for five-and-twenty years – was *he* to come and go at a wife's bidding? And at length the thought seemed so utterly preposterous that he sped northward as fast as possible, determined to right himself this very evening.

Mrs Jordan sat alone. He marched into the room with muddy boots, flung his hat and overcoat into a chair, and poked the fire violently. His wife's eye was fixed on him, and she first spoke – in the quiet voice that he dreaded.

'What do you mean by carrying on like this, Archibald?'

'I shall carry on as I like in my own house – hear that?'

'I do hear it, and I'm very sorry too. It gives me a very bad opinion of you. You will *not* do as you like in your own house. Rage as you please. You will *not* do as you like in your own house.'

There was a contemptuous anger in her eye which the man could not face. He lost all control of himself, uttered coarse oaths, and stood quivering. Then the woman began to lecture him; she talked steadily, acrimoniously, for more than an hour, regardless of his interruptions. Nervously exhausted, he fled at length from the room. A couple of hours later they met again in the nuptial chamber, and again Mrs Jordan began to talk. Her point, as before, was that he had begun married life about as badly as possible. Why had he married her at all? What fault had she committed to incur such outrageous usage? But, thank goodness, she had a will of her own, and a proper self-respect; behave as he might, *she* would still persevere in the path of womanly duty. If he thought to make her life unbearable he would find his mistake; she simply should not heed him; perhaps he would return to his senses before long – and in this vein Mrs Jordan continued until night was at odds with morning, only becoming silent when her partner had sunk into the oblivion of uttermost fatigue.

The next day Mr Jordan's demeanour showed him, for the moment at all events, defeated. He made no attempt to read at breakfast; he moved about very quietly. And in the afternoon he came home at the regulation hour.

Mrs Jordan had friends in the neighbourhood, but she saw little of them. She was not a woman of ordinary tastes. Everything proved that, to her mind, the possession of a nice house, with the prospects of a comfortable life, was an end in itself; she had no desire to exhibit her well-furnished rooms, or to gad about talking of her advantages. Every moment of her day was taken up in the superintendence of servants, the discharge of an infinitude of housewifely tasks. She had no assistance from her daughter; the girl went to school, and was encouraged to study with the utmost application. The husband's presence in the house seemed a mere accident – save in the still nocturnal season, when Mrs Jordan bestowed upon him her counsel and her admonitions.

After the lapse of a few days Mr Jordan again offered combat, and threw himself into it with a frenzy.

'Look here!' he shouted at length, 'either you or I are going to leave this house. I can't live with you – understand? I hate the sight of you!'

'Go on!' retorted the other, with mild bitterness. 'Abuse me as much as you like, I can bear it. I shall continue to do my duty, and unless you have recourse to personal violence, here I remain. If you go too far, of course the law must defend me!'

This was precisely what Mr Jordan knew and dreaded; the law was on his wife's side, and by applying at a police-court for protection she could overwhelm him with shame and ridicule, which would make life intolerable. Impossible to argue with this woman. Say what he might, the fault always seemed his. His wife was simply doing her duty – in a spirit of admirable thoroughness; he, in the eyes of a third person, would appear an unreasonable and violent curmudgeon. Had it not all sprung out of his obstinacy with regard to reading at breakfast? How explain to anyone what he suffered in his nerves, in his pride, in the outraged habitudes of a lifetime?

That evening he did not return to Wood Green. Afraid of questions if he showed himself in the old resorts, he spent some hours in a billiard-room near King's Cross, and towards midnight took a bedroom under the same roof. On going to business next day, he awaited with tremors either a telegram or a visit from his wife; but the whole day passed, and he heard nothing. After dark he walked once more about the beloved streets, pausing now and then to look up at the windows of this or that well remembered house. Ah, if he durst but enter and engage a lodging! Impossible – for ever impossible!

He slept in the same place as on the night before. And again a day passed without any sort of inquiry from Wood Green. When evening came he went home.

Mrs Jordan behaved as though he had returned from business in the usual way. 'Is it raining?' she asked, with a half-smile. And her husband replied, in as matter-of-fact a tone as he could command, 'No, it isn't.' There was no mention between them of his absence. That night, Mrs Jordan talked for an hour or two of his bad habit of stepping on the paint when he went up and down stairs, then fell calmly asleep.

But Mr Jordan did not sleep for a long time. What! was he, after all, to be allowed his liberty *out* of doors, provided he relinquished it within? Was it really the case that his wife, satisfied with her house and furniture and income, did not care a jot whether he stayed away or came home? There, indeed, gleamed a hope. When Mr Jordan slept, he dreamed that he was back again in lodgings at Islington, tasting an extraordinary bliss. Day dissipated the vision, but still Mrs Jordan spoke not a word of his absence, and with trembling still he hoped.

STORIES OF SUCCESSFUL
MARRIAGES

Elizabeth Gaskell

THE MANCHESTER MARRIAGE

(*Household Words*, Christmas 1858)

Mr and Mrs Openshaw came from Manchester to settle in London. He had been, what is called in Lancashire, a salesman for a large manufacturing firm, who were extending their business, and opening a warehouse in the city; where Mr Openshaw was now to superintend their affairs. He rather enjoyed the change; having a kind of curiosity about London, which he had never yet been able to gratify in his brief visits to the metropolis. At the same time, he had an odd, shrewd contempt for the inhabitants, whom he always pictured to himself as fine, lazy people, caring nothing but for fashion and aristocracy, and lounging away their days in Bond Street, and such places; ruining good English, and ready in their turn to despise him as a provincial. The hours that the men of business kept in the city scandalized him too, accustomed as he was to the early dinners of Manchester folk and the consequently far longer evenings. Still, he was pleased to go to London, though he would not for the world have confessed it, even to himself, and always spoke of the step to his friends as one demanded of him by the interests of his employers, and sweetened to him by a considerable increase of salary. This, indeed, was so liberal that he might have been justified in taking a much larger house than the one he did, had he not thought himself bound to set an example to Londoners of how little a Manchester man of business cared for show. Inside, however, he furnished it with an unusual degree of comfort, and, in the winter-time, he insisted on keeping up as large fires as the grates would allow, in every room where the temperature was in the least chilly. Moreover, his northern sense of hospitality was such that, if he were at home, he could hardly suffer a visitor to leave the house without forcing meat and drink upon him. Every servant in the house was well warmed, well fed, and kindly treated; for their master scorned all petty saving in aught that conduced to comfort; while he amused himself by following out all his accustomed habits and individual ways, in defiance of what any of his new neighbours might think.

His wife was a pretty, gentle woman, of suitable age and character. He was forty-two, she thirty-five. He was loud and decided; she soft and yielding. They had two children; or rather, I should say, she had two; for the elder, a girl of eleven, was Mrs Openshaw's child by Frank Wilson, her first husband. The younger was a little boy, Edwin, who could just prattle, and to whom his father delighted to speak in the broadest and most unintelligible Lancashire dialect, in order to keep up what he called the true Saxon accent.

Mrs Openshaw's Christian name was Alice, and her first husband had been her own cousin. She was the orphan niece of a sea-captain in Liverpool; a quiet, grave little creature, of great personal attraction when she was fifteen or sixteen, with regular features and a blooming complexion. But she was very shy, and believed herself to be very stupid and awkward; and was frequently scolded by her aunt, her own uncle's second wife. So when her cousin, Frank Wilson, came home from a long absence at sea, and first was kind and protective to her; secondly, attentive; and thirdly, desperately in love with her, she hardly knew how to be grateful enough to him. It is true, she would have preferred his remaining in the first or second stages of behaviour; for his violent love puzzled and frightened her. Her uncle neither helped nor hindered the love affair, though it was going on under his own eyes. Frank's stepmother had such a variable temper, that there was no knowing whether what she liked one day she would like the next, or not. At length she went to such extremes of crossness that Alice was only too glad to shut her eyes and rush blindly at the chance of escape from domestic tyranny offered her by a marriage with her cousin; and, liking him better than any one in the world, except her uncle (who was at this time at sea), she went off one morning and was married to him, her only bridesmaid being the housemaid at her aunt's. The consequence was that Frank and his wife went into lodgings, and Mrs Wilson refused to see them, and turned away Norah, the warm-hearted housemaid, whom they accordingly took into their service. When Captain Wilson returned from his voyage he was very cordial with the young couple, and spent many an evening at their lodgings, smoking his pipe and sipping his grog; but he told them, for quietness' sake, he could not ask them to his own house; for his wife was bitter against them. They were not, however, very unhappy about this.

The seed of future unhappiness lay rather in Frank's vehement, passionate disposition, which led him to resent his wife's shyness and want of demonstrativeness as failures in conjugal duty. He was already tormenting himself, and her too in a slighter degree, by apprehensions and imaginations of what might befall her during his approaching absence at sea. At last, he went to his father and urged him to insist upon Alice's being once more received under his roof; the more especially as there was now a prospect of her confinement while her husband was away on his voyage. Captain Wilson was, as he himself expressed it, 'breaking up', and unwilling to undergo the excitement of a scene; yet he felt that what his son said was true. So he went to his wife. And before Frank set sail, he had the comfort of seeing his wife installed in her old little garret in his father's house. To have placed her in the one best spare room was a step beyond Mrs Wilson's powers of submission or generosity. The worst part about it, however, was that the faithful Norah had to be dismissed. Her place as housemaid had been filled up; and, even if it had not, she had forfeited Mrs Wilson's good opinion for ever. She comforted her young master and mistress by pleasant prophecies of the time when they would have a household of their own; of which, whatever service she might be in meanwhile, she should be sure to form a part. Almost the last action Frank did, before setting sail, was going with Alice to see Norah once more at her mother's house; and then he went away.

Alice's father-in-law grew more and more feeble as winter advanced. She was of great use to her stepmother in nursing and amusing him; and although there was anxiety enough in the household, there was, perhaps, more of peace than there had been for years, for Mrs Wilson had not a bad heart, and was softened by the visible approach of death to one whom she loved, and touched by the lonely condition of the young creature expecting her first confinement in her husband's absence. To this relenting mood Norah owed the permission to come and nurse Alice when her baby was born, and to remain and attend on Captain Wilson.

Before one letter had been received from Frank (who had sailed for the East Indies and China), his father died. Alice was always glad to remember that he had held her baby in his arms, and kissed and blessed it before his death. After that, and the consequent examination into the state of his affairs, it was found that he had left far less property than people had been led by his style of living to expect; and what money there was, was settled all upon his wife, and at her disposal after her death. This did not signify much to Alice, as Frank was now first mate of his ship, and, in another voyage or two, would be captain. Meanwhile he had left her rather more than two hundred pounds (all his savings) in the bank.

It became time for Alice to hear from her husband. One letter from the Cape she had already received. The next was to announce his arrival in India. As week after week passed over, and no intelligence of the ship having got there reached the office of the owners, and the captain's wife was in the same state of ignorant suspense as Alice herself, her fears grew most oppressive. At length the day came when, in reply to her inquiry at the shipping office, they told her that the owners had given up hope of ever hearing more of the *Betsy-Jane*, and had sent in their claim upon the underwriters. Now that he was gone for ever, she first felt a yearning, longing love for the kind cousin, the dear friend, the sympathizing protector, whom she should never see again; — first felt a passionate desire to show him his child, whom she had hitherto rather craved to have all to herself — her own sole possession. Her grief was, however, noiseless and quiet — rather to the scandal of Mrs Wilson who bewailed her stepson as if he and she had always lived together in perfect harmony, and who evidently thought it her duty to burst into fresh tears at every strange face she saw; dwelling on his poor young widow's desolate state, and the helplessness of the fatherless child, with an unction as if she liked the excitement of the sorrowful story.

So passed away the first days of Alice's widowhood. By and by things subsided into their natural and tranquil course. But, as if the young creature was always to be in some heavy trouble, her ewe-lamb began to be ailing, pining, and sickly. The child's mysterious illness turned out to be some affection of the spine, likely to affect health but not to shorten life — at least, so the doctors said. But the long, dreary suffering of one whom a mother loves as Alice loved her only child, is hard to look forward to. Only Norah guessed what Alice suffered; no one but God knew.

And so it fell out, that when Mrs Wilson, the elder, came to her one day, in violent distress, occasioned by a very material diminution in the value of the property that her husband had left her – a diminution which made her income barely enough to support herself, much less Alice – the latter could hardly understand how anything which did not touch health or life could cause such grief; and she received the intelligence with irritating composure. But when, that afternoon, the little sick child was brought in, and the grandmother – who, after all, loved it well – began a fresh moan over her losses to its unconscious ears – saying how she had planned to consult this or that doctor, and to give it this or that comfort or luxury in after years, but that now all chance of this had passed away – Alice's heart was touched, and she drew near to Mrs Wilson with unwonted caresses, and, in a spirit not unlike to that of Ruth, entreated that, come what would, they might remain together. After much discussion in succeeding days, it was arranged that Mrs Wilson should take a house in Manchester, furnishing it partly with what furniture she had, and providing the rest with Alice's remaining two hundred pounds. Mrs Wilson was herself a Manchester woman, and naturally longed to return to her native town; some connexions of her own, too, at that time required lodgings, for which they were willing to pay pretty handsomely. Alice undertook the active superintendence and superior work of the household; Norah – willing, faithful Norah – offered to cook, scour, do anything in short, so that she might but remain with them.

The plan succeeded. For some years their first lodgers remained with them, and all went smoothly – with that one sad exception of the little girl's increasing deformity. How that mother loved that child, it is not for words to tell!

Then came a break of misfortune. Their lodgers left, and no one succeeded to them. After some months, it became necessary to remove to a smaller house; and Alice's tender conscience was torn by the idea that she ought not to be a burden to her mother-in-law, but to go out and seek her own maintenance. And leave her child! The thought came like the sweeping boom of a funeral-bell over her heart.

By and by, Mr Openshaw came to lodge with them. He had started in life as the errand-boy and sweeper-out of a warehouse; had struggled up through all the grades of employment in it, fighting his way through the hard, striving Manchester life with strong, pushing energy of character. Every spare moment of time had been sternly given up to self-teaching. He was a capital accountant, a good French and German scholar, a keen, far-seeing tradesman – understanding markets and the bearing of events, both near and distant, on trade; and yet, with such vivid attention to present details, that I do not think he ever saw a group of flowers in the fields without thinking whether their colour would, or would not, form harmonious contrasts in the coming spring muslins and prints. He went to debating societies, and threw himself with all his heart and soul into politics; esteeming, it must be owned, every man a fool or a knave who differed from him, and overthrowing his opponents rather by the loud strength of his language than the calm strength of his logic. There was something of the Yankee in all this. Indeed, his theory ran parallel to the famous Yankee motto – 'England flogs creation, and Manchester flogs England.' Such a man, as may be fancied, had had no time for falling in love, or any such nonsense. At the age when most young men go through their courting and matrimony, he had not the means of keeping a wife, and was far too practical to think of having one. And now that he was in easy circumstances, a rising man, he considered women almost as encumbrances to the world, with whom a man had better have as little to do as possible. His first impression of Alice was indistinct, and he did not care enough about her to make it distinct. 'A pretty, yea-nay kind of woman', would have been his description of her, if he had been pushed into a corner. He was rather afraid, in the beginning, that her quiet ways arose from a listlessness and laziness of character, which would have been exceedingly discordant to his active, energetic nature. But, when he found out the punctuality with which his wishes were attended to, and her work was done; when he was called in the morning at the very stroke of the clock, his shaving-water scalding hot, his fire bright, his coffee made exactly as his peculiar fancy dictated (for he was a man who had his theory about everything based upon what he knew of science, and often perfectly original) – then he began to think: not that Alice had any particular merit, but that he had got into remarkably good lodgings; his restlessness wore away, and he began to consider himself as almost settled for life in them.

Mr Openshaw had been too busy, all his days, to be introspective. He did not know that he had any tenderness in his nature; and if he had become conscious of its abstract existence he would have considered it as a manifestation of disease in some part of him. But he was decoyed into pity unawares; and pity led on to tenderness. That little helpless child – always carried about by one of the three busy women of the house, or else patiently threading coloured beads in the chair from which, by no effort of its own, could it ever move – the great grave blue eyes, full of serious, not uncheerful, expression, giving to the small delicate face a look beyond its years – the soft plaintive voice dropping out but few words, so unlike the continual prattle of a child – caught Mr Openshaw's attention in spite of himself. One day – he half scorned himself for doing so – he cut short his dinner-hour to go in search of some toy, which should take the place of those eternal beads. I forget what he bought; but, when he gave the present (which he took care to do in a short abrupt manner, and when no one was by to see him), he was almost thrilled by the flash of delight that came over that child's face, and he could not help, all through that afternoon, going over and over again the picture left on his memory, by the bright effect of unexpected joy on the little girl's face. When he returned home, he found his slippers placed by his sitting-room fire; and even more careful attention paid to his fancies than was habitual in those model lodgings. When Alice had taken the last of his tea-things away – she had been silent as usual till then – she stood for an instant with the door in her hand. Mr Openshaw looked as if he were deep in his book, though in fact he did not see a line; but was heartily wishing the woman would go, and not make any palaver of gratitude. But she only said:

'I am very much obliged to you, sir. Thank you very much,' and was gone, even before he could send her away with a 'There, my good woman, that's enough!'

For some time longer he took no apparent notice of the child. He even hardened his heart into disregarding her sudden flush of colour and little timid smile of recognition, when he saw her by chance. But, after all, this could not last for ever; and, having a second time given way to tenderness, there was no relapse. The insidious enemy having thus entered his heart, in the guise of compassion to the child, soon assumed the more dangerous form of interest in the mother. He was aware of this change of feeling – despised himself for it – struggled with it; nay, internally yielded to it and cherished it, long before he suffered the slightest expression of it, by word, action, or look to escape him. He watched Alice's docile, obedient ways to her stepmother; the love which she had inspired in the rough Norah (roughened by the wear and tear of sorrow and years); but, above all, he saw the wild, deep, passionate affection existing between her and her child. They spoke little to anyone else, or when anyone else was by; but, when alone together, they talked, and murmured, and cooed, and chattered so continually, that Mr Openshaw first wondered what they could find to say to each other, and next became irritated because they were always so grave and silent with him. All this time he was perpetually devising small new pleasures for the child. His thoughts ran, in a pertinacious way, upon the desolate life before her; and often he came back from his day's work loaded with the very thing Alice had been longing for, but had not been able to procure. One time, it was a little chair for drawing the little sufferer along the streets; and, many an evening that following summer, Mr Openshaw drew her along himself, regardless of the remarks of his acquaintances. One day in autumn, he put down his newspaper, as Alice came in with the breakfast, and said, in as indifferent a voice as he could assume:

'Mrs Frank, is there any reason why we two should not put up our horses together?'

Alice stood still in perplexed wonder. What did he mean? He had resumed the reading of his newspaper, as if he did not expect any answer; so she found silence her safest course, and went on quietly arranging his breakfast, without another word passing between them. Just as he was leaving the house, to go to the warehouse as usual, he turned back and put his head into the bright, neat, tidy kitchen, where all the women breakfasted in the morning:

'You'll think of what I said, Mrs Frank' (this was her name with the lodgers), 'and let me have your opinion upon it tonight.'

Alice was thankful that her mother and Norah were too busy talking together to attend much to this speech. She determined not to think about it at all through the day; and, of course, the effort not to think made her think all the more. At night she sent up Norah with his tea. But Mr Openshaw almost knocked Norah down as she was going out at the door, by pushing past her and calling out, 'Mrs Frank!' in an impatient voice, at the top of the stairs.

Alice went up, rather than seem to have affixed too much meaning to his words.

'Well, Mrs Frank,' he said, 'what answer? Don't make it too long; for I have lots of office work to get through tonight.'

'I hardly know what you meant, sir,' said truthful Alice.

'Well! I should have thought you might have guessed. You're not new at this sort of work, and I am. However, I'll make it plain this time. Will you have me to be thy wedded husband, and serve me, and love me, and honour me, and all that sort of thing? Because, if you will, I will do as much by you, and be a father to your child – and that's more than is put in the prayer-book. Now, I'm a man of my word; and what I say, I feel; and what I promise, I'll do. Now, for your answer!'

Alice was silent. He began to make the tea, as if her reply was a matter of perfect indifference to him; but, as soon as that was done, he became impatient.

'Well?' said he.

'How long, sir, may I have to think over it?'

'Three minutes!' (looking at his watch). 'You've had two already – that makes five. Be a sensible woman, say Yes, and sit down to tea with me, and we'll talk it over together; for, after tea, I shall be busy; say No' (he hesitated a moment to try and keep his voice in the same tone), 'and I shan't say another word about it, but pay up a year's rent for my rooms tomorrow, and be off. Time's up! Yes or no?'

'If you please, sir – you have been so good to little Ailsie –'

'There, sit down comfortably by me on the sofa, and let's have our tea together. I am glad to find you are as good and sensible as I took you for.'

And this was Alice Wilson's second wooing.

Mr Openshaw's will was too strong, and his circumstances too good, for him not to carry all before him. He settled Mrs Wilson in a comfortable house of her own, and made her quite independent of lodgers. The little that Alice said with regard to future plans was in Norah's behalf.

'No,' said Mr Openshaw. 'Norah shall take care of the old lady as long as she lives; and, after that, she shall either come and live with us, or, if she likes it better, she shall have a provision for life – for your sake, missus. No one who has been good to you or the child shall go unrewarded. But even the little one will be better for some fresh stuff about her. Get her a bright, sensible girl as a nurse; one who won't go rubbing her with calf's-foot jelly as Norah does; wasting good stuff outside that ought to go in, but will follow doctors' directions; which, as you must see pretty clearly by this time, Norah won't; because they give the poor little wench pain. Now, I'm not above being nesh for other folks myself. I can stand a good blow, and never change colour; but, set me in the operating room in the infirmary, and I turn as sick as a girl. Yet, if need were, I would hold the little wench on my knees while she screeched with pain, if it were to do her poor back good. Nay, nay, wench! keep your white looks for the time when it comes – I don't say it ever will. But this I know, Norah will spare the child and cheat the doctor, if she can. Now, I say, give the bairn a year or two's chance, and then, when the pack of doctors have done their best – and, maybe, the old lady has gone – we'll have Norah back or do better for her.'

The pack of doctors could do no good to little Ailsie. She was beyond their power. But her father (for so he insisted on being called, and also on Alice's no longer retaining the appellation of Mamma, but becoming henceforward Mother), by his healthy cheerfulness of manner, his clear decision of purpose, his odd turns and quirks of humour, added to his real strong love for the helpless little girl, infused a new element of brightness and confidence into her life; and, though her back remained the same, her general health was strengthened, and Alice – never going beyond a smile herself – had the pleasure of seeing her child taught to laugh.

As for Alice's own life, it was happier than it had ever been before. Mr Openshaw required no demonstration, no expressions of affection from her. Indeed, these would rather have disgusted him. Alice could love deeply, but could not talk about it. The perpetual requirement of loving words, looks, and caresses, and misconstruing their absence into absence of love, had been the great trial of her former married life. Now, all went on clear and straight, under the guidance of her husband's strong sense, warm heart, and powerful will. Year by year their worldly prosperity increased. At Mrs Wilson's death, Norah came back to them as nurse to the newly-born little Edwin; into which post she was not installed without a pretty strong oration on the part of the proud and happy father, who declared that if he found out that Norah ever tried to screen the boy by a falsehood, or to make him nesh either in body or mind, she should go that very day. Norah and Mr Openshaw were not on the most thoroughly cordial terms; neither of them fully recognizing or appreciating the other's best qualities.

This was the previous history of the Lancashire family who had now removed to London.

They had been there about a year, when Mr Openshaw suddenly informed his wife that he had determined to heal long-standing feuds, and had asked his uncle and aunt Chadwick to come and pay them a visit and see London. Mrs Openshaw had never seen this uncle and aunt of her husband's. Years before she had married him, there had been a quarrel. All she knew was, that Mr Chadwick was a small manufacturer in a country town in South Lancashire. She was extremely pleased that the breach was to be healed, and began making preparations to render their visit pleasant.

They arrived at last. Going to see London was such an event to them, that Mrs Chadwick had made all new linen fresh for the occasion — from night-caps downwards; and as for gowns, ribbons, and collars, she might have been going into the wilds of Canada where never a shop is, so large was her stock. A fortnight before the day of her departure for London, she had formally called to take leave of all her acquaintance; saying she should need every bit of the intermediate time for packing up. It was like a second wedding in her imagination; and, to complete the resemblance which an entirely new wardrobe made between the two events, her husband brought her back from Manchester, on the last market-day before they set off, a gorgeous pearl and amethyst brooch, saying, 'Lunnon should see that Lancashire folks knew a handsome thing when they saw it.'

For some time after Mr and Mrs Chadwick arrived at the Openshaws' there was no opportunity for wearing this brooch; but at length they obtained an order to see Buckingham Palace, and the spirit of loyalty demanded that Mrs Chadwick should wear her best clothes in visiting the abode of her sovereign. On her return she hastily changed her dress; for Mr Openshaw had planned that they should go to Richmond, drink tea, and return by moonlight. Accordingly, about five o'clock, Mr and Mrs Openshaw and Mr and Mrs Chadwick set off.

The housemaid and cook sat below, Norah hardly knew where. She was always engrossed in the nursery in tending her two children, and in sitting by the restless, excitable Ailsie till she fell asleep. By and by the housemaid Bessy tapped gently at the door. Norah went to her, and they spoke in whispers.

'Nurse! there's someone downstairs wants you.'

'Wants me! who is it?'

'A gentleman –'

'A gentleman? Nonsense!'

'Well! a man, then, and he asks for you, and he rang at the front-door bell, and has walked into the dining-room.'

'You should never have let him,' exclaimed Norah. 'Master and missus out –'

'I did not want him to come in; but, when he heard you lived here, he walked past me, and sat down on the first chair, and said, "Tell her to come and speak to me." There is no gas lighted in the room, and supper is all set out.'

'He'll be off with the spoons!' exclaimed Norah, putting the housemaid's fear into words, and preparing to leave the room; first, however, giving a look to Ailsie, sleeping soundly and calmly.

Downstairs she went, uneasy fears stirring in her bosom. Before she entered the dining-room she provided herself with a candle, and, with it in her hand, she went in, looking around her in the darkness for her visitor.

He was standing up, holding by the table. Norah and he looked at each other; gradual recognition coming into their eyes.

'Norah?' at length he asked.

'Who are you?' asked Norah, with the sharp tones of alarm and incredulity. 'I don't know you'; trying, by futile words of disbelief, to do away with the terrible fact before her.

'Am I so changed?' he said pathetically. 'I dare say I am. But, Norah, tell me!' he breathed hard, 'where is my wife? Is she – is she alive?'

He came nearer to Norah, and would have taken her hand; but she backed away from him; looking at him all the time with staring eyes, as if he were some horrible object. Yet he was a handsome, bronzed, good-looking fellow, with beard and moustache, giving him a foreign-looking aspect; but his eyes! there was no mistaking those eager, beautiful eyes – the very same that Norah had watched not half an hour ago, till sleep stole softly over them.

'Tell me, Norah – I can bear it – I have feared it so often. Is she dead?' Norah still kept silence. 'She is dead!' He hung on Norah's words and looks, as if for confirmation or contradiction.

'What shall I do?' groaned Norah. 'Oh, sir! why did you come? how did you find me out? where have you been? We thought you dead, we did indeed!' She poured out words and questions to gain time, as if time would help her.

'Norah! answer me this question straight, by yes or no – Is my wife dead?'

'No, she is not,' said Norah, slowly and heavily.

'Oh, what a relief! Did she receive my letters? But perhaps you don't know. Why did you leave her? Where is she? Oh, Norah, tell me all quickly!'

'Mr Frank!' said Norah at last, almost driven to bay by her terror lest her mistress should return at any moment and find him there – unable to consider what was best to be done or said – rushing at something decisive, because she could not endure her present state: 'Mr Frank! we never heard a line from you, and the shipowners said you had gone down, you and everyone else. We thought you were dead, if ever man was, and poor Miss Alice and her little sick, helpless child! Oh, sir, you must guess it,' cried the poor creature at last, bursting out into a passionate fit of crying, 'for indeed I cannot tell it. But it was no one's fault. God help us all this night!'

Norah had sat down. She trembled too much to stand. He took her hands in his. He squeezed them hard, as if, by physical pressure, the truth could be wrung out.

'Norah.' This time his tone was calm, stagnant as despair. 'She has married again!'

Norah shook her head sadly. The grasp slowly relaxed. The man had fainted.

There was brandy in the room. Norah forced some drops into Mr Frank's mouth, chafed his hands, and – when mere animal life returned, before the mind poured in its flood of memories and thoughts – she lifted him up, and rested his head against her knees. Then she put a few crumbs of bread taken from the supper-table, soaked in brandy, into his mouth. Suddenly he sprang to his feet.

'Where is she? Tell me this instant.' He looked so wild, so mad, so desperate, that Norah felt herself to be in bodily danger; but her time of dread had gone by. She had been afraid to tell him the truth, and then she had been a coward. Now, her wits were sharpened by the sense of his desperate state. He must leave the house. She would pity him afterwards; but now she must rather command and upbraid; for he must leave the house before her mistress came home. That one necessity stood clear before her.

'She is not here: that is enough for you to know. Nor can I say exactly where she is' (which was true to the letter if not to the spirit). 'Go away, and tell me where to find you tomorrow, and I will tell you all. My master and mistress may come back at any minute, and then what would become of me, with a strange man in the house?'

Such an argument was too petty to touch his excited mind.

'I don't care for your master and mistress. If your master is a man, he must feel for me – poor shipwrecked sailor that I am – kept for years a prisoner amongst savages, always, always, always thinking of my wife and my home – dreaming of her by night, talking to her though she could not hear, by day. I loved her more than all heaven and earth put together. Tell me where she is, this instant, you wretched woman, who salved over her wickedness to her, as you do to me!'

The clock struck ten. Desperate positions require desperate measures.

'If you will leave the house now, I will come to you tomorrow and tell you all. What is more, you shall see your child now. She lies sleeping upstairs. Oh, sir, you have a child, you do not know that as yet – a little weakly girl – with just a heart and soul beyond her years. We have reared her up with such care! We watched her, for we thought for many a year she might die any day, and we tended her, and no hard thing has come near her, and no rough word has ever been said to her. And now you come and will take her life into your hand, and will crush it. Strangers to her have been kind to her; but her own father – Mr Frank, I am her nurse, and I love her, and I tend her, and I would do anything for her that I could. Her mother's heart beats as hers beats; and, if she suffers a pain, her mother trembles all over. If she is happy, it is her mother that smiles and is glad. If she is growing stronger, her mother is healthy: if she dwindles, her mother languishes. If she dies – well, I don't know; it is not everyone can lie down and die when they wish it. Come upstairs, Mr Frank, and see your child. Seeing her will do good to your poor heart. Then go away, in God's name, just this one night; tomorrow, if need be, you can do anything – kill us all if you will, or show yourself a great, grand man, whom God will bless for ever and ever. Come, Mr Frank, the look of a sleeping child is sure to give peace.'

She led him upstairs; at first almost helping his steps, till they came near the nursery door. She had wellnigh forgotten the existence of little Edwin. It struck upon her with affright as the shaded light fell over the other cot; but she skilfully threw that corner of the room into darkness, and let the light fall on the sleeping Ailsie. The child had thrown down the coverings, and her deformity, as she lay with her back to them, was plainly visible through her slight nightgown. Her little face, deprived of the lustre of her eyes, looked wan and pinched, and had a pathetic expression in it, even as she slept. The poor father looked and looked with hungry, wistful eyes, into which the big tears came swelling up slowly and dropped heavily down, as he stood trembling and shaking all over. Norah was angry with herself for growing impatient of the length of time that long lingering gaze lasted. She thought that she waited for full half an hour before Frank stirred. And then – instead of going away – he sank down on his knees by the bedside, and buried his face in the clothes. Little Ailsie stirred uneasily. Norah pulled him up in terror. She could afford no more time, even for prayer, in her extremity of fear; for surely the next moment would bring her mistress home. She took him forcibly by the arm; but, as he was going, his eye lighted on the other bed; he stopped. Intelligence came back into his face. His hands clenched.

'His child?' he asked.

'Her child,' replied Norah. 'God watches over him,' she said instinctively; for Frank's looks excited her fears, and she needed to remind herself of the Protector of the helpless.

'God has not watched over me,' he said, in despair; his thoughts apparently recoiling on his own desolate, deserted state. But Norah had no time for pity. Tomorrow she would be as compassionate as her heart prompted. At length she guided him downstairs, and shut the outer door, and bolted it – as if by bolts to keep out facts.

Then she went back into the dining-room, and effaced all traces of his presence, as far as she could. She went upstairs to the nursery and sat there, her head on her hand, thinking what was to come of all this misery. It seemed to her very long before her master and mistress returned; yet it was hardly eleven o'clock. She heard the loud, hearty Lancashire voices on the stairs; and, for the first time, she understood the contrast of the desolation of the poor man who had so lately gone forth in lonely despair.

It almost put her out of patience to see Mrs Openshaw come in, calmly smiling, handsomely dressed, happy, easy, to inquire after her children.

'Did Ailsie go to sleep comfortably?' she whispered to Norah. 'Yes.'

Her mother bent over her, looking at her slumbers with the soft eyes of love. How little she dreamed who had looked on her last! Then she went to Edwin, with perhaps less wistful anxiety in her countenance, but more of pride. She took off her things, to go down to supper. Norah saw her no more that night.

Beside having a door into the passage, the sleeping-nursery opened out of Mr and Mrs Openshaw's room, in order that they might have the children more immediately under their own eyes. Early the next summer's morning, Mrs Openshaw was awakened by Ailsie's startled call of 'Mother! mother!' She sprang up, put on her dressing-gown, and went to her child. Ailsie was only half awake, and in a not unusual state of terror.

'Who was he, mother? Tell me!'

'Who, my darling? No one is here. You have been dreaming, love. Waken up quite. See, it is broad daylight.'

'Yes,' said Ailsie, looking round her; then clinging to her mother, 'but a man was here in the night, mother.'

'Nonsense, little goose. No man has ever come near you!'

'Yes, he did. He stood there. Just by Norah. A man with hair and a beard. And he knelt down and said his prayers. Norah knows he was here, mother' (half angrily, as Mrs Openshaw shook her head in smiling incredulity).

'Well! we will ask Norah when she comes,' said Mrs Openshaw, soothingly. 'But we won't talk any more about him now. It is not five o'clock; it is too early for you to get up. Shall I fetch you a book and read to you?'

'Don't leave me, mother,' said the child, clinging to her. So Mrs Openshaw sat on the bedside talking to Ailsie, and telling her of what they had done at Richmond the evening before, until the little girl's eyes slowly closed and she once more fell asleep.

'What was the matter?' asked Mr Openshaw, as his wife returned to bed.

'Ailsie wakened up in a fright, with some story of a man having been in the room to say his prayers – a dream, I suppose.' And no more was said at the time.

Mrs Openshaw had almost forgotten the whole affair when she got up about seven o'clock. But, by and by, she heard a sharp altercation going on in the nursery – Norah speaking angrily to Ailsie, a most unusual thing. Both Mr and Mrs Openshaw listened in astonishment.

'Hold your tongue, Ailsie! let me hear none of your dreams; never let me hear you tell that story again!'

Ailsie began to cry.

Mr Openshaw opened the door of communication, before his wife could say a word.

'Norah, come here!'

The nurse stood at the door, defiant. She perceived she had been heard, but she was desperate.

'Don't let me hear you speak in that manner to Ailsie again,' he said sternly, and shut the door.

Norah was infinitely relieved; for she had dreaded some questioning; and a little blame for sharp speaking was what she could well bear, if cross-examination was let alone.

Downstairs they went, Mr Openshaw carrying Ailsie; the

sturdy Edwin coming step by step, right foot foremost, always holding his mother's hand. Each child was placed in a chair by the breakfast-table, and then Mr and Mrs Openshaw stood together at the window, awaiting their visitors' appearance and making plans for the day. There was a pause. Suddenly Mr Openshaw turned to Ailsie, and said:

'What a little goosy somebody is with her dreams, wakening up poor, tired mother in the middle of the night, with a story of a man being in the room.'

'Father! I'm sure I saw him,' said Ailsie, half-crying. 'I don't want to make Norah angry; but I was not asleep, for all she says I was. I had been asleep – and I wakened up quite wide awake, though I was so frightened. I kept my eyes nearly shut, and I saw the man quite plain. A great brown man with a beard. He said his prayers. And then looked at Edwin. And then Norah took him by the arm and led him away, after they had whispered a bit together.'

'Now, my little woman must be reasonable,' said Mr Openshaw, who was always patient with Ailsie. 'There was no man in the house last night at all. No man comes into the house, as you know, if you think; much less goes up into the nursery. But sometimes we dream something has happened, and the dream is so like reality, that you are not the first person, little woman, who has stood out that the thing has really happened.'

'But, indeed, it was not a dream!' said Ailsie, beginning to cry.

Just then Mr and Mrs Chadwick came down, looking grave and discomposed. All during breakfast-time they were silent and uncomfortable. As soon as the breakfast things were taken away, and the children had been carried upstairs, Mr Chadwick began, in an evidently preconcerted manner, to inquire if his nephew was certain that all his servants were honest; for, that Mrs Chadwick had that morning missed a very valuable brooch, which she had worn the day before. She remembered taking it off when she came home from Buckingham Palace. Mr Openshaw's face contracted into hard lines; grew like what it was before he had known his wife and her child. He rang the bell, even before his uncle had done speaking. It was answered by the housemaid.

'Mary, was anyone here last night, while we were away?'

'A man, sir, came to speak to Norah.'

'To speak to Norah! Who was he? How long did he stay?'

'I'm sure I can't tell, sir. He came – perhaps about nine. I went up to tell Norah in the nursery, and she came down to speak to him. She let him out, sir. She will know who he was, and how long he stayed.'

She waited a moment to be asked any more questions, but she was not, so she went away.

A minute afterwards Mr Openshaw made as though he were going out of the room; but his wife laid her hand on his arm.

'Do not speak to her before the children,' she said, in her low, quiet voice. 'I will go up and question her.'

'No! I must speak to her. You must know,' said he, turning to his uncle and aunt, 'my missus has an old servant, as faithful as ever woman was, I do believe, as far as love goes, – but at the same time, who does not speak truth, as even the missus must allow. Now, my notion is, that this Norah of ours has been come over by some good-for-nothing chap (for she's at the time o' life when they say women pray for husbands – "any, good Lord, any") and has let him into our house, and the chap has made off with your brooch, and m'appen many another thing beside. It's only saying that Norah is soft-hearted and doesn't stick at a white lie – that's all, missus.'

It was curious to notice how his tone, his eyes, his whole face was changed, as he spoke to his wife; but he was the resolute man through all. She knew better than to oppose him; so she went upstairs, and told Norah that her master wanted to speak to her, and that she would take care of the children in the meanwhile.

Norah rose to go, without a word. Her thoughts were these:

'If they tear me to pieces, they shall never know through me. He may come – and then, just Lord have mercy upon us all! for some of us are dead folk to a certainty. But *he* shall do it; not me.'

You may fancy, now, her look of determination, as she faced her master alone in the dining-room; Mr and Mrs Chadwick having left the affair in their nephew's hands, seeing that he took it up with such vehemence.

'Norah! Who was that man that came to my house last night?'

'Man, sir!' As if infinitely surprised; but it was only to gain time.

'Yes; the man that Mary let in; that she went upstairs to the nursery to tell you about; that you came down to speak to; the same chap, I make no doubt, that you took into the nursery to have your talk out with; the one Ailsie saw, and afterwards dreamed about; thinking, poor wench! she saw him say his prayers, when nothing, I'll be bound, was further from his thoughts; the one that took Mrs Chadwick's brooch, value ten pounds. Now, Norah! Don't go off. I'm as sure as my name's Thomas Openshaw that you knew nothing of this robbery. But I do think you've been imposed on, and that's the truth. Some good-for-nothing chap has been making up to you, and you've been just like all other women, and have turned a soft place in your heart to him; and he came last night a-lovyering, and you had him up in the nursery, and he made use of his opportunities, and made off with a few things on his way down! Come, now, Norah; it's no blame to you, only you must not be such a fool again! Tell us,' he continued, 'what name he gave you, Norah. I'll be bound, it was not the right one; but it will be a clue for the police.'

Norah drew herself up. 'You may ask that question, and taunt me with my being single, and with my credulity, as you will, Master Openshaw. You'll get no answer from me. As for the brooch, and the story of theft and burglary; if any friend ever came to see me (which I defy you to prove, and deny), he'd be just as much above doing such a thing as you yourself, Mr Openshaw – and more so, too; for I'm not at all sure as everything you have is rightly come by, or would be yours long, if every man had his own.' She meant, of course, his wife; but he understood her to refer to his property in goods and chattels.

'Now, my good woman,' said he, 'I'll just tell you truly, I never trusted you out and out; but my wife liked you, and I thought you had many a good point about you. If you once begin to sauce me, I'll have the police to you, and get out the truth in a court of justice, if you'll not tell it me quietly and civilly here. Now, the best thing you can do is quietly to tell me who the fellow is. Look here! a man comes to my house; asks for you; you take him upstairs; a valuable brooch is missing next day; we know that you, and Mary, and cook, are honest; but you refuse to tell us who the man is. Indeed, you've told me one lie already about him, saying no one was here last night. Now, I just put it to you, what do you think a policeman would say to this, or a magistrate? A magistrate would soon make you tell the truth, my good woman.'

'There's never the creature born that should get it out of me,' said Norah. 'Not unless I choose to tell.'

'I've a great mind to see,' said Mr Openshaw, growing angry at the defiance. Then, checking himself, he thought before he spoke again:

'Norah, for your missus' sake I don't want to go to extremities. Be a sensible woman, if you can. It's no great disgrace, after all, to have been taken in. I ask you once more – as a friend – who was this man that you let into my house last night?'

No answer. He repeated the question in an impatient tone. Still no answer. Norah's lips were set in determination not to speak.

'Then there is but one thing to be done. I shall send for a policeman.'

'You will not,' said Norah, starting forward. 'You shall not, sir! No policeman shall touch me. I know nothing of the brooch, but I know this: ever since I was four-and-twenty, I have thought more of your wife than of myself: ever since I saw her, a poor motherless girl, put upon in her uncle's house, I have thought more of serving her than of serving myself! I have cared for her and her child, as nobody ever cared for me. I don't cast blame on you, sir, but I say it's ill giving up one's life to anyone; for, at the end, they will turn round upon you, and forsake you. Why does not my missus come herself to suspect me? Maybe, she is gone for the police? But I don't stay here, either for police, or magistrate, or master. You're an unlucky lot. I believe there's a curse on you. I'll leave you this very day. Yes! I'll leave that poor Ailsie, too. I will! No good ever will come to you!'

Mr Openshaw was utterly astonished at this speech; most of which was completely unintelligible to him, as may easily be supposed. Before he could make up his mind what to say, or what to do, Norah had left the room. I do not think he had ever really intended to send for the police to this old servant of his wife's; for he had never for a moment doubted her perfect honesty. But he had intended to compel her to tell him who the man was, and in this he was baffled. He was, consequently, much irritated. He returned to his uncle and aunt in a state of great annoyance and perplexity, and told them he could get nothing out of the woman; that some man had been in the house the night before; but that she refused to tell who he was. At this moment his wife came in, greatly agitated, and asked what had happened to Norah; for that she had put on her things in passionate haste, and left the house.

'This looks suspicious,' said Mr Chadwick. 'It is not the way in which an honest person would have acted.'

Mr Openshaw kept silence. He was sorely perplexed. But Mrs Openshaw turned round on Mr Chadwick, with a sudden fierceness no one ever saw in her before.

'You don't know Norah, uncle! She is gone because she is deeply hurt at being suspected. Oh, I wish I had seen her – that I had spoken to her myself. She would have told me anything.' Alice wrung her hands.

'I must confess,' continued Mr Chadwick to his nephew, in a lower voice, 'I can't make you out. You used to be a word and a blow, and oftenest the blow first; and now, when there is every cause for suspicion, you just do nought. Your missus is a very good woman, I grant; but she may have been put upon as well as other folk, I suppose. If you don't send for the police, I shall.'

'Very well,' replied Mr Openshaw, surlily. 'I can't clear Norah. She won't clear herself, as I believe she might if she would. Only I wash my hands of it; for I am sure the woman herself is honest, and she's lived a long time with my wife, and I don't like her to come to shame.'

'But she will then be forced to clear herself. That, at any rate, will be a good thing.'

'Very well, very well! I am heart-sick of the whole business. Come, Alice, come up to the babies; they'll be in a sore way. I tell you, uncle,' he said, turning round once more to Mr Chadwick, suddenly and sharply, after his eye had fallen on Alice's wan, tearful, anxious face, 'I'll have no sending for the police, after all. I'll buy my aunt twice as handsome a brooch this very day; but I'll not have Norah suspected, and my missus plagued. There's for you!'

He and his wife left the room. Mr Chadwick quietly waited till he was out of hearing, and then said to his wife, 'For all Tom's heroics, I'm just quietly going for a detective, wench. Thou need'st know nought about it.'

He went to the police-station and made a statement of the case. He was gratified by the impression which the evidence against Norah seemed to make. The men all agreed in his opinion, and steps were to be immediately taken to find out where she was. Most probably, as they suggested, she had gone at once to the man, who, to all appearance, was her lover. When Mr Chadwick asked how they would find her out, they smiled, shook their heads, and spoke of mysterious but infallible ways and means. He returned to his nephew's house with a very comfortable opinion of his own sagacity. He was met by his wife with a penitent face.

'Oh, master, I've found my brooch! It was just sticking by its pin in the flounce of my brown silk, that I wore yesterday. I took it off in a hurry, and it must have caught in it; and I hung up my gown in the closet. Just now, when I was going to fold it up, there was the brooch! I am very vexed, but I never dreamt but what it was lost!'

Her husband, muttering something very like 'Confound thee and thy brooch too! I wish I'd never given it thee,' snatched up his hat, and rushed back to the station, hoping to be in time to stop the police from searching for Norah. But a detective was already gone off on the errand.

Where was Norah? Half mad with the strain of the fearful secret, she had hardly slept through the night for thinking what must be done. Upon this terrible state of mind had come Ailsie's questions, showing that she had seen the Man, as the unconscious child called her father. Lastly came the suspicion of her honesty. She was little less than crazy as she ran upstairs and dashed on her bonnet and shawl; leaving all else, even her purse, behind her. In that house she would not stay. That was all she knew or was clear about. She would not even see the children again, for fear it should weaken her. She dreaded above everything Mr Frank's return to claim his wife. She could not tell what remedy there was for a sorrow so tremendous, for her to stay to witness. The desire of escaping from the coming event was a stronger motive for her departure, than her soreness about the suspicions directed against her; although this last had been the final goad to the course she took. She walked away almost at headlong speed; sobbing as she went, as she had not dared to do during the past night for fear of exciting wonder in those who might hear her. Then she stopped. An idea came into her mind that she would leave London altogether, and betake herself to her native town of Liverpool. She felt in her pocket for her purse as she drew near the Euston Square station with this intention. She had left it at home. Her poor head aching, her eyes swollen with crying, she had to stand still, and think, as well as she could, where next she should bend her steps. Suddenly the thought flashed into her mind that she would go and find out poor Mr Frank. She had been hardly kind to him the night before, though her heart had bled for him ever since. She remembered his telling her, when she inquired for his address, almost as she had pushed him out of the door, of some hotel in a street not far distant from Euston Square. Thither she went: with what intention she scarcely knew, but to assuage her conscience by telling him how much she pitied him. In her present state she felt herself unfit to counsel, or restrain, or assist, or do aught else but sympathize and weep. The people of the inn said such a person had been there; had arrived only the day before; had gone out soon after arrival, leaving his luggage in their care; but had never come back. Norah asked for leave to sit down, and await the gentleman's return. The landlady – pretty secure in the deposit of luggage against any probable injury – showed her into a room, and quietly locked the door on the outside. Norah was utterly worn out, and fell asleep – a shivering, starting, uneasy slumber, which lasted for hours.

The detective, meanwhile, had come up with her some time before she entered the hotel, into which he followed her. Asking the landlady to detain her for an hour or so, without giving any reason beyond showing his authority (which made the landlady applaud herself a good deal for having locked her in), he went back to the police-station to report his proceedings. He could have taken her directly; but his object was, if possible, to trace out the man who was supposed to have committed the robbery. Then he heard of the discovery of the brooch; and consequently did not care to return.

Norah slept till even the summer evening began to close in. Then started up. Someone was at the door. It would be Mr Frank; and she dizzily pushed back her ruffled grey hair which had fallen over her eyes, and stood looking to see him. Instead, there came in Mr Openshaw and a policeman.

'This is Norah Kennedy,' said Mr Openshaw.

'Oh, sir,' said Norah, 'I did not touch the brooch; indeed I did not. Oh, sir, I cannot live to be thought so badly of'; and very sick and faint, she suddenly sank down on the ground. To her surprise,

Mr Openshaw raised her up very tenderly. Even the policeman helped to lay her on the sofa; and, at Mr Openshaw's desire, he went for some wine and sandwiches; for the poor gaunt woman lay there almost as if dead with weariness and exhaustion.

'Norah,' said Mr Openshaw, in his kindest voice, 'the brooch is found. It was hanging to Mrs Chadwick's gown. I beg your pardon. Most truly I beg your pardon, for having troubled you about it. My wife is almost broken-hearted. Eat, Norah – or, stay, first drink this glass of wine,' said he, lifting her head, and pouring a little down her throat.

As she drank, she remembered where she was, and who she was waiting for. She suddenly pushed Mr Openshaw away, saying, 'Oh, sir, you must go. You must not stop a minute. If he comes back, he will kill you.'

'Alas, Norah! I do not know who "he" is. But someone is gone away who will never come back: someone who knew you, and whom I am afraid you cared for.'

'I don't understand you, sir,' said Norah, her master's kind and sorrowful manner bewildering her yet more than his words. The policeman had left the room at Mr Openshaw's desire, and they two were alone.

'You know what I mean, when I say someone is gone who will never come back. I mean that he is dead!'

'Who?' said Norah, trembling all over.

'A poor man has been found in the Thames this morning – drowned.'

'Did he drown himself?' asked Norah, solemnly.

'God only knows,' replied Mr Openshaw, in the same tone. 'Your name and address at our house were found in his pocket; that, and his purse, were the only things that were found upon him. I am sorry to say it, my poor Norah; but you are required to go and identify him.'

'To what?' asked Norah.

'To say who it is. It is always done, in order that some reason may be discovered for the suicide – if suicide it was. I make no doubt, he was the man who came to see you at our house last night. It is very sad, I know.' He made pauses between each little clause, in order to try and bring back her senses, which he feared were wandering – so wild and sad was her look.

'Master Openshaw,' said she, at last, 'I've a dreadful secret to tell you – only you must never breathe it to anyone, and you and I must hide it away for ever. I thought to have done it all by myself, but I see I cannot. Yon poor man – yes! the dead, drowned creature is, I fear, Mr Frank, my mistress's first husband!'

Mr Openshaw sat down, as if shot. He did not speak; but, after a while, he signed to Norah to go on.

'He came to me the other night, when – God be thanked! – you were all away at Richmond. He asked me if his wife was dead or alive. I was a brute, and thought more of your all coming home than of his sore trial; I spoke out sharp, and said she was married again, and very content and happy. I all but turned him away: and now he lies dead and cold.'

'God forgive me!' said Mr Openshaw.

'God forgive us all!' said Norah. 'Yon poor man needs forgiveness, perhaps, less than any one among us. He had been among the savages – shipwrecked – I know not what – and he had written letters which had never reached my poor missus.'

'He saw his child!'

'He saw her – yes! I took him up, to give his thoughts another start; for I believed he was going mad on my hands. I came to seek him here, as I more than half promised. My mind misgave me when I heard he never came in. Oh, sir, it must be him!'

Mr Openshaw rang the bell. Norah was almost too much stunned to wonder at what he did. He asked for writing materials, wrote a letter, and then said to Norah:

'I am writing to Alice, to say I shall be unavoidably absent for a few days; that I have found you; that you are well, and send her your love, and will come home tomorrow. You must go with me to the police court; you must identify the body; I will pay high to keep names and details out of the papers.'

'But where are you going, sir?'

He did not answer her directly. Then he said:

'Norah! I must go with you, and look on the face of the man whom I have so injured – unwittingly, it is true; but it seems to me as if I had killed him. I will lay his head in the grave as if he were my only brother: and how he must have hated me! I cannot go home to my wife till all that I can do for him is done. Then I go with a dreadful secret on my mind. I shall never speak of it again, after these days are over. I know you will not, either.' He shook hands with her; and they never named the subject again, the one to the other.

Norah went home to Alice the next day. Not a word was said on the cause of her abrupt departure a day or two before. Alice had been charged by her husband, in his letter, not to allude to the supposed theft of the brooch; so she, implicitly obedient to those whom she loved both by nature and habit, was entirely silent on the subject, only treated Norah with the most tender respect, as if to make up for unjust suspicion.

Nor did Alice inquire into the reason why Mr Openshaw had been absent during his uncle and aunt's visit, after he had once said that it was unavoidable. He came back grave and quiet; and from that time forth was curiously changed. More thoughtful, and perhaps less active; quite as decided in conduct, but with new and different rules for the guidance of that conduct. Towards Alice he could hardly be more kind than he had always been; but he now seemed to look upon her as someone sacred, and to be treated with reverence, as well as tenderness. He throve in business, and made a large fortune, one half of which was settled upon her.

Long years after these events – a few months after her mother died – Ailsie and her 'father' (as she always called Mr Openshaw) drove to a cemetery a little way out of town, and she was carried to a certain mound by her maid, who was then sent back to the carriage. There was a headstone, with F. W. and a date upon it. That was all. Sitting by the grave, Mr Openshaw told her the story; and for the sad fate of that poor father whom she had never seen, he shed the only tears she ever saw fall from his eyes.

A MERE INTERLUDE

(*The Bolton Weekly Journal*, 17 and 24 October 1885)

I

The traveller in school-books, who vouched in dryest tones for the fidelity to fact of the following narrative, used to add a ring of truth to it by opening with a nicety of criticism on the heroine's personality. People were wrong, he declared, when they surmised that Baptista Trewthen was a young woman with scarcely emotions or character. There was nothing in her to love, and nothing to hate – so ran the general opinion. That she showed few positive qualities was true. The colours and tones which changing events paint on the faces of active womankind were looked for in vain upon hers. But still waters run deep; and no crisis had come in the years of her early maidenhood to demonstrate what lay hidden within her, like metal in a mine.

She was the daughter of a small farmer in St Maria's, one of the Isles of Lyonesse beyond Off-Wessex, who had spent a large sum, as there understood, on her education, by sending her to the mainland for two years. At nineteen she was entered at the Training College for Teachers, and at twenty-one nominated to a school in the country, near Tor-upon-Sea, whither she proceeded after the Christmas examination and holidays.

The months passed by from winter to spring and summer, and Baptista applied herself to her new duties as best she could, till an uneventful year had elapsed. Then an air of abstraction pervaded her bearing as she walked to and fro, twice a day, and she showed the traits of a person who had something on her mind. A widow, by name Mrs Wace, in whose house Baptista Trewthen had been provided with a sitting-room and bedroom till the schoolhouse should be built, noticed this change in her youthful tenant's manner, and at last ventured to press her with a few questions.

'It has nothing to do with the place, nor with you,' said Miss Trewthen.

'Then it is the salary?'

'No, nor the salary.'

'Then it is something you have heard from home, my dear.'

Baptista was silent for a few moments. 'It is Mr Heddegan,' she murmured. 'Him they used to call David Heddegan before he got his money.'

'And who is the Mr Heddegan they used to call David?'

'An old bachelor at Giant's Town, St Maria's, with no relations whatever, who lives about a stone's throw from father's. When I was a child he used to take me on his knee and say he'd marry me some day. Now I am a woman the jest has turned earnest, and he is anxious to do it. And father and mother say I can't do better than have him.'

'He's well off?'

'Yes – he's the richest man we know – as a friend and neighbour.'

'How much older did you say he was than yourself?'

'I didn't say. Twenty years at least.'

'And an unpleasant man in the bargain perhaps?'

'No – he's not unpleasant.'

'Well, child, all I can say is that I'd resist any such engagement if it's not palatable to 'ee. You are comfortable here, in my little house, I hope. All the parish like 'ee: and I've never been so cheerful, since my poor husband left me to wear his wings, as I've been with 'ee as my lodger.'

The schoolmistress assured her landlady that she could return the sentiment. 'But here comes my perplexity,' she said. 'I don't like keeping school. Ah, you are surprised – you didn't suspect it. That's because I've concealed my feeling. Well, I simply hate school. I don't care for children – they are unpleasant, troublesome little things, whom nothing would delight so much as to hear that you had fallen down dead. Yet I would even put up with them if it was not for the inspector. For three months before his visit I didn't sleep soundly. And the Committee of Council are always changing the Code, so that you don't know what to teach, and what to leave untaught. I think father and mother are right. They say I shall never excel as a schoolmistress if I dislike the work so, and that therefore I ought to get settled by marrying Mr Heddegan. Between us two, I like him better than school; but I don't like him quite so much as to wish to marry him.'

These conversations, once begun, were continued from day to day; till at length the young girl's elderly friend and landlady threw in her opinion on the side of Miss Trewthen's parents. All things considered, she declared, the uncertainty of the school, the labour, Baptista's natural dislike for teaching, it would be as well to take what fate offered, and make the best of matters by wedding her father's old neighbour and prosperous friend.

The Easter holidays came round, and Baptista went to spend them as usual in her native isle, going by train into Off-Wessex and crossing by packet from Pen-zephyr. When she returned in the middle of April her face wore a more settled aspect.

'Well?' said the expectant Mrs Wace.

'I have agreed to have him as my husband,' said Baptista, in an off-hand way. 'Heaven knows if it will be for the best or not. But I have agreed to do it, and so the matter is settled.'

Mrs Wace commended her; but Baptista did not care to dwell on the subject; so that allusion to it was very infrequent between them. Nevertheless, among other things, she repeated to the widow from time to time in monosyllabic remarks that the wedding was really impending; that it was arranged for the summer, and that she had given notice of leaving the school at the August holidays. Later on she announced more specifically that her marriage was to take place immediately after her return home at the beginning of the month aforesaid.

She now corresponded regularly with Mr Heddegan. Her letters from him were seen, at least on the outside, and in part within, by Mrs Wace. Had she read more of their interiors than the occasional sentences shown her by Baptista she would have perceived that the scratchy, rusty handwriting of Miss Trewthen's betrothed conveyed little more matter than details of their future housekeeping, and his preparations for the same, with innumerable 'my dears' sprinkled in disconnectedly, to show the depth of his affection without the inconveniences of syntax.

II

It was the end of July — dry, too dry, even for the season, the delicate green herbs and vegetables that grew in this favoured end of the kingdom tasting rather of the watering-pot than of the pure fresh moisture from the skies. Baptista's boxes were packed, and one Saturday morning she departed by a waggonette to the station, and thence by train to Pen-zephyr, from which port she was, as usual, to cross the water immediately to her home, and become Mr Heddegan's wife on the Wednesday of the week following.

She might have returned a week sooner. But though the wedding day had loomed so near, and the banns were out, she delayed her departure till this last moment, saying it was not necessary for her to be at home long beforehand. As Mr Heddegan was older than herself, she said, she was to be married in her ordinary summer bonnet and grey silk frock, and there were no preparations to make that had not been amply made by her parents and intended husband.

In due time, after a hot and tedious journey, she reached Pen-zephyr. She here obtained some refreshment, and then went towards the pier, where she learnt to her surprise that the little steamboat plying between the town and the islands had left at eleven o'clock; the usual hour of departure in the afternoon having been forestalled in consequence of the fogs which had for a few days prevailed towards evening, making twilight navigation dangerous.

This being Saturday, there was now no other boat till Tuesday, and it became obvious that here she would have to remain for the three days, unless her friends should think fit to rig out one of the island sailing-boats and come to fetch her — a not very likely contingency, the sea distance being nearly forty miles.

Baptista, however, had been detained in Pen-zephyr on more than one occasion before, either on account of bad weather or some such reason as the present, and she was therefore not in any personal alarm. But, as she was to be married on the following Wednesday, the delay was certainly inconvenient to a more than ordinary degree, since it would leave less than a day's interval between her arrival and the wedding ceremony.

Apart from this awkwardness she did not much mind the accident. It was indeed curious to see how little she minded. Perhaps it would not be too much to say that, although she was going to do the critical deed of her life quite willingly, she experienced an indefinable relief at the postponement of her meeting with Heddegan. But her manner after making discovery of the hindrance was quiet and subdued, even to passivity itself; as was instanced by her having, at the moment of receiving information that the steamer had sailed, replied 'Oh', so coolly to the porter with her luggage, that he was almost disappointed at her lack of disappointment.

The question now was, should she return again to Mrs Wace, in the village of Lower Wessex, or wait in the town at which she had arrived. She would have preferred to go back, but the distance was too great; moreover, having left the place for good, and somewhat dramatically, to become a bride, a return, even for so short a space, would have been a trifle humiliating.

Leaving, then, her boxes at the station, her next anxiety was to secure a respectable, or rather genteel, lodging in the popular seaside resort confronting her. To this end she looked about the town, in which, though she had passed through it half-a-dozen times, she was practically a stranger.

Baptista found a room to suit her over a fruiterer's shop; where she made herself at home, and set herself in order after her journey. An early cup of tea having revived her spirits she walked out to reconnoitre.

Being a schoolmistress she avoided looking at the schools, and having a sort of trade connection with books, she avoided looking at the booksellers; but wearying of the other shops she inspected the churches; not that for her own part she cared much about ecclesiastical edifices; but tourists looked at them, and so would she – a proceeding for which no one would have credited her with any great originality, such, for instance, as that she subsequently showed herself to possess. The churches soon oppressed her. She tried the Museum, but came out because it seemed lonely and tedious.

Yet the town and the walks in this land of strawberries, these headquarters of early English flowers and fruit, were then, as always, attractive. From the more picturesque streets she went to the town gardens, and the Pier, and the Harbour, and looked at the men at work there, loading and unloading as in the time of the Phoenicians.

'Not Baptista? Yes, Baptista it is!'

The words were uttered behind her. Turning round she gave a start, and became confused, even agitated, for a moment. Then she said in her usual undemonstrative manner, 'O – is it really you, Charles?'

Without speaking again at once, and with a half-smile, the newcomer glanced her over. There was much criticism, and some resentment – even temper – in his eye.

'I am going home,' continued she. 'But I have missed the boat.'

He scarcely seemed to take in the meaning of this explanation, in the intensity of his critical survey. 'Teaching still? What a fine schoolmistress you make, Baptista, I warrant!' he said with a slight flavour of sarcasm, which was not lost upon her.

'I know I am nothing to brag of,' she replied. 'That's why I have given up.'

'O – given up? You astonish me.'

'I hate the profession.'

'Perhaps that's because I am in it.'

'O no, it isn't. But I am going to enter on another life altogether. I am going to be married next week to Mr David Heddegan.'

The young man – fortified as he was by a natural cynical pride and passionateness – winced at this unexpected reply, notwithstanding.

'Who is Mr David Heddegan?' he asked, as indifferently as lay in his power.

She informed him the bearer of the name was a general merchant of Giant's Town, St Maria's Island – her father's nearest neighbour and oldest friend.

'Then we shan't see anything more of you on the mainland?' inquired the schoolmaster.

'O, I don't know about that,' said Miss Trewthen.

'Here endeth the career of the belle of the boarding-school your father was foolish enough to send you to. A "general merchant's" wife in the Lyonesse Isles. Will you sell pounds of soap and pennyworths of tin tacks, or whole bars of saponaceous matter, and great tenpenny nails?'

'He's not in such a small way as that!' she almost pleaded. 'He owns ships, though they are rather little ones!'

'O, well, it is much the same. Come, let us walk on; it is tedious to stand still. I thought you would be a failure in education,' he continued, when she obeyed him and strolled ahead. 'You never showed power that way. You remind me much of some of those women who think they are sure to be great actresses if they go on the stage, because they have a pretty face, and forget that what we require is acting. But you found your mistake, didn't you?'

'Don't taunt me, Charles.' It was noticeable that the young schoolmaster's tone caused her no anger or retaliatory passion; far otherwise: there was a tear in her eye. 'How is it you are at Pen-zephyr?' she inquired.

'I don't taunt you. I speak the truth, purely in a friendly way, as I should to anyone I wished well. Though for that matter I might have some excuse even for taunting you. Such a terrible hurry as you've been in. I hate a woman who is in such a hurry.'

'How do you mean that?'

'Why – to be somebody's wife or other – anything's wife rather than nobody's. You couldn't wait for me, O, no. Well, thank God, I'm cured of all that!'

'How merciless you are!' she said bitterly. 'Wait for you? What does that mean, Charley? You never showed – anything to wait for – anything special towards me.'

'O come, Baptista dear; come!'

'What I mean is, nothing definite,' she expostulated. 'I suppose you liked me a little; but it seemed to me to be only a pastime on your part, and that you never meant to make an honourable engagement of it.'

'There, that's just it! You girls expect a man to mean business at the first look. No man when he first becomes interested in a woman has any definite scheme of engagement to marry her in his mind, unless he is meaning a vulgar mercenary marriage. However, I *did* at last mean an honourable engagement, as you call it, come to that.'

'But you never said so, and an indefinite courtship soon injures a woman's position and credit, sooner than you think.'

'Baptista, I solemnly declare that in six months I should have asked you to marry me.'

She walked along in silence, looking on the ground, and appearing very uncomfortable. Presently he said, 'Would you have waited for me if you had known?' To this she whispered in a sorrowful whisper, 'Yes!'

They went still farther in silence – passing along one of the beautiful walks on the outskirts of the town, yet not observant of scene or situation. Her shoulder and his were close together, and he clasped his fingers round the small of her arm – quite lightly, and without any attempt at impetus; yet the act seemed to say, 'Now I hold you, and my will must be yours.'

Recurring to a previous question of hers he said, 'I have merely run down here for a day or two from school near Trufal, before going off to the north for the rest of my holiday. I have seen my relations at Redrutin quite lately, so I am not going there this time. How little I thought of meeting you! How very different the circumstances would have been if, instead of parting again as we must in half-an-hour or so, possibly for ever, you had been now just going off with me, as my wife, on our honeymoon trip. Ha – ha – well – so humorous is life!'

She stopped suddenly. 'I must go back now – this is altogether too painful, Charley! It is not at all a kind mood you are in today.'

'I don't want to pain you – you know I do not,' he said more gently. 'Only it just exasperates me – this you are going to do. I wish you would not.'

'What?'

'Marry him. There, now I have showed you my true sentiments.'

'I must do it now,' said she.

'Why?' he asked, dropping the off-hand masterful tone he had hitherto spoken in, and becoming earnest; still holding her arm, however, as if she were his chattel to be taken up or put down at will. 'It is never too late to break off a marriage that's distasteful to you. Now I'll say one thing; and it is truth: I wish you would marry me instead of him, even now, at the last moment, though you have served me so badly.'

'O, it is not possible to think of that!' she answered hastily, shaking her head. 'When I get home all will be prepared – it is ready even now – the things for the party, the furniture, Mr Heddegan's new suit, and everything. I should require the courage of a tropical lion to go home there and say I wouldn't carry out my promise!'

'Then go, in Heaven's name! But there would be no necessity for you to go home and face them in that way. If we were to marry, it would have to be at once, instantly; or not at all. I should think your affection not worth the having unless you agreed to come back with me to Trufal this evening, where we could be married by licence on Monday morning. And then no Mr David Heddegan or anybody else could get you away from me.'

'I must go home by the Tuesday boat,' she faltered. 'What would they think if I did not come?'

'You could go home by that boat just the same. All the difference would be that I should go with you. You could leave me on the quay, where I'd have a smoke, while you went and saw your father and mother privately; you could then tell them what you had done, and that I was waiting not far off; that I was a schoolmaster in a fairly good position, and a young man you had known when you were at the Training College. Then I would come boldly forward; and they would see that it could not be altered, and so you wouldn't suffer a lifelong misery by being the wife of a wretched old gaffer you don't like at all. Now, honestly; you do like me best, don't you, Baptista?'

'Yes.'

'Then we will do as I say.'

She did not pronounce a clear affirmative. But that she consented to the novel proposition at some moment or other of that walk was apparent by what occurred a little later.

III

An enterprise of such pith required, indeed, less talking than consideration. The first thing they did in carrying it out was to return to the railway station, where Baptista took from her luggage a small trunk of immediate necessaries which she would in any case have required after missing the boat. That same afternoon they travelled up the line to Trufal.

Charles Stow (as his name was), despite his disdainful indifference to things, was very careful of appearances, and made the journey independently of her though in the same train. He told her where she could get board and lodgings in the city; and with merely a distant nod to her of a provisional kind, went off to his own quarters, and to see about the licence.

On Sunday she saw him in the morning across the nave of the pro-cathedral. In the afternoon they walked together in the fields, where he told her that the licence would be ready next day, and would be available the day after, when the ceremony could be performed as early after eight o'clock as they should choose.

His courtship, thus renewed after an interval of two years, was as impetuous, violent even, as it was short. The next day came and passed, and the final arrangements were made. Their agreement was to get the ceremony over as soon as they possibly could the next morning, so as to go on to Pen-zephyr at once, and reach that place in time for the boat's departure the same day. It was in obedience to Baptista's earnest request that Stow consented thus to make the whole journey to Lyonesse by land and water at one heat, and not break it at Pen-zephyr; she seemed to be oppressed with a dread of lingering anywhere, this great first act of disobedience to her parents once accomplished, with the weight on her mind that her home had to be convulsed by the disclosure of it. To face her difficulties over the water immediately she had created them was, however, a course more desired by Baptista than by her lover; though for once he gave way.

The next morning was bright and warm as those which had preceded it. By six o'clock it seemed nearly noon, as is often the case in that part of England in the summer season. By nine they were husband and wife. They packed up and departed by the earliest train after the service; and on the way discussed at length what she should say on meeting her parents, Charley dictating the turn of each phrase. In her anxiety they had travelled so early that when they reached Pen-zephyr they found there were nearly two hours on their hands before the steamer's time of sailing.

Baptista was extremely reluctant to be seen promenading the streets of the watering-place with her husband till, as above stated, the household at Giant's Town should know the unexpected course of events from her own lips; and it was just possible, if not likely, that some Lyonessian might be prowling about there, or even have come across the sea to look for her. To meet anyone to whom she was known, and to have to reply to awkward questions about the strange young man at her side before her well-framed announcement had been delivered at proper time and place, was a thing she could not contemplate with equanimity. So, instead of looking at the shops and harbour, they went along the coast a little way.

The heat of the morning was by this time intense. They clambered up on some cliffs, and while sitting there, looking around at St Michael's Mount and other objects, Charles said to her that he thought he would run down to the beach at their feet, and take just one plunge into the sea.

Baptista did not much like the idea of being left alone; it was gloomy, she said. But he assured her he would not be gone more than a quarter of an hour at the outside, and she passively assented.

Down he went, disappeared, appeared again, and looked back. Then he again proceeded, and vanished, till, as a small waxen object, she saw him emerge from the nook that had screened him, cross the white fringe of foam, and walk into the undulating mass of blue. Once in the water he seemed less inclined to hurry than before; he remained a long time; and, unable either to appreciate his skill or criticize his want of it at that distance, she withdrew her eyes from the spot, and gazed at the still outline of St Michael's – now beautifully toned in grey.

Her anxiety for the hour of departure, and to cope at once with the approaching incidents that she would have to manipulate as best she could, sent her into a reverie. It was now Tuesday; she would reach home in the evening – a very late time they would say; but, as the delay was a pure accident, they would deem her marriage to Mr Heddegan tomorrow still practicable. Then Charles would have to be produced from the background. It was a terrible undertaking to think of, and she almost regretted her temerity in wedding so hastily that morning. The rage of her father would be so crushing; the reproaches of her mother so bitter; and perhaps Charles would answer hotly, and perhaps cause estrangement till death. There had obviously been no alarm about her at St Maria's, or somebody would have sailed across to inquire for her. She had, in a letter written at the beginning of the week, spoken of the hour at which she intended to leave her country schoolhouse; and from this her friends had probably perceived that by such timing she would run a risk of losing the Saturday boat. She had missed it, and as a consequence sat here on the shore as Mrs Charles Stow.

This brought her to the present, and she turned from the outline of St Michael's Mount to look about for her husband's form. He was, as far as she could discover, no longer in the sea. Then he was dressing. By moving a few steps she could see where his clothes lay. But Charles was not beside them.

Baptista looked back again at the water in bewilderment, as if her senses were the victim of some sleight of hand. Not a speck or spot resembling a man's head or face showed anywhere. By this time she was alarmed, and her alarm intensified when she perceived a little beyond the scene of her husband's bathing a small area of water, the quality of whose surface differed from that of the surrounding expanse as the coarse vegetation of some foul patch in a mead differs from the fine green of the remainder. Elsewhere it looked flexuous, here it looked vermiculated and lumpy, and her marine experiences suggested to her in a moment that two currents met and caused a turmoil at this place.

She descended as hastily as her trembling limbs would allow. The way down was terribly long, and before reaching the heap of clothes it occurred to her that, after all, it would be best to run first for help. Hastening along in a lateral direction she proceeded inland till she met a man, and soon afterwards two others. To them she exclaimed, 'I think a gentleman who was bathing is in some danger. I cannot see him as I could. Will you please run and help him, at once, if you will be so kind?'

She did not think of turning to show them the exact spot, indicating it vaguely by the direction of her hand, and still going on her way with the idea of gaining more assistance. When she deemed, in her faintness, that she had carried the alarm far enough, she faced about and dragged herself back again. Before reaching the now dreaded spot she met one of the men.

'We can see nothing at all, Miss,' he declared.

Having gained the beach, she found the tide in, and no sign of Charley's clothes. The other men whom she had besought to come had disappeared, it must have been in some other direction, for she had not met them going away. They, finding nothing, had probably thought her alarm a mere conjecture, and given up the quest.

Baptista sank down upon the stones near at hand. Where Charley had undressed was now sea. There could not be the least doubt that he was drowned, and his body sucked under by the current; while his clothes, lying within high-water mark, had probably been carried away by the rising tide.

She remained in a stupor for some minutes, till a strange sensation succeeded the aforesaid perceptions, mystifying her intelligence, and leaving her physically almost inert. With his personal disappearance, the last three days of her life with him seemed to be swallowed up, also his image, in her mind's eye, waned curiously, receded far away, grew stranger and stranger, less and less real. Their meeting and marriage had been so sudden, unpremeditated, adventurous, that she could hardly believe that she had played her part in such a reckless drama. Of all the few hours of her life with Charles, the portion that most insisted in coming back to memory was their fortuitous encounter on the previous Saturday, and those bitter reprimands with which he had begun the attack, as it might be called, which had piqued her to an unexpected consummation.

A sort of cruelty, an imperiousness, even in his warmth, had characterized Charles Stow. As a lover he had ever been a bit of a tyrant; and it might pretty truly have been said that he had stung her into marriage with him at last. Still more alien from her life did these reflections operate to make him; and then they would be chased away by an interval of passionate weeping and mad regret. Finally, there returned upon the confused mind of the young wife the recollection that she was on her way homeward, and that the packet would sail in three-quarters of an hour.

Except the parasol in her hand, all she possessed was at the station awaiting her onward journey.

She looked in that direction; and, entering one of those undemonstrative phases so common with her, walked quietly on.

At first she made straight for the railway; but suddenly turning she went to a shop and wrote an anonymous line announcing his death by drowning to the only person she had ever heard Charles mention as a relative. Posting this stealthily, and with a fearful look around her, she seemed to acquire a terror of the late events, pursuing her way to the station as if followed by a spectre.

When she got to the office she asked for the luggage that she had left there on the Saturday as well as the trunk left on the morning just lapsed. All were put in the boat, and she herself followed. Quickly as these things had been done, the whole proceeding, nevertheless, had been almost automatic on Baptista's part, ere she had come to any definite conclusion on her course.

Just before the bell rang she heard a conversation on the pier, which removed the last shade of doubt from her mind, if any had existed, that she was Charles Stow's widow. The sentences were but fragmentary, but she could easily piece them out.

'A man drowned – swam out too far – was a stranger to the place – people in boat – saw him go down – couldn't get there in time.'

The news was little more definite than this as yet; though it may as well be stated once for all that the statement was true. Charley, with the over-confidence of his nature, had ventured out too far for his strength, and succumbed in the absence of assistance, his lifeless body being at the moment suspended in the transparent mid-depths of the bay. His clothes, however, had merely been gently lifted by the rising tide, and floated into a nook hard by, where they lay out of sight of the passers-by till a day or two after.

IV

In ten minutes they were steaming out of the harbour for their voyage of four or five hours, at whose ending she would have to tell her strange story.

As Pen-zephyr and all its environing scenes disappeared behind Mousehole and St Clement's Isle, Baptista's ephemeral, meteor-like husband impressed her yet more as a fantasy. She was still in such a trance-like state that she had been an hour on the little packet-boat before she became aware of the agitating fact that Mr Heddegan was on board with her. Involuntarily she slipped from her left hand the symbol of her wifehood.

'Hee-hee! Well, the truth is, I wouldn't interrupt 'ee. "I reckon she don't see me, or won't see me," I said, "and what's the hurry? She'll see enough o' me soon!" I hope ye be well, mee deer?'

He was a hale, well-conditioned man of about five and fifty, of the complexion common to those whose lives are passed on the bluffs and beaches of an ocean isle. He extended the four quarters of his face in a genial smile, and his hand for a grasp of the same magnitude. She gave her own in surprised docility, and he continued:

'I couldn't help coming across to meet 'ee. What an unfortunate thing you missing the boat and not coming Saturday! They meant to have warned 'ee that the time was changed, but forgot it at the last moment. The truth is that I should have informed 'ee myself, but I was that busy finishing up a job last week, so as to have this week free, that I trusted to your father for attending to these little things. However, so plain and quiet as it is all to be, it really do not matter so much as it might otherwise have done, and I hope ye haven't been greatly put out. Now, if you'd sooner that I should not be seen talking to 'ee – if 'ee feel shy at all before strangers – just say. I'll leave 'ee to yourself till we get home.'

'Thank you much. I am indeed a little tired, Mr Heddegan.'

He nodded urbane acquiescence, strolled away immediately, and minutely inspected the surface of the funnel, till some female passengers of Giant's Town tittered at what they must have thought a rebuff – for the approaching wedding was known to many on St Maria's Island, though to nobody elsewhere. Baptista coloured at their satire, and called him back, and forced herself to commune with him in at least a mechanically friendly manner.

The opening event had been thus different from her expectation, and she had adumbrated no act to meet it. Taken aback she passively allowed circumstances to pilot her along; and so the voyage was made.

It was near dusk when they touched the pier of Giant's Town, where several friends and neighbours stood awaiting them. Her father had a lantern in his hand. Her mother, too, was there, reproachfully glad that the delay had at last ended so simply. Mrs Trewthen and her daughter went together along the Giant's Walk, or promenade, to the house, rather in advance of her husband and Mr Heddegan, who talked in loud tones which reached the women over their shoulders.

Some would have called Mrs Trewthen a good mother; but though well meaning she was maladroit, and her intentions missed their mark. This might have been partly attributable to the slight deafness from which she suffered. Now, as usual, the chief utterances came from her lips.

'Ah, yes, I'm so glad, my child, that you've got over safe. It is all ready, and everything so well arranged, that nothing but misfortune could hinder you settling as, with God's grace, becomes 'ee. Close to your mother's door a'most, 'twill be a great blessing, I'm sure; and I was very glad to find from your letters that you'd held your word sacred. That's right – make your word your bond always. Mrs Wace seems to be a sensible woman. I hope the Lord will do for her as he's doing for you no long time hence. And how did 'ee get over the terrible journey from Tor-upon-Sea to Pen-zephyr? Once you'd done with the railway, of course, you seemed quite at home. Well, Baptista, conduct yourself seemly, and all will be well.'

Thus admonished, Baptista entered the house, her father and Mr Heddegan immediately at her back. Her mother had been so didactic that she had felt herself absolutely unable to broach the subjects in the centre of her mind.

The familiar room, with the dark ceiling, the well-spread table, the old chairs, had never before spoken so eloquently of the times ere she knew or had heard of Charley Stow. She went upstairs to take off her things, her mother remaining below to complete the disposition of the supper, and attend to the preparation of tomorrow's meal, altogether composing such an array of pies, from pies of fish to pies of turnips, as was never heard of outside the Western Duchy. Baptista, once alone, sat down and did nothing; and was called before she had taken off her bonnet.

'I'm coming,' she cried, jumping up, and speedily disapparelling herself, brushed her hair with a few touches and went down.

Two or three of Mr Heddegan's and her father's friends had dropped in, and expressed their sympathy for the delay she had been subjected to. The meal was a most merry one except to Baptista. She had desired privacy, and there was none; and to break the news was already a greater difficulty than it had been at first. Everything around her, animate and inanimate, great and small, insisted that she had come home to be married; and she could not get a chance to say nay.

One or two people sang songs, as overtures to the melody of the morrow, till at length bedtime came, and they all withdrew, her mother having retired a little earlier. When Baptista found herself again alone in her bedroom the case stood as before: she had come home with much to say, and she had said nothing.

It was now growing clear even to herself that Charles being dead, she had not determination sufficient within her to break tidings which, had he been alive, would have imperatively announced themselves. And thus with the stroke of midnight came the turning of the scale; her story should remain untold. It was not that upon the whole she thought it best not to attempt to tell it; but that she could not undertake so explosive a matter. To stop the wedding now would cause a convulsion in Giant's Town little short of volcanic. Weakened, tired, and terrified as she had been by the day's adventures, she could not make herself the author of such a catastrophe. But how refuse Heddegan without telling? It really seemed to her as if her marriage with Mr Heddegan were about to take place as if nothing had intervened.

Morning came. The events of the previous days were cut off from her present existence by scene and sentiment more completely than ever. Charles Stow had grown to be a special being of whom, owing to his character, she entertained rather fearful than loving memory. Baptista could hear when she awoke that her parents were already moving about downstairs. But she did not rise till her mother's rather rough voice resounded up the staircase as it had done on the preceding evening.

'Baptista! Come, time to be stirring! The man will be here, by Heaven's blessing, in three-quarters of an hour. He has looked in already for a minute or two – and says he's going to the church to see if things be well forward.'

Baptista arose, looked out of the window, and took the easy course. When she emerged from the regions above she was arrayed in her new silk frock and best stockings, wearing a linen jacket over the former for breakfasting, and her common slippers over the latter, not to spoil the new ones on the rough precincts of the dwelling.

It is unnecessary to dwell at any great length on this part of the morning's proceedings. She revealed nothing; and married Heddegan, as she had given her word to do, on that appointed August day.

V

Mr Heddegan forgave the coldness of his bride's manner during and after the wedding ceremony, full well aware that there had been considerable reluctance on her part to acquiesce in this neighbourly arrangement, and, as a philosopher of long standing, holding that whatever Baptista's attitude now, the conditions would probably be much the same six months hence as those which ruled among other married couples.

An absolutely unexpected shock was given to Baptista's listless mind about an hour after the wedding service. They had nearly finished the midday dinner when the now husband said to her father, 'We think of starting about two. And the breeze being so fair we shall bring up inside Pen-zephyr new pier about six at least.'

'What – are we going to Pen-zephyr?' said Baptista. 'I don't know anything of it.'

'Didn't you tell her?' asked her father of Heddegan.

It transpired that, owing to the delay in her arrival, this proposal too, among other things, had in the hurry not been mentioned to her, except some time ago as a general suggestion that they would go somewhere. Heddegan had imagined that any trip would be pleasant, and one to the mainland the pleasantest of all.

She looked so distressed at the announcement that her husband willingly offered to give it up, though he had not had a holiday off the island for a whole year. Then she pondered on the inconvenience of staying at Giant's Town, where all the inhabitants were bonded, by the circumstances of their situation, into a sort of family party, which permitted and encouraged on such occasions as these oral criticism that was apt to disturb the equanimity of newly married girls, and would especially worry Baptista in her strange situation. Hence, unexpectedly, she agreed not to disorganize her husband's plans for the wedding jaunt, and it was settled that, as originally intended, they should proceed in a neighbour's sailing boat to the metropolis of the district.

In this way they arrived at Pen-zephyr without difficulty or mishap. Bidding adieu to Jenkin and his man, who had sailed them over, they strolled arm in arm off the pier, Baptista silent, cold, and obedient. Heddegan had arranged to take her as far as Plymouth before their return, but to go no further than where they had landed that day. Their first business was to find an inn; and in this they had unexpected difficulty, since for some reason or other – possibly the fine weather – many of the nearest at hand were full of tourists and commercial travellers. He led her on till he reached a tavern which, though comparatively unpretending, stood in as attractive a spot as any in the town; and this, somewhat to their surprise after their previous experience, they found apparently empty. The considerate old man, thinking that Baptista was educated to artistic notions, though he himself was deficient in them, had decided that it was most desirable to have, on such an occasion as the present, an apartment with 'a good view' (the expression being one he had often heard in use among tourists); and he therefore asked for a favourite room on the first floor, from which a bow-window protruded, for the express purpose of affording such an outlook.

The landlady, after some hesitation, said she was sorry that particular apartment was engaged; the next one, however, or any other in the house, was unoccupied.

'The gentleman who has the best one will give it up tomorrow, and then you can change into it,' she added, as Mr Heddegan hesitated about taking the adjoining and less commanding one.

'We shall be gone tomorrow, and shan't want it,' he said.

Wishing not to lose customers, the landlady earnestly continued that since he was bent on having the best room, perhaps the other gentleman would not object to move at once into the one they despised, since, though nothing could be seen from the window, the room was equally large.

'Well, if he doesn't care for a view,' said Mr Heddegan, with the air of a highly artistic man who did.

'O no – I am sure he doesn't,' she said. 'I can promise that you shall have the room you want. If you would not object to go for a walk for half an hour, I could have it ready, and your things in it, and a nice tea laid in the bow-window by the time you come back?'

This proposal was deemed satisfactory by the fussy old tradesman, and they went out. Baptista nervously conducted him in an opposite direction to her walk of the former day in other company, showing on her wan face, had he observed it, how much she was beginning to regret her sacrificial step for mending matters that morning.

She took advantage of a moment when her husband's back was turned to inquire casually in a shop if anything had been heard of the gentleman who was sucked down in the eddy while bathing.

The shopman said, 'Yes, his body has been washed ashore,' and had just handed Baptista a newspaper on which she discerned the heading, 'A Schoolmaster drowned while bathing', when her husband turned to join her. She might have pursued the subject without raising suspicion; but it was more than flesh and blood could do, and completing a small purchase almost ran out of the shop.

'What is your terrible hurry, mee deer?' said Heddegan, hastening after.

'I don't know – I don't want to stay in shops,' she gasped.

'And we won't,' he said. 'They are suffocating this weather. Let's go back and have some tay!'

They found the much desired apartment awaiting their entry. It was a sort of combination bed and sitting-room, and the table was prettily spread with high tea in the bow-window, a bunch of flowers in the midst, and a best-parlour chair on each side. Here they shared the meal by the ruddy light of the vanishing sun. But though the view had been engaged, regardless of expense, exclusively for Baptista's pleasure, she did not direct any keen attention out of the window. Her gaze as often fell on the floor and walls of the room as elsewhere, and on the table as much as on either, beholding nothing at all.

But there was a change. Opposite her seat was the door, upon which her eyes presently became riveted like those of a little bird upon a snake. For, on a peg at the back of the door, there hung a hat; such a hat – surely, from its peculiar make, the actual hat – that had been worn by Charles. Conviction grew to certainty when she saw a railway ticket sticking up from the band. Charles had put the ticket there – she had noticed the act.

Her teeth almost chattered; she murmured something incoherent. Her husband jumped up and said, 'You are not well! What is it? What shall I get 'ee?'

'Smelling salts!' she said, quickly and desperately; 'at the chemist's shop you were in just now.'

He jumped up like the anxious old man that he was, caught up his own hat from a back table, and without observing the other hastened out and downstairs.

Left alone she gazed and gazed at the back of the door, then spasmodically rang the bell. An honest-looking country maid-servant appeared in response.

'A hat!' murmured Baptista, pointing with her finger. 'It does not belong to us.'

'O yes, I'll take it away,' said the young woman with some hurry 'It belongs to the other gentleman.'

She spoke with a certain awkwardness, and took the hat out of the room. Baptista had recovered her outward composure. 'The other gentleman?' she said. 'Where is the other gentleman?'

'He's in the next room, ma'am. He removed out of this to oblige 'ee.'

'How can you say so? I should hear him if he were there,' said Baptista, sufficiently recovered to argue down an apparent untruth.

'He's there,' said the girl, hardily.

'Then it is strange that he makes no noise,' said Mrs Heddegan, convicting the girl of falsity by a look.

'He makes no noise; but it is not strange,' said the servant.

All at once a dread took possession of the bride's heart, like a cold hand laid thereon; for it flashed upon her that there was a possibility of reconciling the girl's statement with her own knowledge of facts.

'Why does he make no noise?' she weakly said.

The waiting-maid was silent, and looked at her questioner. 'If I tell you, ma'am, you won't tell missis?' she whispered.

Baptista promised.

'Because he's a-lying dead!' said the girl. 'He's the schoolmaster that was drowned yesterday.'

'O!' said the bride, covering her eyes. 'Then he was in this room till just now?'

'Yes,' said the maid, thinking the young lady's agitation natural enough. 'And I told missis that I thought she oughtn't to have done it, because I don't hold it right to keep visitors so much in the dark where death's concerned; but she said the gentleman didn't die of anything infectious; she was a poor, honest, innkeeper's wife, she says, who had to get her living by making hay while the sun sheened. And owing to the drowned gentleman being brought here, she said, it kept so many people away that we were empty, though all the other houses were full. So when your good man set his mind upon the room, and she would have lost good paying folk if he'd not had it, it wasn't to be supposed, she said, that she'd let anything stand in the way. Ye won't say that I've told ye, please, m'm? All the linen has been changed, and as the inquest won't be till tomorrow, after you are gone, she thought you wouldn't know a word of it, being strangers here.'

The returning footsteps of her husband broke off further narration. Baptista waved her hand, for she could not speak. The waiting-maid quickly withdrew, and Mr Heddegan entered with the smelling salts and other nostrums.

'Any better?' he questioned.

'I don't like the hotel,' she exclaimed, almost simultaneously. 'I can't bear it – it doesn't suit me!'

'Is that all that's the matter?' he returned pettishly (this being the first time of his showing such a mood). 'Upon my heart and life such trifling is trying to any man's temper, Baptista! Sending me about from here to yond, and then when I come back saying 'ee don't like the place that I have sunk so much money and words to get for 'ee. 'Od dang it all, 'tis enough to – But I won't say any more at present, mee deer, though it is just too much to expect to turn out of the house now. We shan't get another quiet place at this time of the evening – every other inn in the town is bustling with rackety folk of one sort and t'other, while here 'tis as quiet as the grave – the country, I would say. So bide still, d'ye hear, and tomorrow we shall be out of the town altogether – as early as you like.'

The obstinacy of age had, in short, overmastered its complaisance, and the young woman said no more. The simple course of telling him that in the adjoining room lay a corpse which had lately occupied their own might, it would have seemed, have been an effectual one without further disclosure, but to allude to *that* subject, however it was disguised, was more than Heddegan's young wife had strength for. Horror broke her down. In the contingency one thing only presented itself to her paralysed regard – that here she was doomed to abide, in a hideous contiguity to the dead husband and the living, and her conjecture did, in fact, bear itself out. That night she lay between the two men she had married – Heddegan on the one hand, and on the other through the partition against which the bed stood, Charles Stow.

VI

Kindly time had withdrawn the foregoing event three days from the present of Baptista Heddegan. It was ten o'clock in the morning; she had been ill, not in an ordinary or definite sense, but in a state of cold stupefaction, from which it was difficult to arouse her so much as to say a few sentences. When questioned she had replied that she was pretty well.

Their trip, as such, had been something of a failure. They had gone on as far as Falmouth, but here he had given way to her entreaties to return home. This they could not very well do without repassing through Pen-zephyr, at which place they had now again arrived.

In the train she had seen a weekly local paper, and read there a paragraph detailing the inquest on Charles. It was added that the funeral was to take place at his native town of Redrutin on Friday.

After reading this she had shown no reluctance to enter the fatal neighbourhood of the tragedy, only stipulating that they should take their rest at a different lodging from the first; and now comparatively braced up and calm – indeed a cooler creature altogether than when last in the town, she said to David that she wanted to walk out for a while, as they had plenty of time on their hands.

'To a shop as usual, I suppose, mee deer?'

'Partly for shopping,' she said. 'And it will be best for you, dear, to stay in after trotting about so much, and have a good rest while I am gone.'

He assented; and Baptista sallied forth. As she had stated, her first visit was made to a shop, a draper's. Without the exercise of much choice she purchased a black bonnet and veil, also a black stuff gown; a black mantle she already wore. These articles were made up into a parcel which, in spite of the saleswoman's offers, her customer said she would take with her. Bearing it on her arm she turned to the railway, and at the station got a ticket for Redrutin.

Thus it appeared that, on her recovery from the paralysed mood of the former day, while she had resolved not to blast utterly the happiness of her present husband by revealing the history of the departed one, she had also determined to indulge a certain odd, inconsequent, feminine sentiment of decency, to the small extent to which it could do no harm to any person. At Redrutin she emerged from the railway carriage in the black attire purchased at the shop, having during the transit made the change in the empty compartment she had chosen. The other clothes were now in the bandbox and parcel. Leaving these at the cloak-room she proceeded onward, and after a wary survey reached the side of a hill whence a view of the burial ground could be obtained.

It was now a little before two o'clock. While Baptista waited a funeral procession ascended the road. Baptista hastened across, and by the time the procession entered the cemetery gates she had unobtrusively joined it.

In addition to the schoolmaster's own relatives (not a few), the paragraph in the newspapers of his death by drowning had drawn together many neighbours, acquaintances, and onlookers. Among them she passed unnoticed, and with a quiet step pursued the winding path to the chapel, and afterwards thence to the grave. When all was over, and the relatives and idlers had withdrawn, she stepped to the edge of the chasm. From beneath her mantle she drew a little bunch of forget-me-nots, and dropped them in upon the coffin. In a few minutes she also turned and went away from the cemetery. By five o'clock she was again in Pen-zephyr.

'You have been a mortal long time!' said her husband, crossly. 'I allowed you an hour at most, mee deer.'

'It occupied me longer,' said she.

'Well – I reckon it is wasting words to complain. Hang it, ye look so tired and wisht that I can't find heart to say what I would!'

'I am – weary and wisht, David; I am. We can get home tomorrow for certain, I hope?'

'We can. And please God we will!' said Mr Heddegan heartily, as if he too were weary of his brief honeymoon. 'I must be into business again on Monday morning at latest.'

They left by the next morning steamer, and in the afternoon took up their residence in their own house at Giant's Town.

The hour that she reached the island it was as if a material weight had been removed from Baptista's shoulders. Her husband attributed the change to the influence of the local breezes after the hot-house atmosphere of the mainland. However that might be, settled here, a few doors from her mother's dwelling, she recovered in no very long time much of her customary bearing, which was never very demonstrative. She accepted her position calmly, and faintly smiled when her neighbours learned to call her Mrs Heddegan, and said she seemed likely to become the leader of fashion in Giant's Town.

Her husband was a man who had made considerably more money by trade than her father had done: and perhaps the greater profusion of surroundings at her command than she had hereto-fore been mistress of, was not without an effect upon her. One week, two weeks, three weeks passed; and, being pre-eminently a young woman who allowed things to drift, she did nothing whatever either to disclose or conceal traces of her first marriage; or to learn if there existed possibilities – which there undoubtedly did – by which that hasty contract might become revealed to those about her at any unexpected moment.

While yet within the first month of her marriage, and on an evening just before sunset, Baptista was standing within her garden adjoining the house, when she saw passing along the road a personage clad in a greasy black coat and battered tall hat, which, common enough in the slums of a city, had an odd appearance in St Maria's. The tramp, as he seemed to be, marked her at once – bonnetless and unwrapped as she was her features were plainly recognizable – and with an air of friendly surprise came and leant over the wall.

'What! don't you know me?' said he.

She had some dim recollection of his face, but said that she was not acquainted with him.

'Why, your witness to be sure, ma'am. Don't you mind the man that was mending the church-window when you and your intended husband walked up to be made one; and the clerk called me down from the ladder, and I came and did my part by writing my name and occupation?'

Baptista glanced quickly around; her husband was out of earshot. That would have been of less importance but for the fact that the wedding witnessed by this personage had not been the wedding with Mr. Heddegan, but the one on the day previous.

'I've had a misfortune since then, that's pulled me under,' continued her friend. 'But don't let me damp yer wedded joy by naming the particulars. Yes, I've seen changes since; though 'tis but a short time ago – let me see, only a month next week, I think; for 'twere the first or second day in August.'

'Yes – that's when it was,' said another man, a sailor, who had come up with a pipe in his mouth, and felt it necessary to join in (Baptista having receded to escape further speech). 'For that was the first time I set foot in Giant's Town; and her husband took her to him the same day.'

A dialogue then proceeded between the two men outside the wall, which Baptista could not help hearing.

'Ay, I signed the book that made her one flesh,' repeated the decayed glazier. 'Where's her good-man?'

'About the premises somewhere; but you don't see 'em together much,' replied the sailor in an undertone. 'You see, he's older than she.'

'Older? I should never have thought it from my own observation,' said the glazier. 'He was a remarkably handsome man.'

'Handsome? Well, there he is – we can see for ourselves.'

David Heddegan had, indeed, just shown himself at the upper end of the garden; and the glazier, looking in bewilderment from the husband to the wife, saw the latter turn pale.

Now that decayed glazier was a far-seeing and cunning man – too far-seeing and cunning to allow himself to thrive by simple and straightforward means – and he held his peace, till he could read more plainly the meaning of this riddle, merely added carelessly, 'Well – marriage do alter a man, 'tis true. I should never ha' knowed him!'

He then stared oddly at the disconcerted Baptista, and moving on to where he could again address her, asked her to do him a good turn, since he once had done the same for her. Understanding that he meant money, she handed him some, at which he thanked her, and instantly went away.

VII

She had escaped exposure on this occasion; but the incident had been an awkward one, and should have suggested to Baptista that sooner or later the secret must leak out. As it was, she suspected that at any rate she had not heard the last of the glazier.

In a day or two, when her husband had gone to the old town on the other side of the island, there came a gentle tap at the door, and the worthy witness of her first marriage made his appearance a second time.

'It took me hours to get to the bottom of the mystery – hours!' he said with a gaze of deep confederacy which offended her pride very deeply. 'But thanks to a good intellect I've done it. Now, ma'am, I'm not a man to tell tales, even when a tale would be so good as this. But I'm going back to the mainland again, and a little assistance would be as rain on thirsty ground.'

'I helped you two days ago,' began Baptista.

'Yes – but what was that, my good lady? Not enough to pay my passage to Pen-zephyr. I came over on your account, for I thought there was a mystery somewhere. Now I must go back on my own. Mind this – 'twould be very awkward for you if your old man were to know. He's a queer temper, though he may be fond.'

She knew as well as her visitor how awkward it would be; and the hush-money she paid was heavy that day. She had, however, the satisfaction of watching the man to the steamer, and seeing him diminish out of sight. But Baptista perceived that the system into which she had been led of purchasing silence thus was one fatal to her peace of mind, particularly if it had to be continued.

Hearing no more from the glazier she hoped the difficulty was past. But another week only had gone by, when, as she was pacing the Giant's Walk (the name given to the promenade), she met the same personage in the company of a fat woman carrying a bundle.

'This is the lady, my dear,' he said to his companion. 'This, ma'am, is my wife. We've come to settle in the town for a time, if so be we can find room.'

'That you won't do,' said she. 'Nobody can live here who is not privileged.'

'I am privileged,' said the glazier, 'by my trade.'

Baptista went on, but in the afternoon she received a visit from the man's wife. This honest woman began to depict, in forcible colours, the necessity for keeping up the concealment.

'I will intercede with my husband, ma'am,' she said. 'He's a true man if rightly managed; and I'll beg him to consider your position. 'Tis a very nice house you've got here,' she added, glancing round, 'and well worth a little sacrifice to keep it.'

The unlucky Baptista staved off the danger on this third occasion as she had done on the previous two. But she formed a resolve that, if the attack were once more to be repeated she would face a revelation – worse though that must now be than before she had attempted to purchase silence by bribes. Her tormentors, never believing her capable of acting upon such an intention, came again; but she shut the door in their faces. They retreated, muttering something; but she went to the back of the house, where David Heddegan was.

She looked at him, unconscious of all. The case was serious; she knew that well; and all the more serious in that she liked him better now than she had done at first. Yet, as she herself began to see, the secret was one that was sure to disclose itself. Her name and Charles's stood indelibly written in the registers; and though a month only had passed as yet it was a wonder that his clandestine union with her had not already been discovered by his friends. Thus spurring herself to the inevitable, she spoke to Heddegan.

'David, come indoors. I have something to tell you.'

He hardly regarded her at first. She had discerned that during the last week or two he had seemed preoccupied, as if some private business harassed him. She repeated her request. He replied with a sigh, 'Yes, certainly, mee deer.'

When they had reached the sitting-room and shut the door she repeated, faintly, 'David, I have something to tell you – a sort of tragedy I have concealed. You will hate me for having so far deceived you; but perhaps my telling you voluntarily will make you think a little better of me than you would do otherwise.'

'Tragedy?' he said, awakening to interest. 'Much you can know about tragedies, mee deer, that have been in the world so short a time!'

She saw that he suspected nothing, and it made her task the harder. But on she went steadily. 'It is about something that happened before we were married,' she said.

'Indeed!'

'Not a very long time before – a short time. And it is about a lover,' she faltered.

'I don't much mind that,' he said mildly. 'In truth, I was in hopes 'twas more.'

'In hopes!'

'Well, yes.'

This screwed her up to the necessary effort. 'I met my old sweetheart. He scorned me, chid me, dared me, and I went and married him. We were coming straight here to tell you all what we had done; but he was drowned; and I thought I would say nothing about him: and I married you, David, for the sake of peace and quietness. I've tried to keep it from you, but have found I cannot. There – that's the substance of it, and you can never, never forgive me, I am sure!'

She spoke desperately. But the old man, instead of turning black or blue, or slaying her in his indignation, jumped up from his chair, and began to caper around the room in quite an ecstatic emotion.

'O, happy thing! How well it falls out!' he exclaimed, snapping his fingers over his head. 'Ha-ha – the knot is cut – I see a way out of my trouble – ha-ha!'

She looked at him without uttering a sound, till, as he still continued smiling joyfully, she said, 'O – what do you mean? Is it done to torment me?'

'No – no! O, mee deer, your story helps me out of the most heart-aching quandary a poor man ever found himself in! You see, it is this – *I've* got a tragedy, too; and unless you had had one to tell, I could never have seen my way to tell mine!'

'What is yours – what is it?' she asked, with altogether a new view of things.

'Well – it is a bouncer; mine is a bouncer!' said he, looking on the ground and wiping his eyes.

'Not worse than mine?'

'Well – that depends upon how you look at it. Yours had to do with the past alone; and I don't mind it. You see, we've been married a month, and it don't jar upon me as it would if we'd only been married a day or two. Now mine refers to past, present, and future; so that —'

'Past, present, and future!' she murmured. 'It never occurred to me that *you* had a tragedy too.'

'But I have!' he said, shaking his head. 'In fact, four.'

'Then tell 'em!' cried the young woman.

'I will – I will. But be considerate, I beg 'ee, mee deer. Well – I wasn't a bachelor when I married 'ee, any more than you were a spinster. Just as you was a widow-woman, I was a widow-man.'

'Ah!' said she, with some surprise. 'But is that all? – then we are nicely balanced,' she added, relieved.

'No – it is not all. There's the point. I am not only a widower.'

'O, David!'

'I am a widower with four tragedies – that is to say, four strapping girls – the eldest taller than you. Don't 'ee look so struck – dumb-like! It fell out in this way. I knew the poor woman, their mother, in Pen-zephyr for some years; and – to cut a long story short – I privately married her at last, just before she died. I kept the matter secret, but it is getting known among the people here by degrees. I've long felt for the children – that it is my duty to have them here, and do something for them. I have not had courage to break it to 'ee, but I've seen lately that it would soon come to your ears, and that hev worried me.'

'Are they educated?' said the ex-schoolmistress.

'No. I am sorry to say they have been much neglected; in truth, they can hardly read. And so I thought that by marrying a young schoolmistress I should get some one in the house who could teach 'em, and bring 'em into genteel condition, all for nothing. You see, they are growed up too tall to be sent to school.'

'O, mercy!' she almost moaned. 'Four great girls to teach the rudiments to, and have always in the house with me spelling over their books; and I hate teaching, it kills me. I am bitterly punished – I am, I am!'

'You'll get used to 'em, mee deer, and the balance of secrets – mine against yours – will comfort your heart with a sense of justice. I could send for 'em this week very well – and I will! In faith, I could send this very day. Baptista, you have relieved me of all my difficulty!'

Thus the interview ended, so far as this matter was concerned. Baptista was too stupefied to say more, and when she went away to her room she wept from very mortification at Mr Heddegan's duplicity. Education, the one thing she abhorred; the shame of it to delude a young wife so!

The next meal came round. As they sat, Baptista would not suffer her eyes to turn towards him. He did not attempt to intrude upon her reserve, but every now and then looked under the table and chuckled with satisfaction at the aspect of affairs. 'How very well matched we be!' he said, comfortably.

Next day, when the steamer came in, Baptista saw her husband rush down to meet it; and soon after there appeared at her door four tall, hipless, shoulderless girls, dwindling in height and size from the eldest to the youngest, like a row of Pan pipes; at the head of them standing Heddegan. He smiled pleasantly through the grey fringe of his whiskers and beard, and turning to the girls said, 'Now come forrard, and shake hands properly with your stepmother.'

Thus she made their acquaintance, and he went out, leaving them together. On examination the poor girls turned out to be not only plain-looking, which she could have forgiven, but to have such a lamentably meagre intellectual equipment as to be hopelessly inadequate as companions. Even the eldest, almost her own age, could only read with difficulty words of two syllables; and taste in dress was beyond their comprehension. In the long vista of future years she saw nothing but dreary drudgery at her detested old trade without prospect of reward.

She went about quite despairing during the next few days – an unpromising, unfortunate mood for a woman who had not been married six weeks. From her parents she concealed everything. They had been amongst the few acquaintances of Heddegan who knew nothing of his secret, and were indignant enough when they saw such a ready-made household foisted upon their only child. But she would not support them in their remonstrances.

'No, you don't yet know all,' she said.

Thus Baptista had sense enough to see the retributive fairness of this issue. For some time, whenever conversation arose between her and Heddegan, which was not often, she always said, 'I am miserable, and you know it. Yet I don't wish things to be otherwise.'

But one day when he asked, 'How do you like 'em now?' her answer was unexpected. 'Much better than I did,' she said, quietly. 'I may like them very much some day.'

This was the beginning of a serener season for the chastened spirit of Baptista Heddegan. She had, in truth, discovered, underneath the crust of uncouthness and meagre articulation which was due to their Troglodytean existence, that her unwelcomed daughters had natures that were unselfish almost to sublimity. The harsh discipline accorded to their young lives before their mother's wrong had been righted, had operated less to crush them than to lift them above all personal ambition. They considered the world and its contents in a purely objective way, and their own lot seemed only to affect them as that of certain human beings among the rest, whose troubles they knew rather than suffered.

This was such an entirely new way of regarding life to a woman of Baptista's nature, that her attention, from being first arrested by it, became deeply interested. By imperceptible pulses her heart expanded in sympathy with theirs. The sentences of her tragi-comedy, her life, confused till now, became clearer daily. That in humanity, as exemplified by these girls, there was nothing to dislike, but infinitely much to pity, she learnt with the lapse of each week in their company. She grew to like the girls of unpromising exterior, and from liking she got to love them; till they formed an unexpected point of junction between her own and her husband's interests, generating a sterling friendship at least, between a pair in whose existence there had threatened to be neither friendship nor love.

A FAITHFUL HEART

(The Speaker, 16 April 1892)

Part I

It was a lovely morning, and Major Shepherd walked rapidly, his toes turned well out, his shoulders set well back. Behind him floated the summer foliage of Appleton Park – the family seat of the Shepherds – and at the end of the smooth, white road lay the Major's destination – the small town of Branbury.

The Major was the medium height; his features were regular and cleanly cut. He would have been a handsome man if his eyes had not been two dark mud-coloured dots, set close together, wholly lacking in expression. A long brown moustache swept picturesquely over bright, smoothly shaven cheeks, and the ends of this ornament were beginning to whiten. The Major was over forty. He carried under his arm a brown-paper parcel (the Major was rarely seen without a brown-paper parcel), and in it were things he could not possibly do without – his diary and his letter-book. The brown-paper parcel contained likewise a number of other papers; it contained the Major's notes for a book he was writing on the principal county families in Buckinghamshire. The Major had been collecting information for this book for many years, and with it he hoped to make two or three hundred pounds – money which he stood sorely in need of – and to advance his position in the county, a position which, in his opinion, his father had done little to maintain, and which, to his very deep regret, his sisters were now doing their best to compromise. That very morning, while packing up his brown-paper parcel, some quarter of an hour ago, he had had a somewhat angry interview on this subject with his sisters. For he had thought it his duty to reprove them for keeping company with certain small London folk who had chosen to come to live in the neighbourhood. Ethel had said that they were not going to give up their friends because they were not good enough for him, and Maud had added significantly that they were quite sure that their friends were quite as good as *the* friend he was going to see in Branbury. The Major turned on his heel and left the house.

As he walked towards Branbury he asked himself if it were possible that they knew anything about Charlotte Street; and as he approached the town he looked round nervously, fearing lest some friend might pop down upon him, and, after some hesitation, decided to take a long detour so as to avoid passing by the house of some people he knew. As he made his way through a bye-street his step quickened, and at the corner of Charlotte Street he looked round to make sure he was not followed. He then drew his keys from his pocket and let himself into a small, mean-looking house.

Major Shepherd might have spared himself the trouble of these precautions; no one was minded to watch him, for everyone knew perfectly well who lived in 27, Charlotte Street. It was common talk that the tall, dark woman who lived in 27 was Mrs Charles Shepherd, and that the little girl who ran by Mrs Shepherd's side on the rare occasions when she was seen in the streets – for it was said that the Major did not wish her to walk much about the town, lest she should attract the attention of the curious, who might be tempted to make inquiries – was the Major's little daughter, and it had been noticed that this little girl went forth now and then, basket on her arm, to do the marketing. It was said that Mrs Shepherd had been a servant in some lodging-house where the Major had been staying; other scandal-mongers declared that they knew for certain that the Major had made his wife's acquaintance in the street. Rumour had never wandered far from the truth. The Major had met his wife one night as he was coming home from his club. They seemed to suit one another; he saw her frequently for several months, and then, fearing to lose her, in a sudden access of jealousy – he had some time before been bitterly jilted – he proposed to marry her. The arrival of his parents, who came up to town beseeching of him to do nothing rash, only served to intensify his determination, and, losing his temper utterly, he told his father and mother that he would never set his foot in Appleton Park in their lifetime if they ever again ventured to pry into his private affairs; and, refusing to give any information regarding his intentions, he asked them to leave his lodgings. What he did after they never knew; years went by, and they sighed and wondered, but the matter was never alluded to in Appleton Park.

But the Major had only £400 a year, and though he lived at Appleton Park, never spending a penny more than was necessary, he could not allow her more than £3 a week. He had so many expenses: his club, his clothes, and all the incidental expenses he was put to in the grand houses where he went to stay. By strict economy, however, Mrs Shepherd managed to make two ends meet. Except when she was too ill and had to call in a charwoman to help her with the heaviest part of the work, she undertook the entire housework herself: when times were hardest, she had even taken in a lodger, not thinking herself above cooking and taking up his dinner. She had noticed that her economies endeared her to the Major, and it was pleasant to please him. Hers was a kind-hearted, simple nature, that misfortune had brought down in the world; but, as is not uncommon with persons of weak character, she possessed a clear, sensible mind which allowed her to see things in their true lights, and without difficulty she recognized the unalterable nature of her case. It mattered little whether the Major acknowledged her or not, his family would never have anything to do with her; the doors of Society were for ever closed against her. So within a year of her marriage with the Major she was convinced that her marriage had better be kept a secret; for, by helping to keep it a secret, she could make substantial amends to the man who had married her; by proclaiming it to the world, she would only alienate his affection. She understood this very well, and in all docility and obedience lent herself to the deception, accepting without complaint a mean and clandestine existence. But she would not allow her little girl to carry up a jug of hot water, and it was only rarely, when prostrate with pain, that she allowed Nellie to take the basket and run round to the butcher's and buy a bit of steak for their dinner. The heiress of Appleton Park must be brought up free from all degrading memory. But for herself she had no care. Appleton Park could never be anything to her, even if she outlived the old people, which was hardly probable. What would she, a poor invalid, do there?

She did not wish to compromise her husband's future, and still less the future of her darling daughter. She could only hope that, when dead, her sins would be forgiven her; and that this release might not be long delayed she often prayed. The house was poor, and she was miserable, but any place was good enough to suffer in. So she said when she rose and dragged herself downstairs to do a little cooking; and the same thought came to her when she lay all alone in the little parlour, furnished with what a few pounds could buy – a paraffin-lamp, a round table, a few chairs, an old and ill-padded mahogany armchair, in which it was a torture to lie; not an ornament on the chimney-piece, not a flower, not a book to while away the interminable hours. From the barren little passage, covered with a bit of oil-cloth, all and everything in 27 was meagre and unimaginative. The Major had impressed his personality upon the house. Everything looked as if it had been scraped. There was a time when Mrs Shepherd noticed the barrenness of her life; but she had grown accustomed to it, and she waited for the Major in the terrible armchair, glad when she heard his step, almost happy when he sat by her and told her what was happening 'at home'.

He took her hand and asked her how she was. 'You are looking very tired, Alice.'

'Yes, I'm a little tired. I have been working all the morning. I made up my room, and then I went out to the butcher's and bought a piece of steak. I have made you such a nice pudding for your lunch; I hope you will like it.'

'There's not much fear about my liking any beefsteak pudding you make, dear; I never knew anyone who could make one like you. But you should not tire yourself – and just as you are beginning to get better.'

Mrs Shepherd smiled and pressed her husband's hand. The conversation fell. At the end of a long silence Mrs Shepherd said: 'What has happened to trouble you, dear? I know something has, I can see it by your face.'

Then the Major told how unpleasantly his sisters had answered him when he had ventured to suggest that they saw far too much of their new neighbours, who were merely common sort of Lon-doners, and never would be received by the county. 'I'm sure that someone must have told them of my visi's here; I'm sure they suspect something . . . Girls are very sharp nowadays.'

'I am sorry, but it is no fault of mine. I rarely leave the house, and I never walk in the principal streets if I can possibly help it.'

'I know, dear, I know that no one can be more careful than you; but as people are beginning to smell a rat notwithstanding all our precautions, I suppose there's nothing for it but to go back to London.'

'Oh, you don't think it will be necessary to go back to London, do you? The place suits the child so well, and it is so nice to see you almost every day; and it is such a comfort when you are not here to know you are only a few miles away; and from the top of the hill the trees of the park are visible, and whenever I feel well enough I walk there and think of the time our Nellie will be the mistress of all those broad acres.'

'It is the fault of the busybodies,' he said; 'I cannot think what pleasure people find in meddling in other people's affairs. I never care what anyone else does. I have quite enough to do thinking of my own.'

Mrs Shepherd did not answer. 'I see,' he said, 'you don't like moving, but if you remain here all the trouble we have taken not to get found out these last ten years will go for nothing. There will be more worry and vexations, and I really don't think I could bear much more; I believe I should go off my head.' The little man spoke in a calm, even voice, and stroked his silky moustache gravely.

'Very well, then, my dear, I'll return to town as soon as you like – as soon as it is convenient. I daresay you are right.'

'I'm sure I am. You have never found me giving you wrong advice yet, have you, dear?'

Then they went down to the kitchen to eat the steak pudding; and when the Major had finished his second helping he lit his pipe, and the conversation turned on how they should get rid of their house, and how much the furniture would fetch. When he had decided to sell the furniture, and had fixed the day of their departure, Mrs Shepherd said –

'There's one thing I have to ask you, dear, and I hope you won't refuse my request. I should like to see Appleton Park before I leave. I should like to go there with Nellie and see the house and the lands that will one day belong to her.'

'I don't know how it is to be managed. If you were to meet my mother and sisters they would be sure to suspect something at once.'

'No one will know who I am. I should like to walk about the grounds for half an hour with the child. If I don't see Appleton now I never shall see it.'

The Major stroked his long, silky moustache with his short, crabbed little hand. He remembered that he had heard the carriage ordered for two o'clock – they were all going to a tennis-party some miles distant. Under the circumstances she might walk about the grounds without being noticed. He did not think any of the gardeners would question her, and, if they did, he could trust her to give an evasive answer. And then he would like her to see the place – just to know what she thought of it.

'Won't you say yes?' she said at last, her voice breaking the silence sharply.

'I was just thinking, dear: they have all gone to a tennis-party today. There'll be no one at home.'

'Well! why not today?'

'Well; I was thinking I've been lucky enough to get hold of some very interesting information about the Websters – about their ancestor Sir Thomas, who distinguished himself in the Peninsular – and I wanted to get it copied under the proper heading, but I daresay we can do that another day. The only thing is, how are you to get there? You are not equal to walking so far –'

'I was thinking, dear, that I might take a fly. I know there is the expense, but . . .'

'Yes; five or six shillings, at least. And where will you leave the fly? At the lodge gate? The flyman would be sure to get into conversation with the lodge-keeper or his wife. He'd tell them where he came from, and –'

'Supposing you were to get a two-wheeled trap and drive me yourself; that would be nicer still.'

'I'm so unlucky; someone would be sure to see me.'

The Major puffed at his pipe in silence. Then he said, 'If you were to put on a thick veil, and we were to get out of the town by this end and make our way through the lanes – it would be a long way round; but one hardly meets anyone that way, and the only danger would be going. We should return in the dusk. I don't care how late you make it; my people won't be home till nine or ten o'clock at night, perhaps later still. There will be dancing, and they are sure to stay late.'

Finally the matter was decided, and about four o'clock the Major went to the livery stable to order the trap. Mrs Shepherd and Nellie joined him soon after. Turning from the pony, whose nose he was stroking, he said –

'I hope you have brought a thick shawl; it will be cold coming back in the evening.'

'Yes, dear, here it is, and another for Nellie. What do you think of this veil?'

'It will do very well. I do hope these stablemen won't talk; let's go off at once.' The Major lifted in the child, tucked the rug about them, and cried to the stableman to let go. He drove very nervously, afraid at every moment lest the pony should bolt; and when the animal's extreme docility assured him there was no such danger, he looked round right and left, expecting at every moment some friend to pounce down upon him. But the ways were empty, the breeze that came across the fields was fresh and sweet, and they were all beginning to enjoy themselves, when he suddenly espied a carriage following in his wake. He whipped up the pony, and contrived to distance his imaginary pursuer; and having succeeded, he praised his own driving, and at the cross-roads he said: 'I dare not go any farther, but you can't miss the lodge gate in that clump of trees – the first white gate you come to. Don't ask any questions; it is ten to one you'll find the gate open; walk straight through, and don't forget to go through the beech-wood at the back of the house; the river runs right round the hill. I want to know what you think of the view. But pray don't ask to see the house; there's nothing to see; the housemaids would be sure to talk, and describe you to my sisters. So now goodbye; hope you'll enjoy yourself. I shall have just time to get to Hambrook and back; I want to see my solicitor. You'll have seen everything in a couple of hours, so in a couple of hours I shall be waiting for you here.'

Part II

It was as the Major said. The lodge-keepers asked no questions, and they passed up the drive, through the silence of an overgrowth of laurels and rhododendrons. Then the park opened before their eyes. Nellie rolled on the short, crisp, worn grass, or chased the dragonflies; the spreading trees enchanted her, and, looking at the house – a grey stone building with steps, pillars, and pilasters, hidden amid cedars and evergreen oaks – she said, 'I never saw anything so beautiful; is that where the Major goes when he leaves us? Look at the flowers, Mother, and the roses. May we not go in there – I don't mean into the house? I heard the Major ask you not to go in for fear we should meet the housemaids – but just past this railing, into the garden? Here is the gate.' The child stood with her hand on the wicket, waiting for reply: the mother stood as in a dream, looking at the house, thinking vaguely of the pictures, the corridors, and staircases, that lay behind the plate-glass windows.

'Yes; go in, my child.'

The gardens were in tumult of leaf and bloom, and the little girl ran hither and thither, gathering single flowers, and then everything that came under her hands, binding them together in bouquets – one for mother, one for the Major, and one for herself. Mrs Shepherd only smiled a little bitterly when Nellie came running to her with some new and more splendid rose. She did not attempt to reprove the child. Why should she? Everything here would one day be hers. Why then should the present be denied them? And so did her thoughts run as she walked across the sward following Nellie into the beechwood that clothed the steep hillside. The pathway led by the ruins of some Danish military earthworks, ancient hollows full of leaves and silence. Pigeons cooed in the vast green foliage, and from time to time there came up from the river the chiming sound of oars. Rustic seats were at pleasant intervals, and, feeling a little tired, Mrs Shepherd sat down. She could see the river's silver glinting through the branches, and, beyond the river, the low-lying river lands, dotted with cattle and horses grazing, dim already with blue evening vapours. In the warm solitude of the wood the irreparable misfortune of her own life pressed upon her: and in this hour of lassitude her loneliness seemed more than she could bear. The Major was good and kind, but he knew nothing of the weight of the burden he had laid upon her, and that none should know was in this moment a greater weight than the burden itself. Nellie was exploring the ancient hollows where Danes and Saxons had once fought, and had ceased to call forth her discoveries when Mrs Shepherd's bitter meditation was broken by the sudden sound of a footstep.

The intruder was a young lady. She was dressed in white, her pale gold hair was in itself an aristocracy, and her narrow slippered feet were dainty to look upon. 'Don't let me disturb you,' she said. 'This is my favourite seat; but I pray you not to move, there is plenty of room.' So amiable was she in voice and manner that Mrs Shepherd could not but remain, although she had already recognized the girl as one of the Major's sisters. Fearing to betray herself, greatly nervous, Mrs Shepherd answered briefly Miss Shepherd's allusions to the beauty of the view. At the end of a long silence Miss Shepherd said –

'I think you know my brother, Major Shepherd.'

Mrs Shepherd hesitated, and then she said: 'No. I have never heard the name.'

'Are you sure? Of course, I may be mistaken; but –'

Ethel made pause, and looked Mrs Shepherd straight in the face. Smiling sadly, Mrs Shepherd said –

'Likenesses are so deceptive.'

'Perhaps, but my memory is pretty good for faces . . . It was two or three months ago, we were going up to London, and I saw my brother get into the train with a lady who looked like you. She really was very like you.'

Mrs Shepherd smiled and shook her head.

'I do not know the lady my brother was with, but I've often thought I should like to meet her.'

'Perhaps your brother will introduce you.'

'No, I don't think he will. She has come to live at Branbury, and now people talk more then ever. They say that he is secretly married.'

'And you believe it?'

'I don't see why it shouldn't be true. My brother is a good fellow in many ways, but, like all other men, he is selfish. He is just the man who would keep his wife hidden away in a lonely little lodging rather than admit that he had made a *mésalliance*. What I don't understand is why she consents to be kept out of the way. Just fancy giving up this beautiful place, these woods and fields, these gardens, that house for, for –'

'I suppose this woman gives up these things because she loves your brother. Do you not understand self-sacrifice?'

'Oh yes, if I loved a man . . . But I think a woman is silly to allow a man to cheat and fool her to the top of his bent.'

'What does it matter if she is happy?'

Ethel tossed her head. Then at the end of a long silence she said: 'Would you care to see the house?'

'No, thank you, Miss; I must be getting on. Goodbye.'

'You cannot get back that way, you must return through the pleasure-grounds. I'll walk with you. A headache kept me at home this afternoon. The others have gone to a tennis-party . . . It is a pity I was mistaken. I should like to meet the person my brother goes every day to Branbury to see. I should like to talk with her. My brother has, I'm afraid, persuaded her that we would not receive her. But this is not true; we should only be too glad to receive her. I have heard Father and Mother say so—not to Charles, they dare not speak to him on the subject, but they have to me.'

'Your brother must have some good reason for keeping his marriage secret. This woman may have a past.'

'Yes, they say that—but I should not care if I liked her, if I knew her to be a good woman now.'

To better keep the Major's secret, Mrs Shepherd had given up all friends, all acquaintance. She had not known a woman-friend for years, and the affinities of sex drew her to accept the sympathy with which she was tempted. The reaction of ten years of self-denial surged up within her, and she felt that she must speak, that her secret was being dragged from her. Ethel's eyes were fixed upon her—in another moment she would have spoken, but at that moment Nellie appeared climbing up the steep bank. 'Is that your little girl? Oh, what a pretty child!' Then raising her eyes from the child and looking the mother straight in the face, Ethel said—

'She is like, she is strangely like, Charles.'

Tears glistened in Mrs Shepherd's eyes, and then, no longer doubting that Mrs Shepherd would break down and in a flow of tears tell the whole story of her life, Ethel allowed a note of triumph to creep into her voice, and before she could stop herself she said, 'And that little girl is the heiress of Appleton Park.'

Mrs Shepherd's face changed expression.

'You are mistaken, Miss Shepherd,' she said; 'but if I ever meet your brother I will tell him that you think my little girl like him.'

Mrs Shepherd pursued her way slowly across the park, her long weary figure showing upon the sunset, her black dress trailing on the crisp grass. Often she was obliged to pause; the emotion and exercise of the day had brought back pain, and her whole body thrilled with it. Since the birth of her child she had lived in pain. But as she leaned against the white gate, and looked back on the beautiful park never to be seen by her again, knowledge of her sacrifice quickened within her – the house and the park, and the manner and speech of the young girl, combined to help her to a full appreciation of all she had surrendered. She regretted nothing. However mean and obscure her life had been, it had contained at least one noble moment. Nellie pursued the dragonflies; Mrs Shepherd followed slowly, feeling like a victor in a great battle. She had not broken her trust; she had kept her promise intact; she would return to London tomorrow or next day, or at the end of the week, whenever the Major wished.

He was waiting for them at the corner of the lane, and Nellie was already telling him all she thought of the house, the woods, the flowers, and the lady who had sat down by Mother on the bench above the river. The Major looked at his wife in doubt and fear; her smile, however, reassured him. Soon after, Nellie fell asleep, and while she dreamed of butterflies and flowers Mrs Shepherd told him what had passed between her and his sister in the beechwood above the river.

'You see, what I told you was right. Your appearance has been described to them; they suspect something, and will never cease worrying until they have found out everything. I'm not a bit surprised. Ethel always was the more cunning and the more spiteful of the two.'

Mrs Shepherd did not tell him how nearly she had been betrayed into confession. She felt that he would not understand her explanation of the mood in which his sister had caught her. Men understand women so little. To tell him would be merely to destroy his confidence in her. As they drove through the twilight, with Nellie fast asleep between, he spoke of her departure, which he had arranged for the end of the week, and then, putting his arm round her waist, he said: 'You have always been a good little woman to me.'

THE SOLID GOLD REEF
COMPANY, LIMITED

(*In Deacon's Orders and Other Stories*, New York: Harper and Bros.,
1895)

Act I

'You dear old boy,' said the girl, 'I am sure I wish it could be, with
all my heart, if I have any heart.'

'I don't believe you have,' replied the boy gloomily.

'Well, but, Reg, consider; you've got no money.'

'I've got five thousand pounds. If a man can't make his way
upon that he must be a poor stick.'

'You would go abroad with it and dig, and take your wife with
you – to wash and cook.'

'We would do something with the money here. You should stay
in London, Rosie.'

'Yes. In a suburban villa, at Shepherd's Bush, perhaps. No, Reg,
when I marry, if ever I do – I am in no hurry – I will step out of this
room into one exactly like it.' The room was a splendid drawing-
room in Palace Gardens, splendidly furnished. 'I shall have my
footmen and my carriage, and I shall –'

'Rosie, give me the right to earn all these things for you!' the
young man cried impetuously.

'You can only earn them for me by the time you have one foot in
the grave. Hadn't I better in the meantime marry some old
gentleman with his one foot in the grave, so as to be ready for you
against the time you come home? In two or three years the other
foot, I dare say, would slide into the grave as well.'

'You laugh at my trouble. You feel nothing.'

'If the pater would part, but he won't; he says he wants all his
money for himself, and that I've got to marry well. Besides, Reg' –
here her face clouded and she lowered her voice – 'there are times
when he looks anxious. We didn't always live in Palace Gardens.

Suppose we should lose it all as quickly as we got it. Oh!' she shivered and trembled. 'No, I will never, never marry a poor man. Get rich, my dear boy, and you may aspire even to the valuable possession of this heartless hand.'

She held it out. He took it, pressed it, stooped and kissed her. Then he dropped her hand and walked quickly out of the room.

'Poor Reggie!' she murmured. 'I wish – I wish – but what is the use of wishing?'

Act II

Two men – one young, the other about fifty – sat in the veranda of a small bungalow. It was after breakfast. They lay back in long bamboo chairs, each with a cigar. It looked as if they were resting. In reality they were talking business, and that very seriously.

'Yes, sir,' said the elder man, with something of an American accent, 'I have somehow taken a fancy to this place. The situation is healthy.'

'Well, I don't know; I've had more than one touch of fever here.'

'The climate is lovely —'

'Except in the rains.'

'The soil is fertile —'

'I've dropped five thousand in it, and they haven't come up again yet.'

'They will. I have been round the estate, and I see money in it. Well, sir, here's my offer: five thousand down, hard cash, as soon as the papers are signed.'

Reginald sat up. He was on the point of accepting the proposal, when a pony rode up to the house, and the rider, a native groom, jumped off and gave him a note. He opened it and read. It was from his nearest neighbour, two or three miles away:

Don't sell that man your estate. Gold has been found. The whole country is full of gold. Hold on. He's an assayer. If he offers to buy, be quite sure that he has found gold on your land.

F. G.

He put the note into his pocket, gave a verbal message to the

boy, and turned to his guest, without betraying the least astonishment or emotion.

'I beg your pardon. The note was from Bellamy, my next
neighbour. Well? You were saying —'

'Only that I have taken a fancy – perhaps a foolish fancy – to
this place of yours, and I'll give you, if you like, all that you have
spent upon it.'

'Well,' he replied reflectively, but with a little twinkle in his
eye, 'that seems handsome. But the place isn't really worth the
half that I spent upon it. Anybody would tell you that. Come, let
us be honest, whatever we are. I'll tell you a better way. We will
put the matter into the hands of Bellamy. He knows what a
coffee plantation is worth. He shall name a price, and if we can
agree upon that, we will make a deal of it.'

The other man changed colour. He wanted to settle the thing
at once as between gentlemen. What need of third parties? But
Reginald stood firm, and he presently rode away, quite sure
that in a day or two this planter, too, would have heard the
news.

A month later, the young coffee-planter stood on the deck of a
steamer homeward bound. In his pocket-book was a plan of his
auriferous estate; in a bag hanging round his neck was a small
collection of yellow nuggets; in his boxes was a chosen assort-
ment of quartz.

Act III

'Well, sir,' said the financier, 'you've brought this thing to me.
You want my advice. Well, my advice is, don't fool away the
only good thing that will ever happen to you. Luck such as this
doesn't come more than once in a lifetime.'

'I have been offered ten thousand pounds for my estate.'

'Oh! Have you! Ten thousand? That was very liberal – very
liberal indeed. Ten thousand for a gold reef!'

'But I thought as an old friend of my father you would,
perhaps —'

'Young man, don't fool it away. He's waiting for you, I
suppose, round the corner, with a bottle of fizz, ready to close.'

'He is.'

'Well, go and drink his champagne. Always get whatever you can. And then tell him that you'll see him —'

'I certainly will, sir, if you advise it. And then?'

'And then – leave it to me. And, young man, I think I heard, a year or two ago, something about you and my girl Rosie.'

'There was something, sir. Not enough to trouble you about it.'

'She told me. Rosie tells me all her love affairs.'

'Is she – is she unmarried?'

'Oh, yes! and for the moment I believe she is free. She has had one or two engagements, but, somehow, they have come to nothing. There was the French count, but that was knocked on the head very early in consequence of things discovered. And there was the Boom in Guano, but he fortunately smashed, much to Rosie's joy, because she never liked him. The last was Lord Evergreen. He was a nice old chap when you could understand what he said, and Rosie would have liked the title very much, though his grandchildren opposed the thing. Well, sir, I suppose you couldn't understand the trouble we took to keep that old man alive for his own wedding. Science did all it could, but 'twas of no use —' The financier sighed. 'The ways of Providence are inscrutable. He died, sir, the day before.'

'That was very sad.'

'A dashing of the cup from the lip, sir. My daughter would have been a countess. Well, young gentleman, about this estate of yours. I think I see a way – I think, I am not yet sure – that I do see a way. Go now. See this liberal gentleman, and drink his champagne. And come here in a week. Then, if I still see my way, you shall understand what it means to hold the position in the City which is mine.'

'And – and – may I call upon Rosie!'

'Not till this day week – not till I have made my way plain.'

Act IV

'And so it means this. Oh, Rosie, you look lovelier than ever, and I'm as happy as a king. It means this. Your father is the greatest genius in the world. He buys my property for sixty thousand pounds – sixty thousand. That's over two thousand a year for me, and he makes a company out of it with a hundred and fifty thousand capital. He says that, taking ten thousand out of it for expenses, there will be a profit of eighty thousand. And all that he gives to you – eighty thousand, that's three thousand a year for you; and sixty thousand, that's two more, my dearest Rosie. You remember what you said, that when you married you should step out of one room like this into another just as good?'

'Oh, Reggie,' she sank upon his bosom – 'you know I never could love anybody but you. It's true I was engaged to old Lord Evergreen, but that was only because he had one foot – you know – and when the other foot went in too, just a day too soon, I actually laughed. So the pater is going to make a company of it, is he? Well, I hope he won't put any of his own money into it, I'm sure, because of late all the companies have turned out so badly.'

'But, my child, the place is full of gold.'

'Then why did he turn it into a company, my dear boy? And why didn't he make you stick to it? But you know nothing of the City. Now, let us sit down and talk about what we shall do – don't, you ridiculous boy!'

Act V

Another house just like the first. The bride stepped out of one palace into another. With their five or six thousand a year, the young couple could just manage to make both ends meet. The husband was devoted; the wife had everything that she could wish. Who could be happier than this pair in a nest so luxurious, their life so padded, their days so full of sunshine?

It was a year after marriage. The wife, contrary to her usual custom, was the first at breakfast. A few letters were waiting for her – chiefly invitations. She opened and read them. Among them lay one addressed to her husband. Not looking at the address, she opened and read that as well:

Dear Reginald:

I venture to address you as an old friend of your own and school-fellow of your mother's. I am a widow with four children. My husband was the vicar of your old parish – you remember him and me. I was left with a little income of about two hundred a year. Twelve months ago I was persuaded in order to double my income

– a thing which seemed certain from the prospectus – to invest everything in a new and rich gold mine. Everything. And the mine has never paid anything. The company – it is called the Solid Gold Reef Company, is in liquidation because, though there is really the gold there, it costs too much to get it. I have no relatives anywhere to help me. Unless I can get assistance my children and I must go at once – tomorrow – into the workhouse. Yes, we are paupers. I am ruined by the cruel lies of that prospectus, and the wickedness which deluded me, and I know not how many others, out of my money. I have been foolish, and am punished; but those people, who will punish them? Help me, if you can, my dear Reginald. Oh! for *GOD'S* sake, help my children and me. Help your mother's friend, your own old friend.

'This,' said Rosie meditatively, 'is exactly the kind of thing to make Reggie uncomfortable. Why, it might make him unhappy all day. Better burn it.' She dropped the letter into the fire. 'He's an impulsive, emotional nature, and he doesn't understand the City. If people are so foolish — What a lot of fibs the poor old pater does tell, to be sure! He's a regular novelist — Oh! here you are, you lazy boy!'

'Kiss me, Rosie.' He looked as handsome as Apollo, and as cheerful. 'I wish all the world were as happy as you and me. Heigho! some poor devils, I'm afraid —'

'Tea or coffee, Reg?'

Henry James

THE TREE OF KNOWLEDGE

(*The Soft Side*, London: Methuen and Co., 1900)

I

It was one of the secret opinions, such as we all have, of Peter Brench that his main success in life would have consisted in his never having committed himself about the work, as it was called, of his friend Morgan Mallow. This was a subject on which it was, to the best of his belief, impossible with veracity to quote him, and it was nowhere on record that he had, in the connexion, on any occasion and in any embarrassment, either lied or spoken the truth. Such a triumph had its honour even for a man of other triumphs – a man who had reached fifty, who had escaped marriage, who had lived within his means, who had been in love with Mrs Mallow for years without breathing it, and who, last but not least, had judged himself once for all. He had so judged himself in fact that he felt an extreme and general humility to be his proper portion; yet there was nothing that made him think so well of his parts as the course he had steered so often through the shallows just mentioned. It became thus a real wonder that the friends in whom he had most confidence were just those with whom he had most reserves. He couldn't tell Mrs Mallow – or at least he supposed, excellent man, he couldn't – that she was the one beautiful reason he had never married; any more than he could tell her husband that the sight of the multiplied marbles in that gentleman's studio was an affliction of which even time had never blunted the edge. His victory, however, as I have intimated, in regard to these productions, was not simply in his not having let it out that he deplored them; it was, remarkably, in his not having kept it in by anything else.

The whole situation, among these good people, was verily a marvel, and there was probably not such another for a long way from the spot that engages us – the point at which the soft declivity of Hampstead began at that time to confess in broken accents to Saint John's Wood. He despised Mallow's statues and adored Mallow's wife, and yet was distinctly fond of Mallow, to whom, in turn, he was equally dear. Mrs Mallow rejoiced in the statues – though she preferred, when pressed, the busts; and if she was visibly attached to Peter Brench it was because of his affection for Morgan. Each loved the other moreover for the love borne in each case to Lancelot, whom the Mallows respectively cherished as their only child and whom the friend of their fireside identified as the third – but decidedly the handsomest – of his godsons. Already in the old years it had come to that – that no one, for such a relation, could possibly have occurred to any of them, even to the baby itself, but Peter. There was luckily a certain independence, of the pecuniary sort, all round: the Master could never otherwise have spent his solemn *Wanderjahre* in Florence and Rome, and continued by the Thames as well as by the Arno and the Tiber to add unpurchased group to group and model, for what was too apt to prove in the event mere love, fancy-heads of celebrities either too busy or too buried – too much of the age or too little of it – to sit. Neither could Peter, lounging in almost daily, have found time to keep the whole complicated tradition so alive by his presence. He was massive but mild, the depositary of these mysteries – large and loose and ruddy and curly, with deep tones, deep eyes, deep pockets, to say nothing of the habit of long pipes, soft hats and brownish greyish weather-faded clothes, apparently always the same.

He had 'written', it was known, but had never spoken, never spoken in particular of that; and he had the air (since, as was believed, he continued to write) of keeping it up in order to have something more – as if he hadn't at the worst enough – to be silent about. Whatever his air, at any rate, Peter's occasional unmentioned prose and verse were quite truly the result of an impulse to maintain the purity of his taste by establishing still more firmly the right relation of fame to feebleness. The little green door of his domain was in a garden-wall on which the discoloured stucco made patches, and in the small detached villa behind it everything was old, the furniture, the servants, the books, the prints, the immemorial habits and the new improvements. The Mallows, at

Carrara Lodge, were within ten minutes, and the studio there was on their little land, to which they had added, in their happy faith, for building it. This was the good fortune, if it was not the ill, of her having brought him in marriage a portion that put them in a manner at their ease and enabled them thus, on their side, to keep it up. And they did keep it up – they always had – the infatuated sculptor and his wife, for whom nature had refined on the impossible by relieving them of the sense of the difficult. Morgan had at all events everything of the sculptor but the spirit of Phidias – the brown velvet, the becoming *beretto*, the 'plastic' presence, the fine fingers, the beautiful accent in Italian and the old Italian factotum. He seemed to make up for everything when he addressed Egidio with the 'tu' and waved him to turn one of the rotary pedestals of which the place was full. They were tremendous Italians at Carrara Lodge, and the secret of the part played by this fact in Peter's life was in a large degree that it gave him, sturdy Briton as he was, just the amount of 'going abroad' he could bear. The Mallows were all his Italy, but it was in a measure for Italy he liked them. His one worry was that Lance – to which they had shortened his godson – was, in spite of a public school, perhaps a shade too Italian. Morgan meanwhile looked like somebody's flattering idea of somebody's own person as expressed in the great room provided at the Uffizi Museum for the general illustration of that idea by eminent hands. The Master's sole regret that he hadn't been born rather to the brush than to the chisel sprang from his wish that he might have contributed to that collection.

It appeared with time at any rate to be to the brush that Lance had been born; for Mrs Mallow, one day when the boy was turning twenty, broke it to their friend, who shared, to the last delicate morsel, their problems and pains, that it seemed as if nothing would really do but that he should embrace the career. It had been impossible longer to remain blind to the fact that he was gaining no glory at Cambridge, where Brench's own college had for a year tempered its tone to him as for Brench's own sake. Therefore why renew the vain form of preparing him for the impossible? The impossible – it had become clear – was that he should be anything but an artist.

'Oh dear, dear!' said poor Peter.

'Don't you believe in it?' asked Mrs Mallow, who still, at more than forty, had her violet velvet eyes, her creamy satin skin and her silken chestnut hair.

'Believe in what?'

'Why in Lance's passion.'

'I don't know what you mean by "believing in it". I've never been unaware, certainly, of his disposition, from his earliest time, to daub and draw; but I confess I've hoped it would burn out.'

'But why should it,' she sweetly smiled, 'with his wonderful heredity? Passion is passion – though of course indeed *you*, dear Peter, know nothing of that. Has the Master's ever burned out?'

Peter looked off a little and, in his familiar formless way, kept up for a moment, a sound between a smothered whistle and a subdued hum. 'Do you think he's going to be another Master?'

She seemed scarce prepared to go that length, yet she had on the whole a marvellous trust. 'I know what you mean by that. Will it be a career to incur the jealousies and provoke the machinations that have been at times almost too much for his father? Well – say it may be, since nothing but clap-trap, in these dreadful days, *can*, it would seem, make its way, and since, with the curse of refinement and distinction, one may easily find one's self begging one's bread. Put it at the worst – say he *has* the misfortune to wing his flight further than the vulgar taste of his stupid countrymen can follow. Think, all the same, of the happiness – the same the Master has had. He'll *know*.'

Peter looked rueful. 'Ah but *what* will he know?'

'Quiet joy!' cried Mrs Mallow, quite impatient and turning away.

II

He had of course before long to meet the boy himself on it and to hear that practically everything was settled. Lance was not to go up again, but to go instead to Paris where, since the die was cast, he would find the best advantages. Peter had always felt he must be taken as he was, but had never perhaps found him so much of that pattern as on this occasion. 'You chuck Cambridge then altogether? Doesn't that seem rather a pity?'

Lance would have been like his father, to his friend's sense, had he had less humour, and like his mother had he had more beauty. Yet it was a good middle way for Peter that, in the modern manner, he was, to the eye, rather the young stock-broker than the young artist. The youth reasoned that it was a question of time – there was such a mill to go through, such an awful lot to learn. He had talked with fellows and had judged. 'One has got, today,' he said, 'don't you see? to know.'

His interlocutor, at this, gave a groan. 'Oh hang it, *don't* know!'

Lance wondered. '"Don't"? Then what's the use – ?'

'The use of what?'

'Why of anything. Don't you think I've talent?'

Peter smoked away for a little in silence; then went on: 'It isn't knowledge, it's ignorance that – as we've been beautifully told – is bliss.'

'Don't you think I've talent?' Lance repeated.

Peter, with his trick of queer kind demonstrations, passed his arm round his godson and held him a moment. 'How do I know?'

'Oh,' said the boy, 'if it's your own ignorance you're defending – !'

Again, for a pause, on the sofa, his godfather smoked. 'It isn't. I've the misfortune to be omniscient.'

'Oh well,' Lance laughed again, 'if you know *too* much – !'

'That's what I do, and it's why I'm so wretched.'

Lance's gaiety grew. 'Wretched? Come, I say!'

'But I forgot,' his companion went on – 'you're not to know about that. It would indeed for you too make the too much. Only I'll tell you what I'll do.' And Peter got up from the sofa. 'If you'll go up again I'll pay your way at Cambridge.'

Lance stared, a little rueful in spite of being still more amused. 'Oh Peter! You disapprove so of Paris?'

'Well, I'm afraid of it.'

'Ah I see!'

'No, you don't see – yet. But you will – that is you would. And you mustn't.'

The young man thought more gravely. 'But one's innocence, already – !'

'Is considerably damaged? Ah that won't matter,' Peter persisted – 'we'll patch it up here.'

'Here? Then you want me to stay at home?'

Peter almost confessed to it. 'Well, we're so right – we four together – just as we are. We're so safe. Come, don't spoil it.'

The boy, who had turned to gravity, turned from this, on the real pressure of his friend's tone, to consternation. 'Then what's a fellow to be?'

'My particular care. Come, old man' – and Peter now fairly pleaded – '*I'll* look out for you.'

Lance, who had remained on the sofa with his legs out and his hands in his pockets, watched him with eyes that showed suspicion. Then he got up. 'You think there's something the matter with me – that I can't make a success.'

'Well, what do you call a success?'

Lance thought again. 'Why the best sort, I suppose, is to please one's self. Isn't that the sort that, in spite of cabals and things, is – in his own peculiar line – the Master's?'

There were so much too many things in this question to be answered at once that they practically checked the discussion, which became particularly difficult in the light of such renewed proof that, though the young man's innocence might, in the course of his studies, as he contended, somewhat have shrunken, the finer essence of it still remained. That was indeed exactly what Peter had assumed and what above all he desired; yet perversely enough it gave him a chill. The boy believed in the cabals and things, believed in the peculiar line, believed, to be brief, in the Master. What happened a month or two later wasn't that he went up again at the expense of his godfather, but that a fortnight after he had got settled in Paris this personage sent him fifty pounds.

He had meanwhile at home, this personage, made up his mind to the worst; and what that might be had never yet grown quite so vivid to him as when, on his presenting himself one Sunday night, as he never failed to do, for supper, the mistress of Carrara Lodge met him with an appeal as to – of all things in the world – the wealth of the Canadians. She was earnest, she was even excited. 'Are many of them *really* rich?'

He had to confess he knew nothing about them, but he often thought afterwards of that evening. The room in which they sat was adorned with sundry specimens of the Master's genius, which had the merit of being, as Mrs Mallow herself frequently suggested, of an unusually convenient size. They were indeed of dimensions not customary in the products of the chisel, and they had the singularity that, if the objects and features intended to be small looked too large, the objects and features intended to be large looked too small. The Master's idea, either in respect to this matter or to any other, had in almost any case, even after years, remained undiscoverable to Peter Brench. The creations that so failed to reveal it stood about on pedestals and brackets, on tables and shelves, a little staring white population, heroic, idyllic, allegoric, mythic, symbolic, in which 'scale' had so strayed and lost itself that the public square and the chimney-piece seemed to have changed places, the monumental being all diminutive and the diminutive all monumental; branches at any rate, markedly, of a family in which stature was rather oddly irrespective of function, age and sex. They formed, like the Mallows themselves, poor Brench's own family – having at least to such a degree the note of familiarity. The occasion was one of those he had long ago learnt to know and to name – short flickers of the faint flame, soft gusts of a kinder air. Twice a year regularly the Master believed in his fortune, in addition to believing all the year round in his genius. This time it was to be made by a bereaved couple from Toronto, who had given him the handsomest order for a tomb to three lost children, each of whom they desired to see, in the composition, emblematically and characteristically represented.

Such was naturally the moral of Mrs Mallow's question: if their wealth was to be assumed, it was clear, from the nature of their admiration, as well as from mysterious hints thrown out (they were a little odd!) as to other possibilities of the same mortuary sort, what their further patronage might be; and not less evident that should the Master become at all known in those climes nothing would be more inevitable than a run of Canadian custom. Peter had been present before at runs of custom, colonial and domestic – present at each of those of which the aggregation had left so few gaps in the marble company round him; but it was his habit never at these junctures to prick the bubble in advance. The fond illusion, while it lasted, eased the wound of elections never won, the long ache of medals and diplomas carried off, on every chance, by everyone but the Master; it moreover lighted the lamp that would glimmer through the next eclipse. They lived, however, after all – as it was always beautiful to see – at a height scarce susceptible of ups and downs. They strained a point at times charmingly, strained it to admit that the public was here and there not too bad to buy; but they would have been nowhere without their attitude that the Master was always too good to sell. They were at all events deliciously formed, Peter often said to himself, for their fate; the Master had a vanity, his wife had a loyalty, of which success, depriving these things of innocence, would have diminished the merit and the grace. Anyone could be charming under a charm, and as he looked about him at a world of prosperity more void of proportion even than the Master's museum he wondered if he knew another pair that so completely escaped vulgarity.

'What a pity Lance isn't with us to rejoice!' Mrs Mallow on this occasion sighed at supper.

'We'll drink to the health of the absent,' her husband replied, filling his friend's glass and his own and giving a drop to their companion; 'but we must hope he's preparing himself for a happiness much less like this of ours this evening – excusable as I grant it to be! – than like the comfort we have always (whatever has happened or has not happened) been able to trust ourselves to enjoy. The comfort,' the Master explained, leaning back in the pleasant lamplight and firelight, holding up his glass and looking round at his marble family, quartered more or less, a monstrous brood, in every room – 'the comfort of art in itself!'

Peter looked a little shyly at his wine. 'Well – I don't care what you may call it when a fellow doesn't – but Lance must learn to *sell*, you know. I drink to his acquisition of the secret of a base popularity!'

'Oh yes, *he* must sell,' the boy's mother, who was still more, however, this seemed to give out, the Master's wife, rather artlessly allowed.

'Ah,' the sculptor after a moment confidently pronounced, 'Lance *will*. Don't be afraid. He'll have learnt.'

'Which is exactly what Peter,' Mrs Mallow gaily returned – 'why in the world were you so perverse, Peter? – wouldn't, when he told him, hear of.'

Peter, when this lady looked at him with accusatory affection – a grace on her part not infrequent – could never find a word; but the Master, who was always all amenity and tact, helped him out now as he had often helped him before. 'That's his old idea, you know – on which we've so often differed: his theory that the artist should be all impulse and instinct. *I* go in of course for a certain amount of school. Not too much – but a due proportion. There's where his protest came in,' he continued to explain to his wife, 'against what *might*, don't you see? be in question for Lance.'

'Ah well' – and Mrs Mallow turned the violet eyes across the table at the subject of this discourse – 'he's sure to have meant of course nothing but good. Only that wouldn't have prevented him, if Lance *had* taken his advice, from being in effect horribly cruel.'

They had a sociable way of talking of him to his face as if he had been in the clay or – at most – in the plaster, and the Master was unfailingly generous. He might have been waving Egidio to make him revolve. 'Ah but poor Peter wasn't so wrong as to what it may after all come to that he *will* learn.'

'Oh but nothing artistically bad,' she urged – still, for poor Peter, arch and dewy.

'Why just the little French tricks,' said the Master: on which their friend had to pretend to admit, when pressed by Mrs Mallow, that these æsthetic vices had been the objects of his dread.

III

'I know now,' Lance said to him the next year, 'why you were so much against it.' He had come back supposedly for a mere interval and was looking about him at Carrara Lodge, where indeed he had already on two or three occasions since his expatriation briefly reappeared. This had the air of a longer holiday. 'Something rather awful has happened to me. It *isn't* so very good to know.'

'I'm bound to say high spirits don't show in your face,' Peter was rather ruefully forced to confess. 'Still, are you very sure you do know?'

'Well, I at least know about as much as I can bear.' These remarks were exchanged in Peter's den, and the young man, smoking cigarettes, stood before the fire with his back against the mantel. Something of his bloom seemed really to have left him.

Poor Peter wondered. 'You're clear then as to what in particular I wanted you not to go for?'

'In particular?' Lance thought. 'It seems to me that in particular there can have been only one thing.'

They stood for a little sounding each other. 'Are you quite sure?'

'Quite sure I'm a beastly duffer? Quite – by this time.'

'Oh!' – and Peter turned away as if almost with relief.

'It's *that* that isn't pleasant to find out.'

'Oh I don't care for "that",' said Peter, presently coming round again. 'I mean I personally don't.'

'Yet I hope you can understand a little that I myself should!'

'Well, what do you mean by it?' Peter sceptically asked.

And on this Lance had to explain – how the upshot of his studies in Paris had inexorably proved a mere deep doubt of his means. These studies had so waked him up that a new light was in his eyes; but what the new light did was really to show him too much. 'Do you know what's the matter with me? I'm too horribly intelligent. Paris was really the last place for me. I've learnt what I can't do.'

Poor Peter stared – it was a staggerer; but even after they had had, on the subject, a longish talk in which the boy brought out to the full the hard truth of his lesson, his friend betrayed less pleasure than usually breaks into a face to the happy tune of 'I told you so!' Poor Peter himself made now indeed so little a point of having told him so that Lance broke ground in a different place a day or two after. 'What was it then that – before I went – you were afraid I should find out?' This, however, Peter refused to tell him – on the ground that if he hadn't yet guessed perhaps he never would, and that in any case nothing at all for either of them was to be gained by giving the thing a name. Lance eyed him on this an instant with the bold curiosity of youth – with the air indeed of having in his mind two or three names, of which one or other would be right. Peter nevertheless, turning his back again, offered no encouragement, and when they parted afresh it was with some show of impatience on the side of the boy. Accordingly on their next encounter Peter saw at a glance that he had now, in the interval, divined and that, to sound his note, he was only waiting till they should find themselves alone. This he had soon arranged and he then broke straight out. 'Do you know your conundrum has been keeping me awake? But in the watches of the night the answer came over me – so that, upon my honour, I quite laughed out. Had you been supposing I had to go to Paris to learn *that*?' Even now, to see him still so sublimely on his guard, Peter's young friend had to laugh afresh. 'You won't give a sign till you're sure? Beautiful old Peter!' But Lance at last produced it. 'Why, hang it, the truth about the Master.'

It made between them for some minutes a lively passage, full of wonder for each at the wonder of the other. 'Then how long have you understood –'

'The true value of his work? I understood it,' Lance recalled, 'as soon as I began to understand anything. But I didn't begin fully to do that, I admit, till I got *là-bas*.'

'Dear, dear!' – Peter gasped with retrospective dread.

'But for what have you taken me? I'm a hopeless muff – that I *had* to have rubbed in. But I'm not such a muff as the Master!' Lance declared.

'Then why did you never tell me – ?'

'That I hadn't, after all' – the boy took him up – 'remained such an idiot? Just because I never dreamed *you* knew. But I beg your pardon. I only wanted to spare you. And what I don't now understand is how the deuce then for so long you've managed to keep bottled.'

Peter produced his explanation, but only after some delay and with a gravity not void of embarrassment. 'It was for your mother.'

'Oh!' said Lance.

'And that's the great thing now – since the murder *is* out. I want a promise from you. I mean' – and Peter almost feverishly followed it up – 'a vow from you, solemn and such as you owe me here on the spot, that you'll sacrifice anything rather than let her ever guess –'

'That *I've* guessed?' – Lance took it in. 'I see.' He evidently after a moment had taken in much. 'But what is it you've in mind that I may have a chance to sacrifice?'

'Oh one has always something.'

Lance looked at him hard. 'Do you mean that *you've* had – ?' The look he received back, however, so put the question by that he found soon enough another. 'Are you really sure my mother doesn't know?'

Peter, after renewed reflexion, was really sure. 'If she does she's too wonderful.'

'But aren't we all too wonderful?'

'Yes,' Peter granted – 'but in different ways. The thing's so desperately important because your father's little public consists only, as you know then,' Peter developed – 'well, of how many?'

'First of all,' the Master's son risked, 'of himself. And last of all too. I don't quite see of whom else.'

Peter had an approach to impatience. 'Of your mother, I say – *always*.'

Lance cast it all up. 'You absolutely feel that?'

'Absolutely.'

'Well then with yourself that makes three.'

'Oh *me*!' – and Peter, with a wag of his kind old head, modestly excused himself. 'The number's at any rate small enough for any individual dropping out to be too dreadfully missed. Therefore, to put it in a nutshell, take care, my boy – that's all – that *you're* not!'

'I've got to keep on humbugging?' Lance wailed.

'It's just to warn you of the danger of your failing of that that I've seized this opportunity.'

'And what do you regard in particular,' the young man asked, 'as the danger?'

'Why this certainty: that the moment your mother, who feels so strongly, should suspect your secret – well,' said Peter desperately, 'the fat would be on the fire.'

Lance for a moment seemed to stare at the blaze. 'She'd throw me over?'

'She'd throw *him* over.'

'And come round to us?'

Peter, before he answered, turned away. 'Come round to *you*.' But he had said enough to indicate – and, as he evidently trusted, to avert – the horrid contingency.

IV

Within six months again, none the less, his fear was on more occasions than one all before him. Lance had returned to Paris for another trial; then had reappeared at home and had had, with his father, for the first time in his life, one of the scenes that strike sparks. He described it with much expression to Peter, touching whom (since they had never done so before) it was the sign of a new reserve on the part of the pair at Carrara Lodge that they at present failed, on a matter of intimate interest, to open themselves – if not in joy then in sorrow – to their good friend. This produced perhaps practically between the parties a shade of alienation and a slight intermission of commerce – marked mainly indeed by the fact that to talk at his ease with his old playmate Lance had in general to come to see him. The closest if not quite the gayest relation they had yet known together was thus ushered in. The difficulty for poor Lance was a tension at home – begotten by the fact that his father wished him to be at least the sort of success he himself had been. He hadn't 'chucked' Paris – though nothing appeared more vivid to him than that Paris had chucked him: he would go back again because of the fascination in trying, in seeing, in sounding the depths – in learning one's lesson, briefly, even if the lesson were simply that of one's impotence in the presence of one's larger vision. But what did the Master, all aloft in his senseless fluency, know of impotence, and what vision – to be called such – had he in all his blind life ever had? Lance, heated and indignant, frankly appealed to his godparent on this score.

His father, it appeared, had come down on him for having, after so long, nothing to show, and hoped that on his next return this deficiency would be repaired. *The* thing, the Master complacently set forth was – for any artist, however inferior to himself – at least to 'do' something. 'What can you do? That's all I ask!' *He* had certainly done enough, and there was no mistake about what he had to show. Lance had tears in his eyes when it came thus to letting his old friend know how great the strain might be on the 'sacrifice' asked of him. It wasn't so easy to continue humbugging – as from son to parent – after feeling one's self despised for not grovelling in mediocrity. Yet a noble duplicity was what, as they intimately faced the situation, Peter went on requiring; and it was still for a time what his young friend, bitter and sore, managed loyally to comfort him with. Fifty pounds more than once again, it was true, rewarded both in London and in Paris the young friend's loyalty; none the less sensibly, doubtless, at the moment, that the money was a direct advance on a decent sum for which Peter had long since privately prearranged an ultimate function. Whether by these arts or others, at all events, Lance's just resentment was kept for a season – but only for a season – at bay. The day arrived when he warned his companion that he could hold out – or hold in – no longer. Carrara Lodge had had to listen to another lecture delivered from a great height – an infliction really heavier at last than, without striking back or in some way letting the Master have the truth, flesh and blood could bear.

'And what I don't see is,' Lance observed with a certain irritated eye for what was after all, if it came to that, owing to himself too; 'what I don't see is, upon my honour, how *you*, as things are going, can keep the game up.'

'Oh the game for me is only to hold my tongue,' said placid Peter. 'And I have my reason.'

'Still my mother?'

Peter showed a queer face as he had often shown it before – that is by turning it straight away. 'What will you have? I haven't ceased to like her.'

'She's beautiful – she's a dear of course,' Lance allowed; 'but what is she to you, after all, and what is it to you that, as to anything whatever, she should or she shouldn't?'

Peter, who had turned red, hung fire a little. 'Well – it's all simply what I make of it.'

There was now, however, in his young friend a strange, an adopted insistence. 'What are you after all to *her*?'

'Oh nothing. But that's another matter.'

'She cares only for my father,' said Lance the Parisian.

'Naturally – and that's just why.'

'Why you've wished to spare her?'

'Because she cares so tremendously much.'

Lance took a turn about the room, but with his eyes still on his host. 'How awfully – always – you must have liked her!'

'Awfully. Always,' said Peter Brench.

The young man continued for a moment to muse – then stopped again in front of him. 'Do you know how much she cares?' Their eyes met on it, but Peter, as if his own found something new in Lance's, appeared to hesitate, for the first time in an age, to say he did know. '*I've* only just found out,' said Lance. 'She came to my room last night, after being present, in silence and only with her eyes on me, at what I had had to take from him: she came – and she was with me an extraordinary hour.'

He had paused again and they had again for a while sounded each other. Then something – and it made him suddenly turn pale – came to Peter. 'She *does* know?'

'She does know. She let it all out to me – so as to demand of me no more than "that", as she said, of which she herself had been capable. She has always, always known,' said Lance without pity.

Peter was silent a long time; during which his companion might have heard him gently breathe, and on touching him might have felt within him the vibration of a long low sound suppressed. By the time he spoke at last he had taken everything in. 'Then I do see how tremendously much.'

'Isn't it wonderful?' Lance asked.

'Wonderful,' Peter mused.

'So that if your original effort to keep me from Paris was to keep me from knowledge – !' Lance exclaimed as if with a sufficient indication of this futility.

It might have been at the futility Peter appeared for a little to gaze. 'I think it must have been – without my quite at the time knowing it – to keep *me*!' he replied at last as he turned away.

Select Bibliography

This listing of scholarly books, covering a wide range of topics in history and in literary criticism, provides a perspective on major works written during the past quarter-century with direct relevance to the problems dramatized in the short stories of this anthology.

Nina Auerbach. *Communities of Woman: An Idea in Fiction* (Cambridge, Mass.: Harvard University Press, 1978)

—— *Women and the Demon* (Cambridge, Mass.: Harvard University Press, 1982)

—— *Romantic Imprisonment: Women and Other Glorified Outcasts* (New York: Columbia University Press, 1985)

Mary Ritter Beard. *Women as a Force in History: A Study in Traditions and Realities* (New York: Macmillan, 1946)

Penny Boumelha. *Thomas Hardy and Women: Sexual Ideology and Narrative Form* (Brighton: Harvester Press, 1982)

N. Boyd. *Josephine Butler, Octavia Hill, Florence Nightingale: Three Victorian Women Who Changed Their World* (London: Macmillan, 1982)

P. Branca. *Silent Sisterhood: Middle-Class Women in the Victorian Home* (London: Croom Helm, 1975)

Richard Brickman, Susan McDonald, and Myra Stark, eds. *Corrupt Relations: Dickens, Thackeray, Trollope, Collins and the Victorian Sexual System* (New York: Columbia University Press, 1982)

Rachel M. Brownstein. *Becoming a Heroine: Reading about Women in Novels* (New York: Viking Press, 1982)

M. Bryant. *The Unexpected Revolution: A Study of the Education of Women and Girls in the Nineteenth Century* (London: University of London, 1980)

Joan N. Burstyn. *Victorian Education and the Ideal of Womanhood* (London: Croom Helm, 1980)

Tess Cosslett. *Woman to Woman: Female Friendship in Victorian Fiction* (Brighton: Harvester, 1988)

Gail Cunningham. *The New Woman and the Victorian Novel* (London: Macmillan, 1978)

Deirdre David. *Intellectual Women and Victorian Patriarchy: Harriet Martineau, Elizabeth Barrett Browning and George Eliot* (London and Ithaca, N.Y.: Macmillan and Cornell University Press, 1987)

Leonore Davidoff. *The Best Circles: Women and Society in Victorian England* (London: Croom Helm, 1973)

Sara Delamont and Lorna Duffin. *The Nineteenth-Century Woman: Her Cultural and Physical World* (London: Croom Helm, 1978)

Carol Dyhouse. *Girls Growing up in Late Victorian and Edwardian England* (London: Routledge and Kegan Paul, 1981)

Lee Edwards. *Psyche as Hero: Female Heroism and Fictional Form* (Middletown, CT: Wesleyan University Press, 1984)

Sarah Eisenstein. *Give Us Bread but Give Us Roses* (London: Routledge and Kegan Paul, 1983)

S. Fletcher. *Feminists and Bureaucrats: A Study in the Development of Girls' Education in the Nineteenth Century* (Cambridge: Cambridge University Press, 1980)

Sandra Gilbert and Susan Gubar. *The Madwoman in the Attic: The Woman Writer and the Nineteenth-Century Literary Imagination* (New Haven, CT: Yale University Press, 1979)

Sander L. Gilman. *Difference and Pathology: Stereotypes of Sexuality, Race, and Madness* (Ithaca, N.Y.: Cornell University Press, 1985)

D. Gorhan. *The Victorian Girl and the Feminine Ideal* (London: Croom Helm, 1982)

Mary S. Hartmann and Louis W. Banner, eds. *Clio's Consciousness Raised: New Perspectives on the History of Women* (New York: Harper and Row, 1974)

Carolyn Heilbrun and M. Higgonet. *The Representation of Women in Fiction* (Baltimore, MD: Johns Hopkins University Press, 1982)

E. O. Hellerstein, L. P. Hume, and K. M. Offen. *Victorian Woman: A Documentary Account of Women's Lives in Nineteenth-Century England, France and the United States* (Stanford, CA: Stanford University Press, 1981)

Margaret Hewitt. *Wives and Mothers in Victorian Industry* (London: Rockliff, 1958)

Patricia Hollis. *Women in Public: The Women's Movement 1850–1900* (London: George Allen and Unwin, 1979)

Margaret Homans. *Bearing the Word: Language and Female Experience in Nineteenth-Century Women's Writing* (Chicago: University of Chicago Press, 1986)

Maggie Humm. *An Annotated Critical Bibliography of Feminist Criticism* (Hemel Hempstead and Boston: Harvester Press and G. K. Hall and Co., 1987)

Patricia Ingham. *Thomas Hardy* (Hemel Hempstead: Harvester Wheatsheaf, 1989)

Mary Jacobus, ed. *Women Writing and Writing about Women* (London: Croom Helm, 1979)

Pat Jalland. *Women, Marriage and Politics 1860–1914* (Oxford and New York: Oxford University Press, 1986)

Angela V. John, ed. *Unequal Opportunities: Women's Employment in England 1800–1918* (Oxford and New York: Basil Blackwell, 1986)

Jean Kennard. *Victims of Convention* (Hamden, CT: Archon Books, 1978)

Susan Kingsley Kent. *Sex and Suffrage in Britain, 1860–1914* (Princeton: Princeton University Press, 1987)

S. Lewenhak. *Women and Trade Unions: An Outline History of Women in the British Trade Union Movement* (London: Benn, 1977)

Jane Lewis, ed. *Labour and Love: Women's Experience of Home and Family 1850–1940* (Oxford and New York: Basil Blackwell, 1986)

J. Liddington and J. Norris. *One Hand Tied behind Us: The Rise of the Women's Suffrage Movement* (London: Virago, 1978)

Theresa McBride. *The Domestic Revolution: The Modernization of Household Services in England and France 1820–1920* (London: Croom Helm, 1976)

Rosemarie Morgan. *Women and Sexuality in the Novels of Thomas Hardy* (London: Routledge, 1988)

Deborah D. Morse. *Women in Trollope's Palliser Novels* (Ann Arbor, Michigan: UMI Research Press, 1987)

Adrienne A. Munich, ed. *Browning Institute Studies, An Annual of Victorian Literary and Cultural History, Volume 13: Victorian Women and Men* (New York: The Browning Institute, City University of New York, 1985)

Pauline Nestor. *Female Friendships and Communities: Charlotte Brontë, George Eliot, Elizabeth Gaskell* (Oxford and New York: Oxford University Press, 1985)

L. M. Newman. *Men's Ideas/Women's Realities: Popular Science 1870–1915* (Oxford: Pergamon Press, 1984)

J. L. Newton *et al.*, eds. *Sex and Class in Women's History* (London: Routledge and Kegan Paul, 1983)

J. L. Newton. *Women, Power and Subversion: Social Strategies in British Fiction 1778–1860* (Athens, Georgia: University of Georgia Press, 1981; London: Methuen, 1985)

Alex Owen. *The Darkened Room/Women, Power, and Spiritualism in Late Victorian England* (London: Virago, 1989)

C. Rover. *Love, Morals and the Feminists* (London: Routledge and Kegan Paul, 1970)

Cynthia E. Russett. *Sexual Science/The Victorian Construction of Womanhood* (Cambridge, Mass.: Harvard University Press, 1989)

Valerie Sanders. *The Private Lives of Victorian Women/Autobiography in Nineteenth Century England* (Hemel Hempstead: Harvester

Wheatsheaf, 1989)

Elaine Showalter. *A Literature of Their Own: British Women Novelists from Brontë to Lessing* (London and Princeton, N.J.: Virago and Princeton University Press, 1977)

—— *The Female Malady: Women, Madness, and English Culture, 1830–1980* (New York: Pantheon Books, 1985; London: Virago, 1987)

P. A. M. Spacks. *The Female Imagination* (New York: Knopf, 1975)

Julia Swindells. *Victorian Writing and Working Women: The Other Side of Silence* (Minneapolis, MN: University of Minnesota Press, 1985; London: Polity Press, 1986)

Barbara Taylor. *Eve and the New Jerusalem: Socialism and Feminism in the Nineteenth Century* (London: Virago, 1983)

Martha Vicinus, ed. *Suffer and Be Still: Women in the Victorian Age* (Bloomington, Indiana: Indiana University Press, 1973; London: Methuen, 1980)

—— *A Widening Sphere: Changing Roles of Victorian Women* (Bloomington, Indiana: Indiana University Press, 1977; London: Methuen, 1980)

—— *Independent Women: Work and Community for Single Women 1850–1920* (London and Chicago, IL: Virago and University of Chicago Press, 1985)

Judith R. Walkowitz. *Prostitution and Victorian Society: Women, Class and the State* (Cambridge: Cambridge University Press, 1980)

Judith Weissman. *Half Savage and Hardy and Free: Women and Rural Radicalism in the Nineteenth-Century Novel* (Middletown, CT: Wesleyan University Press, 1987)

G. Whitelegg *et al.*, eds. *The Changing Experience of Women* (Oxford: Martin Robertson, 1982)

Merryn Williams. *Women in the English Novel 1800–1900* (London: Macmillan, 1984)

A. Wohl. *The Victorian Family* (London: Croom Helm, 1978)

Biographical Notes

Walter Besant (1836–1901) was born in Portsmouth, Hampshire, and received his education at King's College, London, and Christ College, Cambridge. Between 1861 and 1867 he was a senior professor in Loyal College, in the British colony of Mauritius. He wrote several studies of French literature. In 1868 he became secretary to the Palestine Exploration Fund, a position he held for seventeen years. The fruits of this interest may be cited as *Jerusalem: The City of Herod and Saladin* (1871), written in collaboration with the Orientalist Edward Palmer, and *The Survey of Western Palestine* (1881–83). His fourteen romantic novels, written in the 1870s with his collaborator James Rice, earned him considerable royalties. The work which had the greatest impact, however, was *All Sorts and Conditions of Men* (1882). It depicted life in the East End slums of London with such force and dismaying detail that Government efforts to ameliorate conditions led to the creation of the People's Palace (1887) in Mile End Road, which in turn provided amusement and educational opportunities to slum-dwellers there. Besant's *The Children of Gibeon* (1886) attacked the 'sweating system', and also had an impact on public opinion. Besant wrote another thirty-two novels after Rice died, a number of biographies (Rabelais, Richard Jefferies, Captain Cook), literary criticism, and topographical studies (London, Westminster, and South London). His work in founding the Society of Authors (1884) and editing its journal for a full decade helped to protect literary property at a time when some publishers were ruthlessly exploitative. Besant's life is the very model of a late Victorian bookman; he may be profitably studied as a spirit akin to Andrew Lang, Robert Louis Stevenson, Edmund Gosse, and George Saintsbury; he wrote prolifically, and perhaps not always on the basis of deep enough research; but everything he published was readable, lucid, and good value for money received. His short stories tend to be straightforward, a little wicked in their flouting of conventional morality, and suggestive of the existence of a wider world of social and political concerns.

Hubert Crackanthorpe (1870–95) lived a short and troubled life. His parents were well educated, his father having earned a reputation in the law, his mother being an authoress and a well-liked hostess. George Gissing tutored him preparatory to his matriculation at Cambridge. However, he left the university within a year because of trouble with the authorities. By 1892 his talents as a writer were sufficient to bring him the editorship of the *Albermarle*, which specialized in the diagnosis of social problems. He married Leila Macdonald, a lineal descendant of Flora Macdonald, the famous heroine of Scottish history. *Wreckage*, a set of realistic 'studies' that carried within themselves the seeds of an experimental attitude toward fiction, preceded *Sentimental Studies and a Set of Village Tales* (1895), which Crackanthorpe dedicated to Henry ('Harry') Harland of *The Yellow Book*. To what extent differences of temperament with Leila led to depression cannot now be determined. The French police were baffled by the manner of his disappearance on 5 November, 1895, and by the discovery of his body some seven weeks later; it remains unclear whether he committed suicide or was murdered on the Quai Voltaire in Paris. A posthumously published collection of short stories, *Last Studies* (1897), carried an 'appreciation' by Henry James. Crackanthorpe was a noble continuator of the kind of fiction pioneered by Guy de Maupassant, though disillusionment is more marked in the Englishman's work. He was intensely interested in improving his style, and his writing became continually more economical and precisely phrased right up until the end.

Ella D'Arcy (?–1939) lived an obscure childhood, although it is known that her parents were Irish, that she received her education in Germany and France, and that several of her short stories exhibited an intimate knowledge of the Channel Islands. Failing eyesight forced her to renounce artistic ambitions (she was a student at the Slade School). Dickens, impressed by her writing, accepted a manuscript for *All the Year Round*; acceptances followed from *Blackwood's* and *Temple Bar*, but most importantly from *The Yellow Book*. Indeed, 'Irremediable' appeared in the first volume of that periodical, after having been rejected by the editor of *Blackwood's* because of its summary treatment of marriage. Henry Harland, editor of *The Yellow Book*, hired her as his assistant. Though she wrote slowly, and was timid in the face of editorial rebuffs, she managed to complete three collections of short stories: *Monochromes* (1895), *The Bishop's Dilemma* and *Modern Instances* (both in 1898). Her novel remained unpublished, even though only one publisher refused it, and Arnold Bennett begged unsuccessfully for the chance to judge it for himself. She completed a translation of André Maurois's *Ariel* at the expense of her own project, a life of Shelley that she never did much with; Maurois thought her translation very fine. Her last major project also never got into print: a biography and translation of Rimbaud, who in 1930 was a scandalously controversial poet. She loved France, and spent her final years in Paris; death came to her in England. Her short stories, though not often read today, are strong dramatizations of the difficulties plaguing Victorian marriage. Unlike most defenders of women, D'Arcy tended to put the blame on her female characters; there are very few, if any, likeable women in her fiction; but that was the truth as she saw it, and hers remains a distinctive voice in *fin de siècle* literature.

Arthur Conan Doyle (1859–1930) lived an extraordinary life. Quite apart from the phenomenal popularity of Sherlock Holmes, Doyle wrote a number of historical novels, outstanding among them *The White Company* (1890), that many thought would last as 'Literature' longer than any of his other works. Those included plays – *The Story of Waterloo* (1894), starring Sir Henry Irving, was much admired; and poems – John Masefield, for one, rated them high. But he was also a first-rate journalist who wrote impressive histories of the Boer War and the Great War, publishing seventy-one books altogether. Since he did not begin writing professionally until he was almost thirty, the record of his productivity is very full indeed. He championed worthy causes, and took special pride in clearing the reputations of innocent men who had been wrongly accused of serious crimes; his work for the Volunteers was instrumental in the later creation of the Home Guard; and he worked hard and long as President of the Divorce Law Reform Union. In addition to the stories in the Holmes canon, he wrote over one hundred other short stories, dealing with piracy, the boxing ring, and 'the exploits of Brigadier Gerard', a hero of various misadventures during the Napoleonic era. Worth mentioning also are his exploits as an athlete; he specialized in games (cricket in particular), and sports (e.g. boxing).

'George Egerton' (Mary Chavelita [Dunne] Bright) (1859–1945) was born in Australia to a Welsh mother and a cashiered Irish army officer. Her early years were spent in Ireland and at a German school; she worked briefly as a nurse in London, and lived for a short time in New York. Her elopement to Norway with a bigamist – a foredoomed affair – had one important beneficial result: she became fascinated by Ibsen and Strindberg, and translated Knut Hamsun's important novel *Hunger* (1899). Indeed, she dedicated her first volume of short stories, *Keynotes* (1893) to Hamsun. The book, illustrated by Aubrey Beardsley, told readers much that they did not know about the New Woman. She contributed to *The Yellow Book* and, in addition to two novels, published *Symphonies* (1896) and *Fantasies* (1898), both collections of short stories. Her marriage to the theatrical agent Reginald Golding Bright involved her with playwriting; even though important stage personalities like Lily Langtry took an interest in her, her work in this direction never proved commercially successful. Her short stories are marked by a shrewd realism and often by a delicacy of touch suggesting that, at her best, she was capable of much richer insights than most of her contemporary short-story practitioners.

Elizabeth Gaskell (1810–65) was born in London at Cheyne Walk, Chelsea. Her father was a Unitarian minister, a farmer, writer, teacher, and Keeper of the Records in the Treasury; he made sure that she had a first-rate education at Stratford-upon-Avon before he died, an invalid in her care, in 1829. She married William Gaskell, also a hard-working Unitarian minister, a philanthropist, and a lecturer in English literature at Manchester College. When one thinks of her busy family life (six children, four of whom survived), her ceaseless rounds of social engagements, her friendships (Ruskin, Dickens, Carlyle, Harriet Beecher Stowe, Charles Eliot Norton), and her ceaseless flow of high-quality sketches, articles, and poems for various periodicals (chief among them Dickens's *Household Words*), one can only marvel that so much of her work remains readable to this day. *Cranford* (1853), *Cousin Phillis* (1864), *Wives and Daughters* (1866), and a superb biography of her good friend Charlotte Brontë (1857), are dignified, serious, and thought-provoking; they never talk down to readers who may have been spoiled by their experience with Mudie's three-deckers. Mrs Gaskell's short stories, all written to earn money for an expensive family, do not disappoint; each story makes an unsentimental and challenging point. It takes some time for a reader to appreciate the chief male figure in 'The Manchester Marriage', for example, but all the evidence for and against his claim to our affection is provided fairly.

William Schwenck Gilbert (1836–1911) was born in London. His father, a naval surgeon, encouraged his early love of literature, which developed further at Ealing School and University College, London. He was not successful as a barrister, but found his bent from 1861 on in light, irreverent journalism. *Bab Ballads* (collected in 1869) established his reputation (they were wildly popular among all social classes) before he moved on to the theatre. *The Palace of Truth* (1870) was the first of a series of fantasies in verse that enjoyed a moderate success. The Victorians, however, gave a much stronger approval to Gilbert's work as a librettist for a series of musical plays composed by Arthur Sullivan, beginning with *Thespis* (1871) and *Trial by Jury* (1875). The Savoy Operas, which ended with the production of *The Gondoliers* (1889), were hugely enjoyed, and have never been off the boards somewhere in the world since their first appearances in London. These witty and inventively musical plays may turn out to be the most enduring contribution of Victorian theatre to world literature. Gilbert's knighthood in 1907 was the first such honour bestowed on an author solely for his services to the theatre. His death, characteristically, was the result of a gallant attempt to save the life of a young woman who was drowning in a pool at his home in Middlesex. Gilbert wrote dozens of short stories for periodicals, and valued them highly (surprisingly, the short story was his favourite genre). Like his verse, his stories are playful, comic in tone but with some dark undercurrents, and not easy to forget once one has read them.

George Gissing (1857–1903) developed an early interest in reading, and was encouraged by his mother, the daughter of a solicitor. His father was a pharmaceutical chemist. He attended a Quaker school in Worcestershire, and then, at Owens college, Manchester, won an astonishing collection of prizes and scholarships. Inspired by the ancient world, a lover of Gibbon's *History*, he seemed destined for an academic career of distinction; but his attempts to reform Marianne Helen Harrison, a prostitute whom he met in Manchester and whom he tried to support by stealing from the College, led to a prison sentence. In 1877 he visited the U.S., and wrote a number of short stories for the Chicago newspapers; he studied in Germany; but his marriage to Marianne (1879), who had turned into a drunkard, and who was eventually to die in a Lambeth slum (1888), dragged him down. In 1891 he picked up and married Edith Underwood, a servant girl, who proved equally disastrous to his life and career; and in 1897 he fled from her. Gissing's unflinching vision of the middle- and lower-classes is recorded, in a style that owes much (surprisingly) to Meredith and Turgenev, in a number of naturalistic stories possessing high literary value. His most important books – of the twenty-four that began with *Workers in the Dawn* (1880) – are *Demos* (1886), *New Grub Street* (1891), *Born in Exile* (1892) and *The Odd Woman* (1893), as well as the pseudo-memoir *Private Papers of Henry Ryecroft* (1903). His love of the classics is enshrined in *By the Ionian Sea: Notes of a Ramble in Southern Italy* (1901). Gissing included twenty-nine short stories, of varying quality (the best are very good indeed), in *Human Odds and Ends* (1898). Influenced by Auguste Comte and Frederic Harrison, he developed a positivistic outlook with an ultimately optimistic tone. His friends included H. G. Wells, W. H. Hudson, and Edward Clodd. Before he died of double pneumonia, he enjoyed a few years of peace and happiness with Gabrielle Fleury, an intelligent Frenchwoman who appreciated his humanness as well as his talents. The number of readers who 'discover' Gissing seems to grow year by year; he may have a larger audience today than he did during his lifetime.

Thomas Hardy (1840–1928) created Wessex (a term not used for centuries) as the locale of both his novels and his poems; it should not be considered conterminous with Dorset or indeed any single part of the Anglo-Saxon Heptarchy. But, no less than Wordsworth's Lake Country or Scott's Border Country, Wessex has become very real to all readers of Hardy's works. The landscape is charged with symbols, and the characters depicted entertain human passions no less intense than those known to any hero of a Greek tragedy or any character in Shakespearian drama. Born in Higher Bockhampton in the parish of Stinsford, Hardy spent most of his life within a twenty-five mile radius of his birthplace. He began as a writer of pastoral fictions (*Under the Greenwood Tree*, 1872, was his second published novel), but his interest in philosophy, history, and science both deepened and darkened his subject-matter within a few years. He retained an abiding interest in the Napoleonic Wars, and his epic-drama *The Dynasts* may well be the finest treatment of the subject in English literature. His forty-six short stories, essentially by-products of an industrious career, fill four substantial volumes; in the Wessex Edition many of them are told as familiar folk tales, with an emphasis on humour, irony, and melodrama. 'A Mere Interlude' is based in part on Hardy's knowledge of his sister Kate's experiences in training for the profession of teaching, and of her long career as a teacher.

Henry James (1843–1916) was born in New York City to a Scottish mother and an Irish father, and enjoyed a liberal upbringing, along with his brother William (who was later a significant definer of the discipline of psychology). Indeed, all the Jameses were remarkable, and formed one of the most distinguished families in American history. James's first contact with Europe came in 1855, and he learned at an early age to appreciate museums, galleries, and the high culture of several nations. There were voids in his life: he had no Civil War experience, he never married, his fiction does not often deal with underprivileged classes. But he probably knew as much about the art of fiction as practised in France, Russia, and England as any American of his time, and his stories on the 'international theme', dealing with the problems created by innocent Americans who visit the Old World and try to mingle with its upper classes, establishes his reputation as an authoritative representative of the New World. *Daisy Miller* (1878) was a popular novella dealing with this theme, though James moved swiftly beyond its limits. His output (literary criticism, plays, ghost stories, travel essays, and autobiographical books and fragments) was prolific. He wrote some of the finest short stories and novelle of the second half of the nineteenth century. All repay re-reading because of their subtlety and masterly control of the language.

Rudyard Kipling (1865–1936) had as his father the son of a Methodist minister, and as his mother the daughter of another Methodist minister.

John Lockwood Kipling, a teacher of technical arts and crafts in a newly founded school of art, and Alice Macdonald, his witty wife, were living in Bombay when their son was born. The childhood of Rudyard Kipling is treated in a horrifying short story about abusive treatment ('Baa, Baa, Black Sheep'), and in several crucial episodes of *The Light That Failed* (1890), his first novel. Fortunately the 'House of Desolation' in Southsea, England, to which he had been sent in 1871 to avoid the illnesses that plague a child growing up in India, was not the only home he knew; he found friends and a warm family atmosphere in 'The Grange' in Fulham, where members of the second wave of Pre-Raphaelites gathered. Kipling's education at Westward Ho! is recounted in the short stories of *Stalky & Co.* (1899). 'Seven years' hard' as a journalist in India, working for newspapers in Lahore and Allahabad, led to his first experiments in the short story, and he was developing a reputation as a journalist who could write rapidly to order. His return to England in 1889 and a rapid-fire series of reprints of Indian publications, including *Departmental Ditties* (1886), *Plain Tales from the Hills* (1888), as well as the new 'ballads' that coined new and wildly popular catch-phrases, transformed Kipling into one of the true celebrities of late Victorian England. *Kim* is reckoned by some to be Kipling's finest single work, but the hundreds of short stories that Kipling published over a span of more than four decades include some of the most picturesque, complex, and startling stories in the language. Their range of subject-matter is extraordinary; Kipling introduced and made respectable themes and character-types that stay-at-home readers had not previously encountered. (One military historian has said that British soldiers began to talk like Tommy Atkins after reading Kipling's descriptions of Army life.) Kipling's record of the heyday of the British Empire has never been bettered. Moreover, Kipling's short stories for and about children became instant classics: *Captains Courageous, Just So Stories, Puck of Pook's Hill*, and *Rewards and Fairies*.

George Moore (1852–1933) was born in Moore Hall, one of the great Georgian homes of County Mayo, Ireland. His father, addicted to horse-racing, served as a Member of Parliament for many years; he sent his son to Oscott, a Catholic college in England. A bronchitis attack, which sent George Moore home, was much appreciated by the boy. From 1873 to 1875, as a young man, he attempted to develop a career as a painter, but this, like his early publication of a book of poems, proved a failure. In the late 1870s his café education in Paris introduced him to Manet, Degas, and other important painters. Keenly aware of literary fashions (then as later), he wrote *A Modern Lover* (1883) as a naturalistic document. It was promptly banned by the circulating libraries. *Confessions of a Young*

Man (1888), about bohemian life, is a richly textured memoir; equally important in Moore's career is *Esther Waters* (1894), one of the key documents in the emergence of a new realism in the English novel. Because he hated the Boer War and imperial jingoism, he moved back to Ireland in 1901, and joined several activities sponsored by the Gaelic League, and, with Edward Martyn, a cousin possessing genuine but minor talents in playwriting, and William Butler Yeats, he helped to push forward the concept of an Irish National Theatre. (For details, see Moore's three-volume *Hail and Farewell*, published between 1911 and 1914, a chatty and sometimes malicious autobiography.) Moore's novels included *The Brook Kerith*, a splendid imagining of the likely consequences of Jesus's survival after being crucified and taken down from the cross. Its 'melodic line', a stylistic innovation of which Moore was justifiably proud, indicated how far he had travelled from his youthful admiration of Zolaistic doctrine. Moore's short stories, contained in *The Untilled Field* (1903), owe a large debt to Turgenev and Dostoyevsky, and *Celibate Lives* (1927), develops some of Flaubert's concepts of language and style, and are among the best of his works. His final years were spent in a Belgravia house (1911–33). He was respected by his contemporaries as a dedicated artist.

Arthur Morrison (1863–1945), though born in Kent, spent much of his life in the East End of London. As a clerk to the trustees charged with the responsibility of administering the People's Palace in Mile End Road, he came to the attention of the novelist Walter Besant, who recommended him for the position of subeditor of *The Palace Journal*. This in turn became the launching-pad for a career as a free-lance journalist. William Ernest Henley asked him to write for the *National Observer*. The sketches and short stories contributed there became the important book *Tales of Mean Streets* (1894), which was swiftly followed by *A Child of the Jago* (1894). Morrison's tough-minded, straightforward depiction of the brutalizing conditions of slum life led to housing legislation that cleared away some of the worst of the slums. Later works include *The Hole in the Wall* (1902) and three collections of short stories about Martin Hewitt, a detective who continued worthily in the Sherlock Holmes tradition. *Cunning Murrell* (1900), dealing with witchcraft and smuggling on the Essex shore of the Thames Estuary, was a bestseller. Morrison developed a passionate interest in collecting art-works of the Orient, and his two-volume work *The Painters of Japan* (1911) became a standard reference. His superb collection was donated to the British Museum after his death. Morrison's short stories are marked by honesty and vigour; though the best are to be found in *Tales of Mean Streets*, his other collections – *Divers Vanities* (1905), *Green Ginger* (1909), and *Fiddle o' Dreams* (1933) – are well worth reading.

Anthony Trollope (1815–82) had as his father an impractical-minded barrister who became bankrupt in 1834; his flare-ups of temper proved hard on the young child. His mother, Frances Trollope, went to America to supervise the building of a great bazaar in Cincinnati, and wrote *Domestic Manners of the Americans* (1832), a notorious book about her adventures in a country that did not entirely please her; she was an industrious author, writing forty-one books to keep her home solvent. Trollope's experiences as a day-boy at Harrow and as a student with unpaid bills at Winchester were recalled, with great unhappiness, in his *Autobiography* (written in 1875–76, but not published until 1883). After a difficult beginning as a junior clerk in the Post Office (1834), Trollope began his real career as a civil servant when he crossed the Irish Sea to Ireland; there he remained until 1867. On various occasions he visited Egypt, the U.S., and the West Indies on postal business, and he is credited with the invention of the English pillar-box. He began his second career, as a professional author, fairly late in life, but writing at the rate of 1.7 books a year, he eventually caught up with the most prolific of his contemporaries, and produced almost fifty novels before he died in 1882. *The Warden* (1855) began a series of five Barsetshire novels, which for many readers mark his greatest achievement; but others will vote for the six 'political novels', starring Plantagenet Palliser and his wife Glencora. All Trollope's fictions do ample justice to the English girl, to whom he gave 'the most serious, the most patient, the most tender, the most copious consideration' (the phrasing is Henry James's); few stories of the Victorian Age equal the quality of the kindly respect with which the Parson's daughter of Oxney Colne is treated. Trollope, laughing at a comic book which he was reading aloud to his family after dinner, suffered a stroke, and died a month later.

Israel Zangwill (1864–1926) may never regain the popularity he enjoyed at the turn of the century, but his stories of Jews in London's East End presented to interested readers a world hitherto untouched by serious writers. His parents were poor immigrants, and his education at schools in Plymouth and Bristol not first-rate; but he became a teacher of some distinction at the Jews' Free School in Spitalfields, London, after earning a B.A. with Honours at the University of London. His real love, developed as part of a rapidly burgeoning journalistic career, was writing about his own people. He edited the humorous periodical *Ariel*, and from 1881 on made his living as an author. He served as President of the Jewish Territorial Organization for the Settlement of Jews within the British Empire, and was a key figure in the growth and development of the Jewish Historical Society and the Jewish Drama League. His *Children of the Ghetto* (1892) was a great success. He was a popular speaker, and he wrote eighteen plays, including adaptations of his own novels. His translation of selected religious poems by Solomon ben Judah Ibn Gabirol (1924) won plaudits from scholars. The best of his fiction, in *Ghetto Tragedies* (1893) and *The King of Schnorrers: Grotesques and Fantasies* (1894), is a collection of indispensable documents for readers who want to learn more about a dynamic, picturesque ethnic group.